Space Weapons—
The Arms Control Dilemma

Space Weapons—
The Arms Control Dilemma

Edited by
Bhupendra Jasani

sipri

Stockholm International Peace Research Institute

Taylor & Francis
London and Philadelphia
1984

UK   Taylor & Francis Ltd, 4 John St, London WC1N 2ET

USA   Taylor & Francis Inc., 232 Cherry St, Philadelphia, PA 19106-1906

Copyright © SIPRI 1984

British Library Cataloguing in Publication Data

Space weapons: the arms control dilemma.
   1. Space warfare
   I. Jasani, Bhupendra   II. Stockholm International
Peace Research Institute
   358′.8   UG1530

   ISBN 0-85066-262-1

Typeset by Mathematical Composition Setters Ltd, Salisbury, Wilts. Printed in Great Britain by Taylor & Francis (Printers) Ltd, Basingstoke, Hants.

Contents

Preface

Less than a year after the launch of the first military-oriented satellites in 1958, tests began on weapons to destroy spacecraft. The militarization of outer space has occurred very rapidly on two fronts: first, by the use of artificial Earth satellites to enhance the performance of Earth-based weapons and, second, by the development of anti-satellite (ASAT) weapons.

The earlier versions of ASAT missiles were crude and indiscriminate in their destructive capabilities. While the ASAT satellites developed by the USSR were also crude weapons, they were an improvement on the US indiscriminate nuclear-tipped ASAT missiles. Now the USA is testing what promises to be a more efficient weapon; on 21 January 1984 it carried out a test of its air-launched ASAT missile, which eventually will be fitted with a non-nuclear warhead. With the relative flexibility of this new ASAT system, an arms race in this field is well on its way.

There are a number of arms control treaties containing paragraphs which deal with controlling some military activities in outer space. Attempts have been made in the past to introduce controls on ASAT weapons but no agreements were reached. Recently, a number of arms control treaties have been proposed, officially and unofficially, to arrest at least the proliferation of anti-satellite weapons; but these are partial measures. The issue is further complicated by the fact that some of the space-based defensive weapons proposed recently could also be used as offensive ASAT weapons.

At the time of printing it was not clear whether there would be any negotiations between the USA and the USSR on arms control in outer space. However, there is no doubt that the international community as a whole considers that this is an urgent matter. The United Nations General Assembly gave a clear mandate in 1984 to the UN Committee on the Peaceful Uses of Outer Space to consider the issue of the militarization of this environment. Moreover, it urged that the Conference on Disarmament in Geneva give priority to discussions on a possible agreement on the prevention of an arms race in outer space, in all its aspects.

In order to contribute to such discussions and also promote public debate on the militarization of outer space, SIPRI organized a symposium on 'Outer Space—Can Militarization Be Checked?' at which 15 eminent scientists, lawyers and diplomats from seven different countries participated. The meeting took place in Stockholm between 21 and 23 September 1983. This book contains the papers presented at the symposium and an introductory section of six chapters in which Bhupendra Jasani has drawn on the discussions at the conference and on other material to present a general background to the issues covered by the symposium papers.

I should like to express my appreciation to Bhupendra Jasani for the contribution he has made over the years to the study of the militarization of outer space, and to Gillian Stanbridge for her invaluable editorial assistance in the preparation of this work.

SIPRI   *Frank Blackaby*
1984   Director

Space Weapons—The Arms Control Dilemma
Edited by Bhupendra Jasani
Taylor & Francis, London and Philadelphia, 1984, 255 pp.
(Stockholm International Peace Research Institute)
ISBN 0-85066-262-1

ABSTRACTS

KARAS, T., 'Military satellites and war-fighting doctrines', in *Space Weapons—The Arms Control Dilemma*, pp. 43–55

This paper examines the implications of satellites only for nuclear war-fighting doctrines. A variety of doctrinal approaches to making nuclear weapons militarily useful have been conceived: discounting the destructive power of the weapons; limited or protracted nuclear war; 'minimum deterrence'; mutual deterrence through 'assured destruction'; and survival through defensive technology. Warning, communications and intelligence satellites would play roles of varying significance in the different scenarios of war envisaged by these doctrines. The significance of anti-satellite weapons would vary accordingly. In the case of space weapons as BMD systems, it is highly questionable whether such weapons will in themselves release the world from the nuclear balance of terror. Paradoxically, large BMD systems make nuclear 'war-fighting' doctrines which stress attacks limited to military targets less feasible and compel redoubled efforts to maintain adequate 'assured destruction capability' towards the defended nation.

SHAPLEY, D.,'Strategic doctrines, the militarization and the 'semi-militarization' of space', in *Space Weapons—The Arms Control Dilemma*, pp. 57–70

1. US nuclear war doctrine has largely evolved independently of technology. Space technology played a role only late in its evolution; in the late 1970s and early 1980s it helped to make nuclear war-fighting seem more practical.
2. Three developments are eroding the arms control goal of a sanctuary: (*a*) improvements to C^3I systems; (*b*) a high-confidence, easy to hide ASAT system now being developed by the USA; and (*c*) a space-based ABM battle station, which, although very remote and unlikely, is getting more public attention. All 3 are creating new instabilities in what used to be the stable sanctuary of space, and arms control policies are needed even for the research phase.
3. The question of whether satellites may be knocked out to gain advantage in a crisis or a conventional war raises new 'grey areas'. These urgently require study, new doctrines and new arms control agreements.

TREZZA, C., 'Advantages and disadvantages of an eventual ban on deployment of military satellites', in *Space Weapons—The Arms Control Dilemma*, pp. 71–76

A distinction has to be made between different kinds of military satellite. Reconnaissance and surveillance satellites, especially those which perform a function within the framework of an arms control agreement, clearly have a stabilizing character. They create confidence through verification and transparency, thus their prohibition would provoke negative consequences. The banning of the other large category of military satellites, the so-called 'auxiliary' satellites, which are instrumental to other military activities, would only make sense if it were coupled with a general ban on the weapon systems of which they are an orbital appendix. Moreover, their prohibition would create great practical problems in view of the dual use, military and civilian, which these satellites normally have. However, ASAT satellites are destabilizing and can generate an arms race in outer space; they should therefore be banned through international agreements.

SCHEFFERS, J., 'Why anti-satellite warfare should be prohibited', in *Space Weapons—The Arms Control Dilemma*, pp. 77–82

Any approach to an ASAT treaty as a means to prohibit ASAT warfare presupposes that satellites should be protected. This means that military satellites, vital for waging war on Earth, will also enjoy protection from attack or other hostile interference, although they constitute valid military targets. After examining whether or not anti-satellite warfare should be prohibited, it is concluded that even on military grounds an ASAT treaty as an instrument for negotiated constraints would be greatly preferable to totally unrestrained competition in ASAT weaponry. The technical complexities involved as well as the question of adequate verification of an ASAT treaty are not insoluble, if an actual prohibition of anti-satellite warfare, strengthened by a number of complementary measures, is considered by the 2 major space powers to be in their mutual long-term security interest, ensuring the maximum possible stability of nuclear deterrence.

SMITH, M., 'Satellite and missile ASAT systems and potential verification problems associated with the existing Soviet systems', in *Space Weapons—The Arms Control Dilemma*, pp. 83–91

The Soviet Union has an operational ASAT device using a co-orbital satellite interceptor. The United States does not, at present, possess an ASAT capability, but it is developing a direct ascent system using an interceptor launched from an F-15 aircraft. There are several different types of device that can be used to destroy the operational capabilities of satellites, if not the satellites themselves. This paper addresses only those systems which rely on either satellite or missile interceptions, not those based on directed-energy weapons or the effects of nuclear explosions in space. BMD systems are not included. Whether an agreement banning ASAT systems can be reached despite the numerous potential verification problems will depend primarily on the determination of the two countries to reach such an accord and therefore on what risks they are willing to accept.

KERR, D., 'Implications of anti-satellite weapons for ABM issues', in *Space Weapons—The Arms Control Dilemma*, pp. 107–125

Present asymmetries in current-generation ASAT forces provide an ominous and destabilizing influence. The deployment of the US miniature homing vehicle ASAT weapon to deter Soviet ASAT use would have little effect on ABM issues. More difficult questions are raised by the possible development, testing and deployment of directed-energy ASAT weapons, for these could seriously affect possibilities for continued adherence to the 1972 ABM Treaty. The successful development of directed-energy ASAT technologies might be the first step towards effective defence against ballistic missiles. Conversely, prohibiting development of these technologies for ASAT applications would reinforce the ban on new ABM technologies and probably preclude their development. The possible constraints on technological development and movement away from a strategic equation dominated by retaliation with offensive nuclear forces must be weighed against the benefits of ASAT limitation.

NAHIN, P., 'Space-based directed energy beam weapons', in *Space Weapons—The Arms Control Dilemma*, pp. 93–105

At issue here are weapons for ASAT use for purely defensive purposes. The ASAT case has the obvious objection of being clearly hostile in intent, and could increase tensions by denying intelligence information during periods of intense crisis. The case is made here that space-based ABM systems, using non-nuclear technology, might actually contribute to a decline in the arms race. A suggestion for revising the ABM Treaty is made that couples each new deployment of space-based ABM systems with a further reduction in fixed land-based ICBMs. This coupling is an essential factor. The argument is made that initial ABM defences make the deployment of multiple warhead missiles unattractive and further weaken the case for a highly accurate counterforce weapon with multiple independently targetable re-entry vehicles, such as the MX. Some elementary calculations are presented on the energy requirements for a laser ASAT system.

GOLDBLAT, J., 'New means of ballistic missile defence: the question of legality and arms control implications', in *Space Weapons—The Arms Control Dilemma*, pp. 127–130

With the increased US interest in developing a space-based BMD with the use of lasers and particle beams, the question arises as to the legality of such weapons. This paper outlines 2 interpretations of the 1972 ABM Treaty: (*a*) the creation of any BMD weapons based on physical principles other than those of the current ABMs is permitted; or (*b*) supported by the author, only fixed, land-based BMD systems and their components, based on 'other physical principles', may be created. Both interpretations would allow research into new means of defence. The author discusses how this research goes against what the ABM Treaty was apparently trying to achieve. He also argues that irrespective of whether or not an effective defence against missiles can be built, the very pursuit of such a goal escalates the arms race and may render nuclear war more probable.

GOTTFRIED, K., 'An ASAT test ban treaty', in *Space Weapons—The Arms Control Dilemma*, pp. 131–144

It is argued that the further growth of ASAT capabilities would significantly decrease crisis stability, and undermine the ABM Treaty, and that these dangers can only be averted by an ASAT test ban. To this end a bilateral Draft Treaty which would forbid the testing of weapons in space, and against space objects, is presented and discussed. Such a test ban would leave the USSR with a residual ASAT capability. The threat that this would pose to the USA is assessed, and compared to the risks that would accompany unrestricted ASAT competition. The problems of verifying compliance with the Draft Treaty are examined.

DANIELSSON, S., 'Approaches to prevent an arms race in outer space', in *Space Weapons—The Arms Control Dilemma*, pp. 157–171

Many military space systems are so important that an attack on them could be a *casus belli*. The effects of the introduction of beam weapons for ABM purposes are such that even research and development could lead to nervousness and tension, and weapons in outer space would have adverse effects on civilian space activities. The author discusses existing rules of international law relevant to the use of weapons in space and analyses 2 proposals to prevent an arms race in outer space presented by Italy (1979) and the Soviet Union (1981). Different approaches to preventing an arms race in outer space are discussed: a ban on all or certain military uses of outer space; a ban on certain arms; and prohibition of hostile acts. The need for verification, openness and a step-by-step approach is stressed. Certain measures are needed as soon as possible: a ban on certain acts in outer space and on systems to be used for such acts, be they based on the ground, in the air or in outer space. This ban should include development, testing and deployment as well as dismantling of existing systems. Furthermore, the ABM prohibition of 1972 should be confirmed.

SLOCOMBE, W., 'Approaches to an ASAT treaty', in *Space Weapons—The Arms Control Dilemma*, pp. 145–155

Because any arms control effort to make satellites absolutely safe from attack in a general nuclear war is infeasible, arms control should focus on reducing the capability and opportunity for precision attacks. For such agreements, verification poses a major problem, because a concealed ability to attack relatively few satellites could be militarily significant and because many means of interference and attack (other than physical intercept) exist. A number of particular agreements could be useful especially if coupled with measures to increase survivability and redundancy of space systems, thereby reducing the significance of small-scale cheating. Such measures include limits on testing (possibly focused on banning tests of ASAT systems able to reach geosynchronous orbit) and restrictions on application of innovative technologies to ASAT purposes.

JANKOWITSCH, P., 'Arms control in outer space: the need for new legal action', in *Space Weapons—The Arms Control Dilemma*, pp. 173–184

Progress in concluding new arms control agreements relating to outer space has been virtually nil for over a decade. The same lack of progress has dogged the various multilateral fora that have been landed with this problem. At the same time an arms race in outer space appears imminent. The author underlines that much of the blame for this development must go to the inadequacy of existing international treaties, resulting not only from insufficient coverage of the area of weapons deployment but also from a number of built-in ambiguities. He explores various steps which might be taken in order to build a coherent new body of space law and suggests a movement towards a multilateral approach. It is concluded that a strong case can be made for a new unified instrument encompassing all relevant provisions of international law. On the way to this new instrument of law a number of contingency measures would have to be taken. With regard to the threat presented by ASAT systems, a bilateral alternative might have to be adopted, even on a temporary basis, with a view to later incorporation in a multilateral system of treaties.

VELIKHOV, E., KOKOSHIN, A. & VASSILIEV, A., 'Averting a new round in the militarization of outer space: an urgent problem and goal', in *Space Weapons—The Arms Control Dilemma*, pp. 185–192

The military use of space has entered a new and dangerous phase. The greatest long-term threat lies in the possible creation by the USA of an anti-missile system based mainly on outer space echelons. The paper outlines findings which indicate that a space-based system cannot be taken as an effective means of defence against a massive first strike, but it would be an important factor in creating a first-strike capability. Another grave danger is presented by ASAT developments. An ASAT attack would justify a massive attack against the side that started military action against satellites; and ASAT developments threaten national technical means of verification. Thus the Soviet Union has presented to the UN a new draft treaty prohibiting the use or threat of force in outer space and by space objects against targets on the Earth. It proposes prohibition of the placing of any kind of weapons in outer space. The new draft prohibits also testing of ASAT systems and creation of new ASAT systems and provides for scrapping of any existing systems.

GUIONNET, M., 'Verification possibilities should an ASAT treaty materialize', in *Space Weapons—The Arms Control Dilemma*, pp. 193–196

Ascertaining that a satellite has been attacked is no easy matter. Making sure that existing first generation ASAT systems (rendezvous type) are not stored on the ground for future use is an impossible task as the systems themselves and the associated ground facilities have no distinctive external features whatsoever. It should, however, be possible to verify that no 'space mines' have been orbited. The testing and deployment of second generation systems (beam weapons) should be verifiable, although such activities could possibly be conducted under cover of other, seemingly harmless, operations.

Part I

The Arms Control Dilemma—
An Overview

Bhupendra Jasani

Chapter 1. Introduction

The militarization of outer space began just over a year after the launching of Sputnik 1 in October 1957 with the launch of the first military-related satellite in December 1958. Less than a year later, the tests of anti-satellite (ASAT) weapons began. Thus, militarization of this environment occurred very rapidly in two stages: first, by the introduction by the military of artificial Earth satellites to enhance the Earth-based weapon systems; and second by beginning development of weapons to be aimed at and used against military satellites. The earlier versions of ASAT missiles and anti-satellite satellites were either crude weapons or indiscriminate in their destructive capability. However, as the development of some new types of anti-ballistic missile (ABM) weapons progressed, their use as ASAT weapons became apparent, thus adding a new dimension to the ASAT arms race.

When discussing ASAT arms control measures, therefore, it is important to be aware of the considerable extent of and the reasons for the militarization of outer space. This has happened in spite of a number of existing bilateral and multilateral legal measures controlling some aspects of activities in this environment.

While there are a number of arms control treaties containing paragraphs which deal with controlling some military activities in outer space, it is the 1967 Treaty on Principles Governing the Activities of States in the Exploration and Use of Outer Space, Including the Moon and Other Celestial Bodies (the 1967 Outer Space Treaty) which specifically deals with activities in this environment. However, in the treaty the only military aspect dealt with explicitly is the prohibition on placing "in orbit around the Earth any objects carrying nuclear weapons or any other kinds of weapons of mass destruction", installing such weapons on celestial bodies, or stationing such weapons in outer space "in any other manner" (article IV).

Elsewhere in the treaty, emphasis is placed on the use of outer space "in the interest of maintaining international peace and security" (article III), and in the preamble there is a vague recognition of "the common interest of all mankind in the progress of the exploration and use of outer space for peaceful purposes". In spite of pledges such as: "the exploration and use of outer space ... shall be carried out for the benefit and in the interests of all countries ... and shall be the province of all mankind" (article I), the two big space powers now seem to be embarking upon an extensive ASAT arms race. How is this possible? Most arms control treaties which have provisions regarding activities in outer space are such that many military satellites are legally protected from harmful interference thus encouraging their extensive use.

The fact that the development of ASAT weapons began and continued is because there is no treaty that prohibits such weapons *per se*. And the Outer Space Treaty is generally seen as a framework of a legal regime which might be complemented by special measures dealing with such issues as ASAT weapons. It was hoped that the United Nations Committee on the Peaceful Uses of Outer Space (COPUOS), together with its legal and technical sub-committees, would propose further measures in the light of the developments in outer space technology. But, unfortunately, there was no follow-up on questions of disarmament and demilitarization of outer space. In fact, when recent attempts have been made, they have resulted in disappointments.

Although the 1967 Outer Space Treaty has demilitarized the Moon and other celestial bodies, outer space as a whole has only been partially demilitarized. This has partly resulted from the interpretation given by the USA and the USSR to the Treaty; they have interpreted the provisions of the Treaty for the peaceful applications of space technology as meaning non-aggressive rather than non-military. Whether the Treaty was ever meant as a significant disarmament measure is not clear.

In view of this, a brief review is given in chapter 2 of the extent to which military satellites are used by various nations.

A brief review of various types of ASAT weapons is given in chapter 3. Chapter 4 provides an overview of the defensive space-based weapons and indicates the commonality between these and the offensive ASAT weapons. The arms control implications of these activities are considered in chapter 5.

A number of arms control treaties, officially and unofficially, have been proposed to arrest the militarization of outer space. In chapter 5, these proposals are examined and some new measures are suggested.

All military satellites launched during 1982 and 1983 are listed in appendix 1.

Further reading

Jasani, B. (ed.), *Outer Space—A New Dimension of the Arms Race* (Taylor & Francis, London, 1982), a SIPRI book.

Jasani, B. and Lunderius, M.A., 'Peaceful uses of outer space—legal fiction and military reality', *Bulletin of Peace Proposals*, Vol. 11, No. 1, March 1980, pp. 57–70.

Report of the Second United Nations Conference on the Exploration and Peaceful Uses of Outer Space, A/CONF.101/10, 31 August 1982.

SIPRI, *Outer Space—Battlefield of the Future*? edited by B. Jasani (Taylor & Francis, London, 1978).

Chapter 2. Targets in space

By the end of 1983 at least 2 114 military oriented satellites had been launched. The functions of military satellites, which constitute about 75 per cent of all satellites orbited, range from navigation, communications, meteorology and geodesy to reconnaissance (see figure 1). Their orbital parameters are summarized in table 1. The functions of these spacecraft are briefly reviewed in the following sections in order to assess which types of satellite could be the

Figure 1. Number of military satellites of different types launched between 1958 and 1983

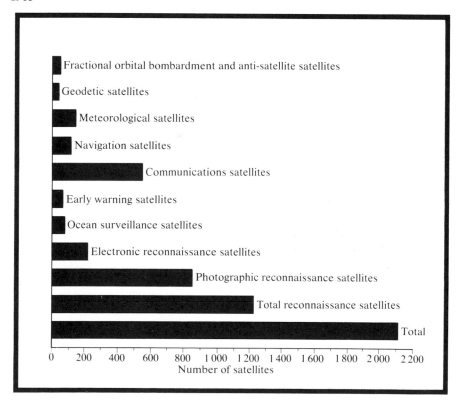

Table 1. Some orbital characteristics of various satellites

Satellite	Altitude (km)	Orbital inclination
Photographic reconnaissance		
Big Bird	180–290	97°
KH-11	240–530	97°
Cosmos	180–350	62°, 72°, 82°, 67°
Electronic reconnaissance		
US	480	97°
Cosmos	{ 500	74°
	{ 650	82°
Ocean surveillance		
US	1 100	63°
Cosmos	250	65°
Early warning		
US	36 000	0°
Cosmos	688 × 39 000	63°
Nuclear explosion detection		
US	110 000	35°
Meteorological		
US	36 000	0°
Meteor	{ 900	81°
	{ 610	98°
Communications		
US-SDS DSCS	250 × 39 000	64°
US-FLTSATCOM	36 000	0°
Molniya	440 × 40 000	63°
Cosmos	1 400	74°
Navigation		
US	20 000	64°
Cosmos	1 000	83°
Geodetic		
US	1 000–6 000	60–115°
Cosmos	1 000–2 000	74°, 83°

targets for the anti-satellite (ASAT) weapons currently being developed by the Soviet Union and the USA.

I. Reconnaissance satellites

Reconnaissance craft are probably the most important type of military satellite since not only are they used for verifying certain arms control agreements but are also primarily used for pin-pointing military targets. These satellites can be divided into four kinds: photographic, electronic, ocean surveillance and early warning satellites (see figure 1).

Photographic reconnaissance satellites

These detect, identify and pin-point military targets. Sensors on board such satellites include television cameras, multispectral scanners and microwave radars.

The USA and the Soviet Union are the leaders in this area of space technology. Several types of US photographic reconnaissance satellite have now been identified. For example, the latest generation of spacecraft is the KH-11 with a lifetime of close to four years and the ability to resolve objects 30 cm in size. This is an improved version of the KH-9, the so-called Big Bird satellite. A new spacecraft, KH-12, is being developed to replace KH-8, -9 and -11 satellites. An important feature of the KH-12 is that it is alleged to carry a radar warning system and a substantial amount of extra fuel in order to manoeuvre out of the path of possible Soviet radar-guided ASAT satellites. The lifetime of the Soviet photographic satellites is also increasing. Most of such satellites are orbited for 14 days but recently their lifespan has increased to 40 days and in 1983 a satellite remained in orbit for 53 days.

The People's Republic of China has also launched at least five such satellites. Of the military satellites launched by these three nations, some 40 per cent have been used for photographic reconnaissance purposes. France has plans to launch such a military satellite called SAMRO (Satellite Militaire de Reconnaissance Optique) in the late 1980s. Currently funding has been approved for research and development for the period 1984–88. Moreover, France and FR Germany are studying the development of a joint military reconnaissance satellite.

Electronic reconnaissance satellites

These are the "ears" in space (see figure 1). They carry equipment designed to detect and monitor radio signals generated by the opponent's military activities. Signals originate, for example, from military communications between bases, from early warning radars, air-defence and missile-defence radars or from those used for missile control. These satellites also gather data on missile testing, new radars and many other types of communications traffic. Not only do they locate systems producing electronic signals but also measure the characteristics of the signals so as to be able to plan penetration of defences.

Ocean surveillance and oceanographic satellites

These detect and track naval ships and determine sea conditions which can, for instance, help in forecasting the weather or, less innocently, in detecting submarines. Space-based sensors include radars that can "see" through clouds and detect even small pleasure boats. The radars on Soviet spacecraft are powered by small nuclear reactors.

Knowledge of what is happening in the ocean—for example the height of waves, the strength and direction of ocean currents, and salinity of the sea water—can help in the design of sensors to determine whether submarines are lurking beneath the surface. These factors also contribute to improving the accuracies of missiles launched from submarines.

Early warning satellites

These have partially replaced the radars that were originally deployed to give warning of a surprise attack by ballistic missiles. The radars provided about 15 minutes during which a response could be worked out. The use of early warning satellites has extended this warning time to some 30 minutes. The US early warning satellites are placed in geostationary orbit 36 000 km above the Earth while such Soviet satellites are orbited in a highly elliptical orbit.

II. Communications satellites

Space-based sensors for surveillance of the Earth, together with land-based surveillance systems, generate a considerable amount of data. The transmission of this and other data for military purposes needs reliable and secure communication systems. Space is an area of vital interest as some 80 per cent of military communications are carried out using artifical Earth satellites. Satellites also play a vital role in the command and control functions for the military forces of the big powers. Even communications between mobile forces such as aircraft, naval ships and soldiers on foot and their commanders is being conducted via satellites. Moreover the communications between the two big powers in a state of emergency would be via satellites.

Most US communications satellites are placed in geostationary orbit, while the Soviets still use a highly elliptical orbit. However, some of their civilian satellites are placed in geostationary orbit. Moreover, communication between the superpowers in a state of emergency would be via satellites.

III. Navigation satellites

For many weapon systems it is important to know the exact position and speed of the weapon. This is particularly so for missiles launched from sea-based platforms. Satellites are beginning to fulfil these requirements. Naval surface ships as well as submarines, aircraft and missiles determine their positions and velocities using signals emitted continuously by satellites. A constellation of 18 satellites would, for example, determine positions with an accuracy of about 20 m.

Both the USA and the USSR have developed satellite navigation systems. In the USA, an added mission is planned for such satellites. Although the USA has launched satellites specifically to detect nuclear explosions in the atmosphere and in outer space, it is now planned that US navigation satellites will carry sensors for this purpose also. Moreover, this is intended to provide damage assessment both within the USA and within enemy territories during and after a nuclear attack. This effort is in support of nuclear war doctrines which require early warning of attack, information for assessing the size of the attack and data on the attacked target so that an appropriate response can be made.

IV. Meteorological satellites

While the knowledge of cloud formation and movements is of importance in the photography of targets of military interest by reconnaissance satellites and in planning bombing missions, the amount of data collected is considerably more than this. For example, there are sensors on board such satellites which measure the oxygen and nitrogen density of the thermosphere, and which determine the temperature and water vapour at various altitudes. One reason for such detailed measurements of the properties of the atmosphere could be that once man has understood the mechanics of weather and climate formation, he may be able to control these for hostile purposes.

However, an immediate application of such data is for improving the accuracies of missiles. Among the factors influencing the accuracy of a missile are the water vapour content in the atmosphere and the wind velocity along the missile's possible trajectory. Not only do the meteorological conditions determine the corrections made to missile trajectories but these conditions are also taken into account when predicting satellite orbital tracks.

V. Geodetic satellites

The knowledge of geophysics is continually being refined and increased. An important aspect of geophysics is geodesy which includes determination of the size and shape of the Earth, its gravitational field, detailed maps and the location on the globe of cities, towns and villages as well as the precise positions of military targets.

With the development of digital data processing, considerable impact is expected on the performance of such weapon systems, such as intercontinental ballistic missiles (ICBMs) and cruise missiles, the accuracy of which is largely dependent on geophysical knowledge in general and geodesy in particular. For example, the knowledge of target positions, the ability to correct the trajectory of missiles and determine accurately their launch orientation, and extensive knowledge of the values of the Earth's gravitational field over the globe are vital to the improved accuracies of delivery vehicles used for warheads. Satellites are used considerably to increase the knowledge of these factors.

This brief review of the military encroachment on outer space indicates that the military satellites of the major powers are increasingly becoming part of the world-wide nuclear and conventional weapon systems that threaten the Earth's future. Because of this, such spacecraft could be targets in any major future conflict. In the next chapter, therefore, some of the anti-satellite weapons that may be deployed in the very near future as well as some exotic varieties such as laser beam weapons are briefly reviewed.

Further reading

'French, Germans study recon satellite plan', *Aviation Week and Space Technology*, Vol. 120, No. 23, 4 June 1984, p. 23.

Jasani, B., 'The military use of outer space', in *World Armaments and Disarmament, SIPRI Yearbook 1984* (Taylor & Francis, London, 1984), p. 354.

Pike, J., 'Space weapons race—stop it now', *Journal of the Federation of American Scientists, FAS Public Interest Report*, Vol. 36, No. 9, November 1983.

Statement in the French parliament by the Minister for Defence M. Charles Hernu, *Journal Officiel de la République Francaise*, No. 55 (Q), 2 February 1984, p. 140.

Chapter 3. Anti-satellite weapons

The ASAT arms race began soon after the first military satellite was launched in 1958. The testing of some US air-launched ASAT missiles in late 1959 and the deployment of the US land-based ASAT missiles and their nuclear warheads marked the beginning of the ASAT weapon race. The next to appear on the scene were the Soviet ASAT satellites. While these were crude weapons, they were an improvement on the indiscriminate nuclear-tipped US ASAT missiles. On 21 January 1984, the USA carried out a test of its air-launched ASAT missile which eventually will be fitted with a non-nuclear warhead. Thus, with the relative flexibility of this new ASAT system, the ASAT arms race has been taken a step further. If high-energy beam weapons are made to work, then the ASAT arms race will have reached its goal of ultimate speed.

Actual ASAT weapons are not, however, the only means of carrying out ASAT activities. The ground receiving stations linked, for example, to communications satellites and the space surveillance network are vulnerable to attack also. Thus, in any discussions involving ASAT systems, weapons capable of destroying such ground data-receiving stations and ground-based satellite command and control systems should also be considered. One of the weapons which might be used for this purpose is based on an effect known as the electromagnetic pulse (EMP) associated with any nuclear explosion. This and other types of ASAT weapon are considered briefly below.

I. Conventional ASAT weapons

The 'conventional' weapons are based on missile and satellite technologies. Unconventional weapons are those which use directed electromagnetic radiation as a means of destroying or damaging spacecraft.

The US ASAT missiles

The concept of ASAT missiles in the USA dates back to 1959 when, under a programme called Bold Orion, the US Air Force began testing ASAT missiles launched from B-47 aircraft. Some four tests were conducted.[1] One of these was successfully conducted on 19 October 1959 against the Explorer 6 satellite (launched on 7 August 1959) as a target.[2] The satellite was not damaged and decayed by July 1961. The spacecraft was launched in a highly elliptical orbit with its argument of perigee at about 53° (on 26 October 1959) and a perigee height of 244 km.[3] The satellite's apogee height was 42 200 km so that the interception must have taken place close to its perigee point. This is interesting since the satellite travels with the maximum velocity at its perigee, thus indicating the level of sophistication that might have been achieved at the time.

Under the US Department of Defense (DoD) programme called SPIN (space intercept), all the three services began independently the development of ASAT weapons.[4] The US Air Force, in fact, in 1963 demonstrated an ASAT capability against satellites in low orbits. A Thor booster was launched from Johnston Island against a spent US rocket which was orbiting the Earth at the time.[5] These ASAT missiles were based on Johnston and Kwajalein Islands in the Pacific Ocean. Under this Program 437, earlier systems used the Delta and Agena upper stages.[4] Some 16 tests were carried out using the Thor system but the programme was terminated in 1976.

A second project under the US Air Force was called Program 706. This designation replaced an earlier one, SAINT (satellite interceptor), which was to demonstrate a military rendezvous with unknown or unidentified spacecraft in Earth orbit. The initial launching of the SAINT was to have been made in 1962 by an Atlas-Agena B rocket but the project was abandoned before the flight took place.[6] Under Program 706, however, study continued on a possible manned interceptor craft.

A third US Air Force programme was labelled Program 922, under which it is reported that a direct ascent system with terminal homing ASAT weapon was being investigated. A number of alternatives were considered which included a non-nuclear warhead. One such concept was a launch into space of a warhead containing pellets loaded with chemical explosives which would destroy a satellite in orbit.[4] This was a concept similar to that being investigated by the US Navy.

Under the US Navy ASAT programme called Early Spring, a submarine-launched missile was to have been developed. Such a missile would hover up to some 90 seconds in space waiting for its target to arrive.[4] In another concept, called Skipper, a batch of steel pellets would have been launched by a rocket in the path of a satellite. Under yet another programme called Hi-Ho actual testing of ASAT weapons was carried out. For example, in 1962 the Navy conducted two ASAT missile tests. As in the case of the US Air Force Bold Orion programme, the ASAT missiles were launched from an aircraft, this time from F-14 fighter planes.[1] It is interesting to note that both these tests involved the use of the Altair rocket as a second stage, just as it is used in the new US F-15 launched ASAT missiles.

The US Army was also involved in the development of ASAT weapons in the early 1960s. Under Program 505, Zeus and Nike X missiles were based on the Kwajalein Islands in the Pacific Ocean.[4] These missiles were originally developed as part of the anti-ballistic missile (ABM) system. This system was operational between 1964 and 1968.

By the mid-1970s most of these programmes were cancelled. However, the effort in ASAT weaponry was not lost altogether because some of the earlier ideas have found their way into the current US Air Force programme in which a direct-ascent system is being developed. This system is based almost entirely on well known, well proven and readily available technology. The system consists of a booster with a short-range attack missile (SRAM, AGM-69, first deployed in 1972) as the first stage and a Thiokol Altair rocket as the second stage. A miniature homing vehicle (MHV) with its infra-red heat-seeking homing guidance sensor is mounted on the Altair. A re-entry vehicle from a Minuteman I intercontinental ballistic missile was successfully intercepted by a non-nuclear interceptor on 10 June 1984. This non-nuclear interceptor employed a long-wavelength infra-red sensor for guiding itself to the re-entry vehicle similar to that envisaged for the MHV. The entire ASAT weapon is about 5.5 m long and about 0.5 m in diameter and is mounted under the F-15 fighter aircraft. The MHV warhead, weighing about 1 200 kg, would, with its rocket, be launched from an altitude of 10–15 km. The F-15 has a horizontal range of about 2 500 km which can be increased to 7 500 km if the aircraft is fuelled in the air. The SRAM has a range of 60–160 km. The Thiokol two-stage rocket has a range of up to about 300 km. Thus presumably the system can have a range of up to 475 km. It can be seen from table 1 that the USA could therefore reach Soviet photographic, ocean surveillance and possibly communications satellites with its ASAT weapon.

On 21 January 1984 such a system was tested, but without the warhead or a target. Some 12 tests are planned.[7] The first test carried a simulated MHV but no target was orbited. The US Air Force could not test the weapon against a target since, according to Senator Tsongas' amendment to the FY-1984 Defense Authorization Act, the President is required, before an MHV test against a space object, to certify that the US is endeavouring to negotiate in good faith a verifiable comprehensive ASAT treaty with the Soviet Union. Second, the Congress required a report on the President's arms control policy for ASAT weapons by 31 March 1984, before the Pentagon could spend funds allocated for such weapons.

On 31 March 1984, a report on the US Policy on ASAT Arms Control was presented to the US Congress. During his testimony to the House Foreign Affairs Panel, Kenneth Adelman (Director of the US Arms Control and Disarmament Agency) said that this report indicates that "we are endeavouring to respond to the thrust of the Tsongas Amendment by concentrating, in the ongoing studies, on the more limited arrangement—that would ban or otherwise limit specific weapon systems, types of activities or threats". In June 1984, the Senate voted to continue testing the US ASAT weapon provided the Administration began negotiations with the USSR on an ASAT treaty.

There are some 12 tests of the US F-15 ASAT weapon planned for and, after the initial evaluation flights of the missile, the MHV will be tested against a target satellite called "Tomato Can".[8] Moreover, there are indications that work has already begun on the next generation of ASAT missiles for destroying satellites in higher orbits.

By 1987 some 28 F-15s are expected to be ready for use with two MHVs deployed on each aircraft. A total of two squadrons is expected to be fitted for ASAT missions by 1989. The F-15s need short runways so that virtually any airport could be used to launch the ASAT weapon. Thus, since the system is not confined to any specific launch pad on Earth, the MHV can be used as a direct-ascent system against satellites in any orbital inclination.

Soviet ASAT satellites

Soviet ASAT weapon research may have begun as early as 1963 but rigorous testing with targets and interceptors began in 1968 (see table 2). Until 1970 both the targets and the interceptors were launched from Tyuratam, but since 1971 all the targets have been launched from Plesetsk and the interceptors from Tyuratam. In most cases the interceptions have been made at altitudes between some 200 km and 2 000 km.

The targets have been intercepted in three ways. In one, the interceptor, usually launched at an orbital inclination of 62°, makes several orbital manoeuvres to achieve an eccentric orbit. The interceptor then passes at considerable speed close to the target, near the perigee of the former's orbit. Soon after the pass is made, the interceptor is exploded, presumably to test the kill mechanism for the destruction of the target.

In a second method, the interceptor makes a slower approach to the target. Both the interceptor and the target are usually launched at an orbital inclination of 65° and in the same orbital plane. In the third method, the interceptor climbs close to the target, intercepts it and then is commanded back to the Earth before it has completed a full orbit. The interceptor enters the Earth's atmosphere and disintegrates. In all the tests conducted so far, no target has apparently been destroyed. The terminal guidance may consist of a radar or an infra-red sensor. It appears that since 1976 some six tests have been carried out using the infra-red guidance system but all of these have failed.[9] If the interceptor gets to within one kilometre of its target, then the test is considered to be a successful one. However, the estimates of the success rate vary between about 45 per cent[10] and 65 per cent (see paper 5, page 85).

In most of these tests, the interceptions have been made at altitudes between some 200 and 1 000 km (see table 2). Thus, from table 1 it can be seen that the US photographic, electronic and ocean reconnaissance and the geodetic and some communications satellites could be vulnerable to the Soviet ASAT system. However, the Soviet Union has not tested its ASAT satellites at an orbital inclination of 77°, an orbit used by all the US photographic and electronic reconnaissance satellites.

It can be seen that both the US and Soviet ASAT systems have a limited range. Moreover, they tend to be relatively slow, particularly the Soviet ASAT satellites. In view of this, two other ASAT systems are being considered in order to increase the range and the efficiency with which the destructive energy could be delivered to the target. In one an MHV would be launched by larger launchers from submarines. In this way the advantage of a moving launch

Table 2. The Soviet interceptor-destructor tests: 1968–82[a]

Test number	Target satellite				Interceptor satellite			
	Cosmos number	Launch date	Orbital inclination (deg)	Perigee/apogee height (km)	Cosmos number	Launch date	Orbital inclination (deg)	Perigee/apogee height (km)
1	248	19 Oct 68	62	475/543	249[b]	20 Oct 68	62	493/2157
2					252[b]	1 Nov 68	62	521/2149
3	373	20 Oct 70	63	472/544	374[b]	23 Oct 70	63	521/2141
4					375[b]	30 Oct 70	63	528/2098
5	394	9 Feb 71	66	527/614	397[b]	25 Feb 71	66	574/2202
6	400	18 Mar 71	66	983/1006	404[c]	4 Apr 71	66	802/1010
7	459	29 Nov 71	66	224/260	462[b]	3 Dec 71	66	230/1800
8	803	12 Feb 76	66	554/618	804[d]	16 Feb 76	66	556/615
9					814[d]	13 Apr 76	65	118/480
10	839	9 Jul 76	66	984/2098	843[e]	21 Jul 76	65	132/346
11	880	9 Dec 76	66	560/617	886[b]	27 Dec 76	66	590/2296
12	909	19 May 77	66	990/2109	910[e]	23 May 77	66	300/1774
13					918[c]	17 Jun 77	65	128/243
14	959	21 Oct 77	66	145/850	961[c]	26 Oct 77	66	125/302
15	967	13 Dec 77	66	973/1013	970[b]	21 Dec 77	65	144/854
16					1009[c]	19 May 78	66	996/1364
17	1171	3 Apr 80	66	947/1033	1174[e]	18 Apr 80	66	362/1025
18	1241	21 Jan 81	66	977/1011	1243[c]	2 Feb 81	66	297/1017
19					1258[c]	14 Mar 81	66	303/1026
20	1375	6 Jun 82	66	981/1011	1379[c]	18 Jun 82	65	144/546

[a] Other Cosmos possibly related to the interceptor-destructor programme are numbers 185, 217, 291, 516, 520, 521, 752, 816, 844, 885, 891, 933, 1075, 1146, 1169.
[b] Exploded.
[c] Entered the atmosphere.
[d] Probably recovered.
[e] Probably failed.

Sources: 'Summary log of space launches 1957–81', *TRW Space Log*, Vol. 19, 1982, pp. 27–115.
Jasani, B. (ed.), *Outer Space–A New Dimension of the Arms Race* (Taylor & Francis, London, 1982), pp. 364–365 [a SIPRI book].
SIPRI, *Outer Space–Battlefield of the Future*, edited by B. Jasani (Taylor & Francis, London, 1978), pp. 181–182.
SIPRI, *World Armaments and Disarmament, SIPRI Yearbook 1982* (Taylor & Francis, London, 1982), p. 312.
SIPRI, *World Armaments and Disarmament, SIPRI Yearbook 1983* (Taylor & Francis, London, 1983), p. 453.

platform would be retained and the range of the weapon would be increased to reach geostationary orbit (36 000 km). In the other system, high-energy beam weapons are thought to be useful as ASAT systems, particularly those which use high-energy lasers. These are considered below.

II. High-energy laser weapons

Laser weapons are thought to be attractive not only because they can deliver destructive energy at the speed of light, but also because they have a high fire-

15

power potential per weapon. They could be switched rapidly from one target to another. Not much information is available from the USSR on these directed-energy weapons. However, evidence reported in the West suggests that they are also investigating the potential uses of directed-energy weapons.

In the USA a number of potential devices are being investigated for weapon applications by the Air Force, the Navy and the Defense Advanced Research Project Agency (DARPA). The US Air Force has carried out a number of tests using its airborne laser laboratory (ALL) equipped with a 400 kW carbon dioxide gas dynamic laser.[11] The laser radiation wavelength is 10.6 μm. In such a laser, the rapid expansion of the lasing gas provides the inverted distribution of excited molecular energy states necessary for laser beam emission.

A laser beam can damage the target essentially in two ways. For energies between 10^6 and 10^4 W/cm^2 the incident continuous laser beam melts or evaporates the solid surface. At higher energies (considerably greater than 10^9 W/cm^2) and with shorter pulse lengths, not only does the target surface vaporize but it is also ionized, producing a high density plasma which continues to absorb the incident laser radiation. The very rapid temperature increase at the surface causes the laser-produced plasma to blow off or ablate towards the laser beam. This, in turn, drives an intense hydrodynamic shockwave into the target skin, probably rupturing it.

In order to keep the beam divergence and the size of the optics to a minimum, short-wavelength lasers are preferable. Also, since beam target coupling strongly increases with decreasing wavelength, the need for short-wavelength lasers is further emphasized.

The DARPA, under its Triad programme, is investigating the use of a ground-based chemical laser device to demonstrate the feasibility of a laser suitable for deployment in outer space. In a chemical laser the inverted distribution of excited molecular energy states is obtained by means of chemical reactions. The most commonly used chemical reaction is between hydrogen and fluorine emitting radiation at a relatively short wavelength of 2.7 μm or deuterium and fluorine radiating at 3.8 μm. The Triad programme consists of three elements, code-named *Alpha*, under which the feasibility of generating infra-red chemical high-energy lasers is being investigated; *LODE* (large optical demonstration experiment), under which a large mirror 4 m in diameter is being developed to steer and control the laser beam; and the space-borne *Talon Gold*, under which the target acquisition tracking and precision-pointing techniques are being investigated.[12]

The energy of the laser being investigated under Alpha is classified information. Even if the laser is of the order of 5 MW, it can be seen from figure 2 that there is a considerable range over which the weapon could be useful. For example, at 500 km a 5 MW laser would damage the satellite's skin in one second. However, chemical lasers have a maximum chemical to laser energy efficiency of about 250 kJ kg fuel, so about 20 kg of chemical fuel would be needed assuming conversion efficiency of 25 per cent. For a useful weapon, the range needs to be considerably greater than 100 km, so the large amount of

Figure 2. Laser energy required to damage a satellite at various ranges for lasers of different wavelengths

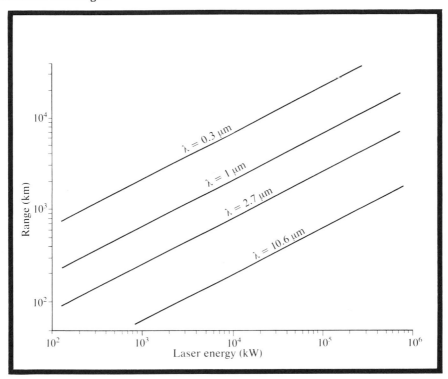

fuel needed must be transported to orbital laser platforms. For details on the theoretical basis of the calculation see paper 6 (page 93).

Four more advanced laser concepts are also being investigated. These are the excited dimer and excimer laser, the free-electron laser, the gamma-ray laser or 'graser' and the X-ray laser. In the excimer laser (emitting radiation of 0.3 μm) electrons are used to bombard noble gases such as xenon or krypton so that the electrons in their shells are removed. The resulting ions, in their excited state, react chemically to form xenon fluoride or krypton fluoride. They constitute the inverted population for lasing. It can be seen from figure 2 that even at a laser energy of 200 kW considerable range can be obtained—of the order of 1 000 km. However, excimer lasers today suffer from low overall efficiencies (1–3 per cent) requiring multi-megawatt input power for weapon application. Moreover, there are problems of severe corrosion and maintaining the purity of the lasing material which make such lasers unsuitable as space-based ASAT weapons.

A relatively new and, in principle, different and tunable laser type is the free-electron laser (FEL). When electrons are accelerated, they radiate. Thus, if a beam of electrons is injected through a magnetic field of suitably changing direction, the electrons can be made to emit coherent radiation. For short-wavelength radiation, the electrons must be highly relativistic. In principle, a wide range of frequencies may be available together with tunability. Such a device could reach a high efficiency but needs a particle accelerator as an electron beam source.

Other potential devices which have entered the high-energy laser weapon debate are the graser and X-ray laser. These have been the subject of theoretical analyses both in the USA and USSR for more than a decade.[13]

In contrast to optical lasers, which derive their beam energy from the stimulated release of energy stored in excited atoms or molecules, the radiative energy emitted by a graser or X-ray laser originates from excited states in the shell structure of the nuclei of atoms such as excited states in the high-energy K and L shells of atoms. The pumping of X-ray lasers requires very intense radiation like that emitted from a nuclear explosion.[14]

An X-ray laser can in principle be pumped by a high intensity flash of X-rays from a conventional X-ray source. However, these are generally not intense enough to achieve the required gain, except for the possibility of optical resonances existing in the nuclei of some isotopes.[15]

X-rays can neither be reflected by mirrors nor refracted in prisms. The normal laser technique to increase the chance of stimulated emission of radiation from the already inverted population of energy states in the lasing material by repeated reflections between mirrors therefore cannot be used in X-ray lasers. Moreover, the X-ray laser radiation cannot be focused using mirrors and lenses as is done in other types of laser. In addition, the lifetime of a high-energy excited state is very short compared with normal excited atomic states. All these factors necessitate the use of copious radiation from a nuclear explosion as the pumping source of the X-ray laser. This means that such an X-ray laser (with wavelengths of 10^{-3}–10^{-4} μm) operates as a single laser pulse device. Its beam properties, particularly the beam divergence, are therefore determined by the geometry of the lasing medium, normally taken to be long rods pumped by the nuclear explosion. It was reported in 1981 that the Lawrence Livermore Laboratory had tested the concept of the X-ray pumped laser during an underground nuclear explosion.[16] The device apparently produced an X-ray laser pulse of 1.4 μm wavelength and several hundred terawatts power (this would correspond to a few hundred joules for a pulse of picosecond duration). A second test of this, the so-called Excalibur (X-ray laser), was also reported and more are planned.[17]

There would be a number of problems even if X-ray lasers were made to work. For example, if they were deployed in geostationary orbit the radiation generated from the nuclear explosive may well damage other friendly satellites in that orbit. Such a weapon at lower altitudes may also affect other satellites by its electromagnetic pulse, which may be extensive enough to affect objects on the Earth's surface. Above all, there are considerable implications for various arms control treaties, which are considered later.

There are three concepts which are worth mentioning here. The idea of a laser powered directly by nuclear energy in the so-called nuclear-pumped lasers was proposed soon after the discovery of lasers. The walls of a chamber containing a lasing gas are either (*a*) coated with ^{10}B or ^{235}U compounds; or (*b*) ^{3}He or gaseous ^{235}UF$_6$ is mixed with the lasing gas. The thermal neutrons from a reactor are then allowed to interact with the gas in the chamber to produce nuclear fission products. When a high-energy fission fragment is absorbed by the lasing gas it loses its energy by inelastic collisions causing ionization and excitation of the lasing medium. The population inversion in a lasing medium by nuclear pumping is thought to occur in several ways, but at present the knowledge is limited. However, using ^{3}He/Ar gas, a laser power output of 1 kW has been achieved at a wavelength of 1.79 μm. This power output has been doubled in the Soviet Union using ^{4}He/Xe mixture. The laser wavelengths in this case have been 2.63 and 2.48 μm.[18]

The second concept, electromagnetic (EM) guns, is not a directed-energy weapon but it could be regarded as a hybrid between conventional weapons and more futuristic directed-energy weapons. This is partly because an EM gun requires the same intense bursts of electric energy as those needed for many types of directed-energy weapon. An EM gun simply accelerates a projectile by using electromagnetic forces rather than those produced by the expanding gases from chemical reaction.[19] The main advantage would be considerably higher projectile velocities. Thus an EM gun would be an important intermediate step towards the possible realization of directed-energy weapons.

The third concept, the electromagnetic pulse weapon, is based on the possibility of producing a directed EMP effect. Only a few nuclear weapons exploded high above the atmosphere could devastate the opponent's satellites and disrupt or even destroy electronic components of communications networks and computers. The EMP from a nuclear explosion 400 km above the Earth, for example, would affect an area as large as the European continent. However, because an EMP weapon with directional property has not yet been devised, it would also destroy the attacker's satellites. This problem might be overcome in the future. For example, production of an EMP effect has been studied using highly relativistic beams of electrons.[20] These have been examined for their applications in laboratories to study the effects of EMP on various components and electronic systems. Using an electron beam with energy of 400 MeV, a current of 250 kA and a pulse with 2 ns rise time, EMP effects have been simulated.

Apart from the high-energy laser beams and EMP weapons, microwave radiation has also been thought to be useful as a weapon. If a burst of radio-frequency or microwave radiation were to be produced using a very high peak-power microwave generator, then such an energy could be directed by an antenna system.[21] This type of radiation could disrupt or even destroy, for example, electronic components of communications networks and computers. Relatively little is known at present about this technology.

Many of the ASAT weapons discussed above share the technology with some of the space-based defensive weapons. These are briefly examined in the next chapter.

References

1. Pike, J., 'Anti-satellite weapons', *Journal of the Federation of American Scientists, FAS Public Interest Report*, Vol. 36, No. 9, November 1983.
2. Stares, P.B., 'Déjà vu: the ASAT debate in historical context', *Arms Control Today*, Vol. 13, No. 11, December 1983
3. King-Hele, D.G., Hiller, H. and Pilkington, J.A., 'Revised table of Earth satellites, volume 1: 1957 to 1968', *Royal Aircraft Establishment, Technical Report 78012*, January 1978, p. 3.
4. "SPIN", *DMS Market Intelligence Report*, January and August 1968.
5. 'Anti-satellite effort decision awaited', *Aviation Week and Space Technology*, Vol. 104, No. 4, 24 January 1977, p. 19.
6. Sheldon, C.S., 'United States and Soviet progress in space. Summary data through 1976 and a forward look', *Congressional Research Service*, Library of Congress, Report No. QB.1C.Gen, 76-32 SP, 2 February 1976.
   McGuire, V., 'AF hoping for cheap SAINT', *Missiles and Rockets*, Vol. 7, No. 20, 14 November 1960, pp. 38–40.
7. 'USAF flight tests asat weapon', *Aviation Week and Space Technology*, Vol. 120, No. 5, 30 January 1984, p. 19.
   'Telemetry data shows US anti-satellite "performed well"', *Defense Electronics*, Vol. 16, No. 2, February 1984, p. 30.
8. 'Controlling space weapons', *Hearings before the Committee on Foreign Relations, United States Senate*, 98th Congress, First Session, 14 April and 18 May 1983, p. 55.
9. 'US DoD developing second-generation ASAT missile', *Interavia Air Letter*, No. 10458, 6 March 1984, p. 4.
10. 'The Soviet ASAT test record', *Defense Daily*, Vol. 134, No. 36, 21 June 1984, pp. 286–287.
11. 'USAF tests high-energy laser weapon', *Flight International*, Vol. 119, No. 3744, 7 February 1981, p. 334.
    'Laser fails to destroy missile', *Aviation Week and Space Technology*, Vol. 114, No. 23, 8 June 1981, p. 63.
    'Second laser laboratory test', *Interavia Air Letter*, No. 9778, 26 June 1981, p. 8.
    'Airborne laser lab downs missiles', *Laser Focus/Electro-Optics*, Vol. 19, No. 9, September 1983, p. 82.
12. 'DoD's space-based laser program—potential progress and problems', *General Accounting Office, Report No. C-MASAD-82-10*, 26 February 1982.
13. Douglas, J. M., 'Russian progress on the nuclear laser', *Science News*, Vol. 105, 5 February 1974, pp. 8–9.
    Baldwin, G. C. and Khokhlov, R. V., 'Prospects for a gamma-ray laser', *Physics Today*, February 1975, pp. 32–39.
    Baldwin, G. C. and Sotem, J. C., 'Approaches to the development of gamma-ray lasers', *Review of Modern Physics*, Vol. 53, No. 4, Part 1, October 1981, pp. 687–744.
14. Winterberg, F., 'Nuclear and thermonuclear directed beam weapons', *Fusion*, August 1981, pp. 52–54.
15. 'New hope for gamma-ray lasers', *Laser Focus*, Vol. 18, No. 10, October 1982, pp. 14–15.
    Chapline, G. and Wood, L., 'X-ray lasers', *Physics Today*, June 1975, pp. 40–48.

Bunkin, F. V., Derzhiev, V. I. and Yakovlenko, S. I., 'Prospects for light amplification in the far ultraviolet', *Soviet Journal of Quantum Electron*, Vol. 11, No. 8, August 1981, pp. 981–997.

16. Robinson, C. A., Jr, 'Advances made on high-energy laser', *Aviation Week & Space Technology*, Vol. 114, No. 8, 23 February 1981, pp. 25–27.

Hecht, J., 'The X-ray laser flap', *Laser Focus*, Vol. 17, No. 5, May 1981, p. 8.

17. 'Laser Wars', *The Economist, Foreign Report No. 1812*, 23 February 1984, pp. 1–2.

18. Jalujka, N. W., 'Direct nuclear-pumped lasers', *NASA Technical Paper 2091*, 1983.

19. Garwin, R. and Pike, J., 'Space weapons', *Bulletin of the Atomic Scientists*, Vol. 40, No. 5, May 1984, pp. 2S–11S.

20. Tumolillo, T. A., Wandra, J. P., Hobbs, W. E. and Smith, K., 'The radiated electromagnetic field from collimated gamma-rays and electron beams in air', *IEEE Transactions on Nuclear Science*, Vol. NS-27, No. 6, December 1980, pp. 1851–1856.

Hobbs, W. E. and Smith K. S., 'Source-region electromagnetic pulse associated with high-energy electron beams', Paper prepared for *1981 Annual Conference on Nuclear and Space Radiation Effects*, Seattle, Washington, 21–24 July 1981.

21. 'Soviet study potential of electromagnetic pulse weapon', *Aerospace Daily*, Vol. 100, 28 November 1979, p. 129.

Chapter 4. Space-based defensive weapons

On 23 March 1983, President Reagan called on US scientists and engineers to find "the means of rendering nuclear weapons impotent and obsolete".[1] This has added a new dimension to the ASAT weapon arms race because some ASAT weapons are envisaged not only for space warfare but also for ballistic missile defence (BMD) systems based in outer space. This dual ASAT role is not a new one. The early US ground-based ASAT system using the US Army's Nike-Zeus missiles, for example, was a slightly modified version of an anti-ballistic missile (ABM) system. Even the present US non-nuclear kill (NNK) ASAT interceptor was originally conceived in the 1960s as an ABM warhead.[2]

I. Ballistic missile defence

The essential elements of any BMD system are target-detection, -recognition, -tracking and -destruction systems. At present these tasks are being performed by ground-based radar sensors and by target interceptors armed with nuclear warheads. However, considerable efforts have been devoted to R & D on new concepts of a BMD system (see paper 7, page 107). While much can be learnt from open literature about US thinking on BMD, an equal amount of information is not available from the Soviet Union. However, there are conventional BMD systems around Moscow and some of their efforts in the field of high-energy lasers could be for BMD applications. It has been suggested that the Soviet Union may be developing a rapidly deployable BMD system which would consist of a phased-array radar, a missile-tracking radar and an interceptor with high-altitude intercept capability.[3]

Land-based BMD

There have been two basic concepts underlying the ABM systems—area defence and point defence. The former involves the defence of large areas and is, usually, associated with protecting cities; point defence involves defending a specific geographic point such as a complex of missile silos.

During the late 1960s and early 1970s the USA had an ABM system deployed but has no such system deployed at present. In September 1967, President Johnson authorized the deployment of the Sentinel ABM area-defence system. The Nike-Zeus missile, with a five-megaton thermonuclear warhead, was to be the basis of this system. The interception would occur above the Earth's atmosphere.

Continued controversy over the ABM issues prompted President Nixon to propose a new plan based on the point-defence concept under a programme renamed Safeguard. Safeguard was to be deployed to protect only some of the intercontinental ballistic missile silos against, for example, a limited attack from the People's Republic of China or an accidental firing of Soviet missiles. Safeguard was approved in August 1969 involving the Spartan (an enlarged and improved Nike-Zeus) and Sprint missiles. The latter was designed as a terminal defence missile with very high acceleration to intercept and destroy incoming re-entry vehicles during the last seconds of their flight. Spartan employed a thermonuclear warhead with a yield of about one megaton and Sprint employed a warhead with a yield of one kiloton.[4]

Two different radar systems were developed for the Safeguard system. A so-called perimeter acquisition radar (PAR) was a large phased-array radar capable of detecting incoming re-entry vehicles at 3 300 km with its 35 m diameter antenna. Once the PAR detected the incoming re-entry vehicles, and tracked them, the data were analysed by computers and passed on to the second radar called the missile site radar (MSR). The MSR controlled the interception by the Spartan missile and the launch of and interception by the Sprint to destroy those warheads which escaped the Spartan.

By October 1975, Safeguard became operational with 28 Sprint and 8 Spartan missiles deployed at Grand Forks, North Dakota. However, shortly after this Safeguard was de-commissioned, although the PAR was retained. This radar is operated by the Air Force and used as an early warning system to detect an attack from submarine-launched missiles.

Since 1975 research and development funding has continued under two BMD programmes known as the Advanced Technology Program (ATP) and the Systems Technology Program (STP).[5] Funding for these R&D programmes prior to fiscal year 1981 was nearly $2.5 billion while for fiscal years 1982, 1983 and 1984 it was just over $460 million, $519 million and $660 million respectively. For fiscal year 1985 $1 288 million was requested, indicating that there is now an active interest in such BMD development.[6]

Under the ATP, advanced radars and optical sensors are being investigated. Radar development includes the investigation of shorter wavelength (millimetre-range) radars to increase resistance to blackouts resulting from nuclear explosions. Such radars may also increase the resolution and accuracy of measurements of the range, angle and speed of targets.

Passive optical sensors using long-range infra-red signals to detect and discriminate large numbers of objects in space are being investigated under the Designating Optical Tracker (DOT) programme. Such a device would be launched by a sounding rocket and would be operated when above the atmosphere. A DOT device has been tested on four occasions: in December 1978, February and September 1980, and June 1981.

Another development underway within the ATP is the so-called Forward

Acquisition Sensor (FAS). The purpose of FAS is to demonstrate the use of a long-range missile-borne target acquisition sensor which might be used in a BMD system and in an early warning system.

The STP is concerned with the integration of systems developed under the ATP and other programmes into a workable BMD system. At present, under the STP two BMD concepts are being considered, Low Altitude Defense (LoAD, designed for defence—below 9 km—of missiles in fixed silos or deployed in a deceptive mode), and Overlay Defense. The use of these two concepts either on their own or combined in a layered defence is being considered.

At the lowest level the layered defence envisages low-altitude defence at heights of up to 9 km and terminal defence at an altitude of between 9 km and 115 km using radar sensors, data processors and interceptor technology being developed under the LoAD programme. The mid-course defence ranges between altitudes of about 45 km and 90 km and the exo-atmospheric defence above about 90 km. At high altitudes the defence would consist of long-range interceptors with non-nuclear warheads and optical, terminal-homing guidance systems to intercept incoming warheads above the atmosphere.

Once a warning of an attack had been received either from an early warning satellite or from forward acquisition systems such as ground-based early warning radars, a sounding rocket would be launched. Optical sensors aboard such a rocket would locate and track the warheads and transmit their trajectory data to interceptors.

Under the layered defence programme, the Homing Overlay Experiment (HOE) has been designed to investigate the non-nuclear kill (NNK) system and optical guidance. One of the aims of HOE is to demonstrate the intercept capability of a single NNK warhead using a long-wavelength infra-red terminal guidance system. A Minuteman I ICBM is launched, followed by an infra-red telescope to detect and track the target, and then the NNK interceptor to kill the target. It is planned that the infra-red telescope and its onboard data processor will eventually replace large ground-based radars and computers for acquisition, assessment, tracking and discrimination of the target.

In another system, the NNK interceptor, instead of destroying the target by collision, ejects metal pellets in a controlled sequence so as to place them in concentric circles in the path of the incoming target warheads. These pellets would then destroy them on impact.[7]

Some four tests were planned for under the HOE programme.[5] Two of these were completed on 7 February and 28 May 1983.[8] In both these tests, the missiles failed to intercept their targets. On 10 June 1984, the last of the four HOE tests was conducted. A Minuteman I ICBM, launched from Vandenberg Air Force Base, released its dummy warhead above the atmosphere. Twenty minutes later an interceptor missile carrying its NNK warhead was launched from Mech Island, the Kwajalein missile test range.[9] Above the atmosphere the missile released the NNK warhead. Its long-wave infra-red sensor and guidance computer locked onto the Minuteman dummy re-entry vehicle. At about 160 km above the Earth's surface the NNK deployed a 4.5 m metal umbrella-shaped device studded with weights, hit the re-entry vehicle and destroyed it. It is interesting to note that, even with the ABM Treaty of 1972, such activities are possible.

Moreover, even as early as the late 1960s and early 1970s the concept of layered defence was evident in the US thinking on ABM systems. A further dimension seems to have been added now to the concept of the layered defence as suggested by President Reagan's 23 March 1983 speech.

The BMD concepts described above do not include methods of early-trajectory or boost-phase interceptions of offensive missiles. High-energy laser devices or other directed-energy weapons are thought to be particularly applicable as BMD non-nuclear interceptors of ICBMs during their boost phase.[10]

Space-based BMD

There are three concepts of a space-based BMD system. The first is that in which high-energy lasers are orbited. These are very similar to the high-energy laser weapons discussed in chapter 3.

The second concept in this scheme is that proposed by the High Frontier Group. In this concept, 432 satellites, each armed with 40–45 missile interceptors, would be placed permanently in orbit round the Earth.[11] The interceptors, each capable of obtaining a velocity of about 1 km/s relative to the carrier satellite, would be guided by infra-red sensors to home in on enemy missile boosters and destroy them by colliding against them at high speed. Owing to the vulnerability of the above space-based systems, a third concept has been put forward.

The third BMD concept which is partly space-based is that supported by US presidential science adviser George A. Kayworth. This system would consist of several hundred lasers each operating at or near the visible light spectrum. The lasers would be dispersed throughout the US land mass and would be fired at large Earth-orbiting mirrors launched in great numbers on warning of an attack by enemy missiles. The laser light would be reflected off and refocused by these mirrors onto targets. While this scheme is only at a conceptual stage, it is difficult to see how problems such as launching and placing the mirrors in their correct orbital positions could be solved in time for enemy missiles to be intercepted by the reflected laser beam. The trajectory of an ICBM can be divided into three parts : the boost phase, during which time the ICBM is most vulnerable since it is easily detectable by observations of the exhaust flame from the booster and the missile structure is under considerable mechanical strain; the mid-course phase, during which the missile releases its warhead or warheads; and the re-entry phase, during which the warheads enter the atmosphere. The time taken by the ICBM during the boost phase above the atmosphere is less than 300 seconds. It is only during this short time that the beam could reliably intercept the ICBM.

Another method which could be classified under the third BMD concept is known as the 'pop-up' system. Anti-missile rockets would be kept ready for immediate launching carrying either conventional or nuclear explosives or X-ray laser devices. The latter would have to be a nuclear explosive laser since the pop-up rocket has to be launched with high acceleration, which could be achieved if a relatively light payload is used. For boost-phase interception such a pop-up system would suffer from the same objection as mentioned above (i.e., the time factor). Moreover, owing to the shortage of time, many of the important decisions may be left to computers thus adding yet another problem, namely that of accidents. The interception of the warheads could be made once they are released after the boost phase but a laser may be ineffective against hardened warheads.

It is important to realize that together with the NNK type of BMD system, a high-energy laser could also be used as an ASAT weapon. The significance of these developments is discussed in the next chapter.

References

1. 'Text of Reagan address on defense policy', *Congressional Quarterly Weekly Reports*, Vol. 41, No. 12, 26 March 1983, pp. 629–633.
2. 'Anti-satellite missile flight test near', *Defense Electronics*, Vol. 12, No. 12, December 1980, pp. 22–24.
   Pike, J., 'Anti-satellite weapons', *Journal of the Federation of American Scientists, FAS Public Interest Report*, Vol. 36, No. 9, November 1983, p. 4.
3. 'The ballistic missile defence research and development programme, Statement by S. C. Mayer', *Department of Defense Authorization for Appropriation for Fiscal Year 1981, Hearings before the Committee on Armed Services*, Part I, US Senate, January–February 1979 (US Government Printing Office, Washington, D.C., 1979), pp. 309–315.
4. Rathjens, G. W., 'The dynamics of the arms race', *Scientific American*, Vol. 220, No. 4, April 1969, pp. 15–25.
5. 'Ballistic missile defense', *Fiscal Year 1983 Arms Control Impact Statements*, March 1982 (US Government Printing Office, Washington, D.C., 1982), pp. 128–145.
6. 'Strategic defense 5-year budget', *Defense Daily*, Vol. 132, No. 23, 3 February 1984, p. 192.
7. Barasch, G. E., Cooper, N. and Pollock, R., 'Ballistic missile defense—a quick-look assessment', *Los Alamos Scientific Laboratory Report* No. LA-UR-80-1578, 1980.
   Aldridge, R. C., *First Strike! The Pentagon's Strategy for Nuclear War* (Southend Press, Boston, MA, 1983), p. 201.
8. 'Ballistic missile interception test', *Interavia Air Letter*, No. 10 197, 21 February 1983, p. 1.
   'HOE fails to intercept target in second test', *Defense Daily*, Vol. 128, No. 23, 2 June 1983, p. 179.
   'Intercepteur HOE', *Air et Cosmos*, No. 961, 2 July 1983, p. 38.
   'Second HOE test fails', *Interavia Air Letter*, No. 10 268, 3 June 1983, p. 4.
9. 'HOE experiment—further details', *Interavia Air Letter*, No. 10 523, 13 June 1984, p. 1.

10. Barasch, G. E., Kerr, D. M., Kupperman, R. H., Pollock, R. and Smith H. A., 'Ballistic missile defense: a potential arms-control initiative', *Los Alamos Report*, No. LA-8632 UC-2, January 1982.
11. Graham, D. O., *High Frontier—A New National Strategy* (High Frontier, Washington, DC, 1982), pp. 119–128.

Chapter 5. The arms control dilemma

I. Introduction

So far we have covered two aspects of the militarization of outer space. First, the military encroachment on outer space has led to a situation where military satellites of the two major powers are becoming vital parts of the world-wide nuclear and conventional weapon systems. As advances are made in military space technology, improvements in the efficiency of weapons occur. This in turn may refine war-fighting tactics as well as give rise to new ones (see papers 1, page 43, and 2, page 57). Over the past two decades or so, nuclear war-fighting tactics have undergone a change from the doctrine of mutual assured destruction (MAD) to doctrines of limited strategic options, flexible response and counterforce doctrines.

In view of the potential role of satellites in waging wars on Earth, it is not surprising that they have become important military targets. Thus began the second phase of the militarization of outer space: the development and even in some cases the deployment of anti-satellite (ASAT) weapons.

A dilemma then is, should there be an ASAT arms control treaty which would protect satellites that contribute to the arms race on Earth? (See papers 3, page 71 and 4, page 77). In any case, several arms control treaties contain pledges not to interfere with the national technical means of verification. This means that effectively reconnaissance satellites are protected by these treaties. In the following sections an attempt is made, therefore, to identify what legal measures exist and their relevance to outer space. The reasons why an ASAT treaty is necessary are also considered.

II. Existing legal measures

The existing legal regime of outer space consists of the 1967 Outer Space Treaty, a handful of other agreements and a number of arms control treaties with provisions which are related to activities in outer space (see table 3 and papers 11, page 157 and 12, page 173).

The 1967 Outer Space Treaty deals very inadequately with the problem of the militarization of outer space. The only limitation placed on military

Table 3. Treaties that contain provisions relevant to outer space with the appropriate articles

Treaty	Date of entry into force	Nature of treaty	Relevant provisions
Treaty banning nuclear weapon tests in the atmosphere, in outer space and under water (PTBT)	10 Oct 1963	Multilateral	*Article I.* Each of the Parties to this Treaty undertakes to prohibit, to prevent, and not to carry out any nuclear weapon test explosion, or any other nuclear explosion, at any place under its jurisdiction or control: (*a*) in the atmosphere; beyond its limits, including outer space; or under water, including territorial water or high seas;
Treaty on principles governing the activities of states in the exploration and use of outer space, including the Moon and other celestial bodies (Outer Space Treaty)	10 Oct 1967	Multilateral	*Article IV.* States Parties to the treaty undertake not to place in orbit around the Earth any objects carrying nuclear weapons or any other kinds of weapons of mass destruction, install such weapons on celestial bodies, or station such weapons in outer space in any other manner.
Treaty between the USA and the USSR on the limitation of anti-ballistic missile systems (ABM Treaty)[a]	3 Oct 1972	Bilateral	*Article II.1.* For the purposes of the Treaty an ABM system is a system to counter strategic ballistic missiles or their elements in flight trajectory, currently consisting of: (*a*) ABM interceptor missiles, which are interceptor missiles constructed and deployed for an ABM role, or a type tested in an ABM mode; *Article V.1.* Each Party undertakes not to develop, test, or deploy ABM systems or components which are sea-based, air-based, space-based, or mobile land-based.
Agreed interpretations and unilateral statements regarding the ABM Treaty			(*a*) *Initial statements. Paragraph D.* ...the Parties agree that in the event ABM systems based on other physical principles and including components capable of substituting for ABM interceptor missiles, ABM launchers, or ABM radars are created in the future, specific limitations on such systems and their components would be subject to discussion ...
Interim agreement between the USA and the USSR on certain measures with respect to the limitations of strategic offensive arms (SALT I agreement)[b]	3 Oct 1972	Bilateral	*Article V.2.* Each Party undertakes not to interfere with the national technical means of verification ...
International Telecommunication Convention (ITU convention)	25 Oct 1973	Multilateral	*Article 35. 135.1.* All stations, whatever their purpose, must be established and operated in such a manner as not to cause harmful interference to the radio services or communications of other Members or of recognized private operating agencies, or of other duly authorized operating agencies which carry on radio services, and which operate in accordance with the provisions of the Radio Regulations.

Table continued

Table 3. Continued

Treaty	Date of entry into force	Nature of treaty	Relevant provisions
Convention on the prohibition of military or any other hostile use of environmental modification techniques	5 Oct 1978	Multilateral	*Article II.* As used in article I, the term 'environmental modification techniques' refers to any technique for changing—through the deliberate manipulation of natural processes—the dynamics, composition or structure of the earth, including its biota, lithosphere, hydrosphere and atmosphere, or of outer space.
Treaty between the USA and the USSR on the limitation of strategic offensive arms (SALT II treaty)[b]	Signed on 18 Jun 1979 but not in force yet	Bilateral	*Article VII.1.* The limitations provided for in Article III shall not apply to ICBM and SLBM test and training launchers or to space vehicle launchers for exploration and use of outer space. *Article VII.2.(c).* There shall be no conversion of ICBM test and training launchers or of space vehicle launchers into ICBM launchers subject to the limitations provided for in Article III. *Article IX.1.* Each Party undertakes not to develop, test, or deploy: (c) Systems for placing into Earth orbit nuclear weapons or any other kind of weapons of mass destruction, including fractional orbital missiles;
Agreement governing the activities of states on the Moon and other celestial bodies	Adopted by the UN General Assembly on 5 Dec 1979; not in force yet	Multilateral	*Article 3. 2.* Any threat or use of force or any other hostile act or threat of hostile act on the Moon is prohibited. It is likewise prohibited to use the Moon in order to commit any such act or to engage in any such threat in relation to the Earth, the Moon spacecraft, the personnel of spacecraft or man-made space objects. 3. States Parties shall not place in orbit around or other trajectory to or around the Moon objects carrying nuclear weapons or any other kinds of weapons of mass destruction or place or use such weapons on or in the Moon. 4. The establishment of military bases, installations and fortifications, the testing of any type of weapons and the conduct of military manoeuvres on the Moon shall be forbidden.
Soviet proposal for a draft treaty on the prohibition of the stationing of weapons of any kind in outer space (UN Document A/36/192, 22 August 1981)[c]	—	Multilateral	*Article 1.1.* States Parties undertake not to place in orbit around the earth objects carrying weapons of any kind, install such weapons on celestial bodies, or station such weapons in outer space in any other manner, including on reusable manned space vehicles of an existing type or of other types which States Parties may develop in the future. *Article 3.* Each State Party undertakes not to destroy, damage, disturb the normal functioning or change the flight trajectory of space objects of other State Parties, if such objects were placed in orbit in strict accordance with Article 1, paragraph 1 of this treaty.

Soviet proposal for a draft treaty on the prohibition of the use of force in outer space and from space against the Earth[c] (UN Document A/38/194, 20 August 1983)

—

Multilateral

Article 1. It is prohibited to resort to the use or threat of force in outer space and the atmosphere and on the Earth through the utilization, as instruments of destruction, of space objects in orbit around the Earth, on celestial bodies or stationed in space in any other manner.

It is further prohibited to resort to the use or threat of force against space objects in orbit around the Earth, on celestial bodies or stationed in outer space in any other manner.

Article 2. In accordance with the provisions of Article 1, States Parties to this Treaty undertake:

1. Not to test or deploy by placing in orbit around the Earth or stationing on celestial bodies or in any other manner any space-based weapons for the destruction of objects on the Earth, in the atmosphere or in outer space.

2. Not to utilize space objects in orbit around the Earth, on celestial bodies or stationed in outer space in any other manner as means to destroy any targets on the Earth, in the atmosphere or in outer space.

3. Not to destroy, damage, disturb the normal functioning or change the flight trajectory of space objects of other states.

4. Not to test or create new anti-satellite systems and to destroy any anti-satellite systems that they may already have.

5. Not to test or use manned spacecraft for military, including anti-satellite, purposes.

---

[a] Article XII.2 contains a pledge "not to interfere with the national technical means of verification …" so that effectively necessary satellites are already protected.

[b] Article XV.2 contains a pledge "not to interfere with the national technical means of verification …" "identical to those in the ABM and SALT I treaties. Questions involving unintended interference with national technical means of verification would be dealt with within the framework of the Standing Consultative Commission (Article XVII.2c) of the SALT II treaty.

[c] Both these draft treaties contain non-interference clauses regarding the national technical means of verification.

activities in this environment is the prohibition of the placing in orbit of nuclear weapons or other weapons of mass destruction (article IV.1). The treaty thus legitimizes other military uses of outer space. Under article IV.2 of the Treaty, the Moon and other celestial bodies are demilitarized, but outer space as a whole has only been partially demilitarized. Indeed, whether the treaty was ever meant as an important arms control measure is doubtful.[1] The use of nuclear weapons and any other weapons of mass destruction in or from orbit is very doubtful from the point of view of their military effectiveness. However, if a total ban on the use of outer space for military purposes had been imposed by the treaty, the question of the extension of the arms race to this environment may not have arisen today. ASAT weapons are being developed because of the existence of military satellites.

With the exception of the 1963 Partial Test Ban Treaty, other subsequent treaties have legitimized the military use of outer space and, in fact, offer protection to the majority of military satellites. For example, the 1972 ABM Treaty and the SALT I and II treaties contain pledges not to interfere with national technical means of verification. This effectively means that photographic, electronic, early warning and ocean-surveillance satellites are protected by these treaties from destruction or interference. The 1973 International Telecommunication Union Convention (see table 3) obligates parties to the Convention to avoid harmful interference with the radio services or communications of other parties.

Thus only military navigation, geodetic, meteorological and most civilian satellites are without any protection. But when devices to detect nuclear explosions are deployed on board the US NAVSTAR satellites, these might also be classified under the category of national technical means of verification and so be protected by some of the above-mentioned arms control treaties. A number of other arms control measures achieved since 1972 would also protect most military satellites under the verification clauses.

However, there is no doubt of the need for an ASAT treaty. There are two main reasons for this. One is that the existing treaties protect only some military satellites leaving civilian satellites totally unprotected. Second, in time of crisis, a nation having ASAT weapons may be tempted to use them, leaving no time for reflection. In the present political climate, a collision with a military satellite could arouse fears that an anti-satellite weapon had been used. It must be remembered that about eight in every ten satellites in space are military, so any collision is very likely to involve a military satellite. In fact on three occasions in May 1980, within a period of two weeks, six satellites, five military and one civilian, were involved in near collisions.[2] All of these were in the geostationary orbit and they all belonged to the USA so that evasive actions were possible.

Some new arms control measures in outer space have been proposed both officially and by non-governmental organizations (for the latter see paper 9, page 131). These are attempts to protect *all* military satellites, to a varying degree. But, of course, they would also protect civilian satellites. These measures are briefly described below.

III. New proposals

In 1981, the Soviet Union proposed the prohibition of objects carrying weapons of any kind "in orbit around the earth" (article 1, paragraph 1).[3] Such a provision may be taken to mean that direct-hit weapons are allowed. Most weapons that are deployed today and may be deployed in the near future are launched either from Earth or from within the atmosphere (such as the US F-15 launched ASAT missile). The protection of some military satellites is further emphasized in article 3 of the proposal in which it is stated "Each State Party undertakes not to destroy ... space objects of other States Parties if such objects were placed in orbit in strict accordance with article 1, paragraph 1 ...". This means that only the *weapons* placed in orbit may be destroyed. It is interesting to note here that the nature of such weapons is not made clear. As can be seen from the above technical description of some ASAT weapons, a satellite can be destroyed by another colliding with it.

A second draft treaty proposed by the Soviet Union in 1983 apparently includes prohibition against all weapons, but the proposal is not without ambiguity.[4] For example, article 1 of the proposed treaty prohibits the "...resort to the use or threat of force in outer space and the atmosphere and on the Earth through the utilization ... of space objects in orbit..." (table 3). While this prohibits weapons which are space-based only, in the article it is further prohibited "to resort to the use or threat of force against space objects...". However, this part of the article does not elaborate on the method by which the force or threat of force is applied. This may also be interpreted as allowing the *possession* of ASAT weapons as long as they are not space-based. Such an ambiguity is carried over in article 2 of the proposal which deals with the prohibition on testing of ASAT weapons but only in orbit. An interesting feature of this proposal, however, is the inclusion of the limited prohibition on anti-ballistic missile weapons or ballistic missile defence systems emphasizing the dual nature of BMD and ASAT systems. (For further details see paper 13, page 185.)

A third proposal was made by the Union of Concerned Scientists in the USA in June 1983.[5] In article I of this proposal it is stated: "Each Party undertakes not to destroy, damage, render inoperable or change the flight trajectory of space objects of other States". Again, under this the possession of ASAT weapons is not prohibited. However, article II, paragraph 1 prohibits the deployment of weapons, but only "in orbit around the Earth". An interesting feature of this article is that it does limit the space-based BMD systems. Moreover, under paragraph 3 of this article, "Each Party undertakes not to test such weapons in space or against space objects". The usefulness of such a measure may be limited since certain weapons need not be tested in space or even against space objects.

It is important to emphasize that because of the dual nature of the ASAT weapons any space-related arms control discussions cannot be conducted without bringing in BMD issues.

Research and development on new methods to counter intercontinental ballistic missiles has been in progress despite the 1972 bilateral ABM Treaty. The question arises as to the legality of such systems (see paper 8, page 127). The treaty could be interpreted in different ways. According to one view, all ABM systems are banned except those which are described in the treaty as permitted (article III). Another view is that apart from ABM systems allowed for in the treaty, fixed land-based BMD systems based on other physical principles may be allowed. A third view, supported by the author, is that the development, testing and deployment of any BMD systems, based on physical principles other than those which existed in 1972, is permitted. Various provisions of the treaty are, therefore, examined below.

IV. 1972 ABM Treaty

The 1972 ABM treaty limits the number and deployment of ABM systems within limited areas. For example, under the treaty "Each Party undertakes to limit anti-ballistic missile (ABM) systems..." (article I.1). Moreover, "Each party undertakes not to deploy ABM systems for a defense of the territory of its country ... except as provided for in Article III of this treaty" (article I.2). For the purpose of the treaty an ABM system is defined as " ... a system ... currently consisting of: (a) ABM interceptor missiles, which are interceptor missiles constructed and deployed for an ABM role ... and (c) ABM radars which are radars conctructed and deployed for an ABM role..." (article II.1). Furthermore, article III of the treaty defines the regions within which a specified number of ABM systems are allowed. Therefore, the deployment of ABM systems is prohibited elsewhere. However, this restriction would seem to apply to ABM interceptor missiles only since, for the purposes of the treaty, an ABM system is defined as consisting of ABM interceptor missiles (article II.1). Thus the deployment of lasers or other directed-energy BMD system would be allowed.

It can be argued that the treaty prohibits the development, testing or deployment of all "ABM systems and components which are sea-based, air-based, space-based or mobile land-based" (article V.1). However, by definition ABM systems are those consisting of ABM interceptor missiles (article II.1) so that a directed-energy BMD system would not be covered by article V of the treaty.

Finally, the treaty needs to be read with the Agreed Interpretations and Unilateral Statements Regarding the ABM Treaty. According to paragraph (a)[D] of the Agreed Interpretations, "In order to insure fulfillment of the obligation not to deploy ABM systems and their components ..., the Parties agree that in the event ABM systems based on other physical principles and including components capable of substituting for ABM interceptor missiles, ABM launchers, or ABM radars are created in the future, specific limitations on such systems and their components would be subject to discussion...". This seems again to suggest that directed-energy BMD systems by themselves are not subject to prohibition under the provisions of the ABM Treaty.

In the early 1970s the significance of the Treaty was seen to lie in the fact that both sides had in effect agreed to maintain mutual vulnerability. The current interest in BMD is thus of special concern because it reflects a change of doctrine away from deterrence. Furthermore, developments in high-energy laser BMD would give impetus to its applications as an ASAT weapon since many of the key problems in both the applications are identical. All this makes it essential to begin negotiations on an ASAT treaty as well as more comprehensive BMD measures. It has been argued that verifying an ASAT treaty would be difficult.[6] Some thoughts on this and other arms control issues are discussed below.

V. Verification

A close examination of the way in which the two superpowers use different orbits for satellites performing various military missions indicates that there are distinct differences in the orbits used (see figure 3). It can be seen that while the USSR launches its satellites in a very narrow range of orbital inclinations (between 45° and about 85°), the USA has used a much wider range of orbital inclinations. Therefore, there is some overlap between the orbital inclinations of the satellites of the two powers (e.g., 50°, 65°, 75° and 85°). However, if the US satellites launched after 1966 are examined, it is found that the majority of them have orbital inclinations greater than 75° and, with the exception of only a few satellites, after 1972, have been launched between 50° and 85° (see figure 3).

Therefore, if there were a ban on ASAT weapons, the USA would be easily alerted to possible violation on the part of the Soviet Union, since it would be rather unusual for them to launch satellites in orbits that are used by the USA. An exception to this, of course, is the geostationary orbit (GSO) where both powers orbit their satellites. However, the present Soviet ASAT system has a maximum range of about 1 000 km; the GSO is at 36 000 km. Moreover, the Soviet Union uses a specific type of launcher to orbit its ASAT satellites. Therefore, a launch of an ASAT weapon could be detected from space by observation of the launcher.

On the other hand, the US ASAT system is very different from that deployed by the USSR at present. The US system is a direct ascent system which can be launched against satellites in any orbit. While this flexibility, together with the small size of the weapon, increases its survivability, the verification of its ban would be very difficult to achieve using the normal space-based surveillance systems.

Verification of the ban on weapons of the more futuristic variety would not present any significant problems since, at least in the early stages, such weapons are likely to be large and therefore easily observable. However, once the US ASAT weapon is fully tested, a ban on its deployment would be very difficult to verify. Thus, if no steps are taken soon, it may be too late to achieve any meaningful arms control in space. (See paper 14, page 193 for further discussion on verification.)

Figure 3. Number of US and Soviet military satellites as a function of their orbital inclinations: ⊏⊐ satellites launched 1958–83; ■■■ satellites launched 1972–83

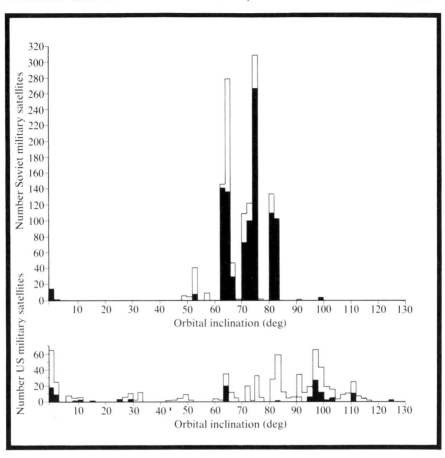

VI. Implications

Even though the technological problems relating to a space-based BMD laser weapon system may not be solved in the foreseeable future, the proposed application of high-energy laser beams raises considerable difficulties from the point of view of arms control at present. For example, the possible use of a ballistic missile defence system may have a considerable destabilizing effect on the relationship between the two superpowers. If one side acquired such a weapon, it might then be tempted to strike first against the other, probably using tactical nuclear weapons, believing that it could still defend itself against the opponent's ICBMs, the release of which might result in escalation from tactical to strategic nuclear weapons. This is to be viewed particularly in the light of the availability of such small-yield, highly accurate nuclear weapons.

Moreover, a very important consequence would be for both the USA and the Soviet Union to embark on yet another round of arms competition. Not only may there be a renewed BMD race, but the two sides would multiply manyfold their offensive nuclear arsenals to ensure that despite the opposing BMD systems some nuclear weapons would reach their targets. This would increase the nuclear arms race instead of checking it.

Perhaps a more serious implication of such a development lies in the fact that it violates the spirit of the 1972 ABM Treaty. The two parties should begin discussion on the limitation of these new systems now. The Treaty provides for such discussions.

Another difficulty the new technology raises is that if X-ray or gamma-ray lasers are deployed, this may jeopardize the 1963 Partial Test Ban Treaty, which bans nuclear weapon tests in the atmosphere, in outer space and under water. As mentioned earlier, X-ray and gamma-ray lasers can be produced using small thermonuclear explosions or small fission or neutron bombs. Moreover, more testing and certainly the deployment of such systems will violate the 1967 Outer Space Treaty which prohibits orbiting nuclear weapons and weapons of mass destruction. X-ray lasers have been called "third generation nuclear weapons".[7] Certainly, the Outer Space Treaty will be violated in spirit since orbiting any BMD system cannot be regarded as a peaceful activity and the Treaty requires parties to use space for peaceful purposes only.

However, perhaps the most important problem raised by the development and possible eventual deployment of BMD weapons is from the point of view of a possible anti-satellite treaty. Both the USA and the Soviet Union began talks on the control of their anti-satellite activities during 1978 and 1979. These did not progress very far and, in fact, the discussions ceased in 1979. However, in August 1981 the USSR proposed to the United Nations a new treaty banning the placement of any kind of weapon in Earth orbit. In August 1983, the USSR proposed to the United Nations another treaty, this time banning the use of force in outer space and from space against the Earth. As a result of the first proposal, the discussion on this has been referred to the Committee on Disarmament (now called the Conference on Disarmament, CD) in Geneva. However, the CD is finding it difficult to establish a working group to consider the issue of the arms race in space. (For some possible approaches to an ASAT treaty see paper 10, page 145.) The possible deployment of a ballistic missile defence system which can be used as an anti-satellite weapon will complicate the discussions at the CD even more.

As mentioned earlier, the international community expressed its concern during the 1982 UNISPACE conference at the continued militarization of outer space. Further attempts to discuss these issues during the UN COPUOS meeting in Vienna in 1984 also ended in failure. The meeting ended on 22 June 1984 with the USA not participating in the discussion on whether COPUOS should be mandated to discuss the militarization of space to supplement the work of the CD in Geneva.

At the end of June 1984, a glimmer of hope appeared when, in response to a call made by the Soviet Union to begin discussions in September 1984 in

Vienna on arms control in space, the USA reacted positively. However, this was on condition that the negotiations on the much broader and, according to the Soviet Union, unrelated subject of nuclear arms control should also resume. The Soviet Union's reaction was negative and the proposal for talks foundered.

References

1. Jasani, B. and Lunderius, M. A., 'Peaceful uses of outer space—legal fiction and military reality', *Bulletin of Peace Proposals*, Vol. 11, No. 1, March 1980, pp. 57–70.
2. Jasani, B., Perek, L., Lála, P. and Sehnal, L., 'Physical nature and technical attributes of the geostationary orbit', *UN Report* No. A/AC.105/203/Add.4, 18 May 1983.
3. 'Soviet proposal for a draft treaty on the prohibition of the stationing of weapons of any kind in outer space', *UN Document* No. A/36/192, 20 August 1981.
4. 'Soviet proposal for a draft treaty on the prohibition of the use of force in outer space and from space against the earth', *UN Document* No. A/38/194, 23 August 1983.
5. 'A treaty limiting anti-satellite weapons', *Anti-satellite Weapons: Arms Control or Arms Race*? (Union of Concerned Scientists, 30 June 1983), pp. 33–35.
6. Report to the Congress on US Policy on ASAT Arms Control, presented 31 March 1984, House Document 98-197, 3 April 1984.
7. Teller, E., Statement made during Hearings before the Committee on Armed Services, United States Senate, *Department of Defense Authorization for Appropriations for Fiscal Year 1984*, Part 5, Strategic and Theater Nuclear Forces, 15, 18, 21, 23 March, 7, 15 April, 2 May 1983 (US Government Printing Office, Washington, DC, 1983), p. 2898.

Chapter 6. Recommendations

It is obvious that there is a dilemma. Military spacecraft have contributed considerably to the formulation of strategies for actually fighting nuclear war rather than just deterring it. On the face of it it would seem a reasonable idea to ban all military satellites. But would it? These same satellites can be used to monitor treaties safeguarding international security, and they can be used to maintain military communications so that war by miscalculation is less likely. But some form of treaty is needed to protect satellites for peaceful and stable use. There must also be other ways of reducing the destabilizing effects of the military use of space.

Considering this the following points are offered for inclusion and consideration in any debate that may lead towards a draft proposal for the protection of outer space vehicles.

1. While all the satellites launched are registered with the United Nations in conformity with General Assembly Resolution 1721 B (XVI), the information given on most spacecraft is scanty. Important details, such as the launch time and site, physical characteristics of satellites, degree of manoeuvrability, satellite lifetime and often the orbital characteristics of satellites, should be given. At present, the purpose of a spacecraft is often difficult to determine.

2. It is important to closely examine the special body of law dealing with activities in outer space so that there is a clear understanding of which satellites really are protected and what further measures are needed.

3. The minimum that the two major powers could do to bring at least some military activities in outer space under control is to agree to an ASAT treaty that will ban not only tests but also possession.

Unless an ASAT treaty is achieved soon the development and deployment of some of the space weapons which could be used for both offensive and defensive purposes could mean an abrogation of the 1972 Anti-Ballistic Missile Treaty. It would probably also involve breach of the 1967 Outer Space Treaty (which is already being violated in spirit) and even the 1963 Partial Test Ban Treaty. New legal instruments submitted as drafts by the USSR and some non-governmental organizations should be taken as a basis for discussion even on an international basis.

A draft multilateral treaty to control space weapons was proposed by the Soviet Union in 1983. While the US Administration had indicated that it will not seek a comprehensive ASAT treaty, mainly because of the verification problems, it may be prepared to consider a limited ASAT treaty. For example, the Administration may consider prohibiting some specific types of weapon or action.

4. As an interim measure countries could impose a moratorium on the testing of ASAT weapons and could also make a declaration of no-first-use of ASAT weapons. In fact, the USSR and the People's Republic of China have made a declaration not to be the first to use nuclear weapons. There is a connection in that certain types of laser weapons are regarded as third generation nuclear weapons. A no-first-use of ASAT weapons declaration may be useful in the case of an incomplete ASAT treaty.

5. The same technologies can be used in both anti-satellite systems and ballistic missile defence. Thus it is no use banning one of these systems and letting the other go ahead. If there were only a ban on ASAT systems, the result would probably be that the technologies which were being developed for ASAT purposes would acquire a new label: we would be told that they were being developed for anti-ballistic missile purposes. It follows that any action against the development or deployment of anti-satellite systems should be accompanied by equivalent action against anti-ballistic missile systems. This may require some renegotiation of the Anti-Ballistic Missile Treaty to ensure that it is water-tight.

6. Since disarmament is a concern for all, it is essential that discussions on the concept of an international satellite monitoring agency are kept alive. A regional satellite monitoring agency can be considered as an interim measure.

7. To ensure availability of satellites during a time of crisis, both the USSR and the USA intend to station spare satellites in orbit. Moreover, for a continuous world-wide availability of accurate navigation capability it is necessary to have a number of spacecraft in a space-based navigation system. Similarly, a world-wide communications system needs at least three satellites in orbit. It may be suggested that the number of military satellites launched per year by a country should be limited so that, at least, the performance of some weapon systems on Earth could be degraded and even the efficiency of performance of effectiveness of military forces could be reduced.

It is crucial to obtain a clear understanding of the military uses of outer space with a view to clearly defining which of the military satellites are to be permitted and for what purposes. While there are still only two countries which are able to enhance the performance of their nuclear arsenals using space technology, a truly comprehensive outer space treaty containing real disarmament measures must be worked out. Another opportunity will be missed if greater control over the militarization of space is not brought about now.

Part II
Militarization of space and arms control

Paper 1.   Military satellites and war-fighting doctrines

Thomas Karas*

Office of Technology Assessment, United States Congress,
Washington, DC 20510, USA

I. Introduction

Military satellites are of increasing importance across the spectrum of military activity, from day-to-day maintenance to all-out war. This paper examines not that whole spectrum, but the most intense—the strategic nuclear war-fighting—end of it. An analysis of the implications of satellites for strategic nuclear war-fighting doctrines requires first some discussion of the contending concepts of nuclear warfare.

II. War-fighting doctrines and nuclear weapons

The possession of arsenals of many thousands of nuclear weapons has caused the United States and the Soviet Union to be known as 'superpowers', yet their possession of such instruments of mass destruction has forced upon them a self-restraint unknown to earlier world powers. The nuclear weapon has posed an insoluble dilemma for military doctrines. On the one hand it is the most powerful—by many orders of magnitude—weapon in history; on the other, it is seemingly too powerful to use.

Nuclear-age military planners, at least in the United States, still grapple with this dilemma. It is the job of the military to plan for war. Granted, those not resigned to the inevitability of war hope that the result of their preparations will be not war but deterrence. By being manifestly ready to fight and win (or at least not to lose) a war if attacked or challenged, one side hopes to dissuade the other side from risking it. How can weapons seemingly too terrible to be

*The views in this paper do not necessarily reflect those of the Office of Technology Assessment, the Technology Advisory Board, or individual members of Congress.

used be subsumed into theories of war-fighting as opposed to mutual suicide? No one, emphatically including military strategists, is comfortable with the idea that superpower national security depends on credibly threatening to slaughter tens of millions of people in a nuclear holocaust. But the weapons are deployed and ready to be used.

Military analysts have taken varied approaches to integrating nuclear weapons into war-fighting doctrines. One is to discount the human scale of their destructiveness, to treat them as bigger 'conventional' weapons. The use in World War II of conventional explosives and incendiary bombs as 'strategic' weapons of mass destruction perhaps laid the psychological groundwork for this approach. After all, more civilians died in non-nuclear fire-bombings than in the Hiroshima and Nagasaki blasts. Such thinking may have lain behind Strategic Air Command strategy in the 1950s, which was to deliver the maximum available firepower in a short time.[1] The view that nuclear weapons are just larger bombs also seems to be implied by those who argue for the effectiveness of civil defence: "If there are enough shovels to go around, everybody's going to make it".[2]

A second approach to fitting nuclear weapons into military doctrine has been to develop theories of limited nuclear war, in which the scale of destruction may be controlled by both sides confining their nuclear strikes to limited numbers or limited sets of targets.[3] A variation on this theme is the concept of protracted nuclear war: nuclear war is conducted not as a one-day spasm of retaliation, but as a more or less controlled military campaign extending over weeks or months.

Limited and protracted nuclear war theories have been given substance by modern weapons technology. Technicians invent new devices to bring the nuclear genie under rational control: smaller nuclear warheads for more confined circles of destruction, more accurate delivery systems for the precise targeting of specifically military installations, improved intelligence systems for the location of those targets and more pervasive command and control systems for the measured and centralized direction of the application of nuclear force.

A recurrent theme in the technological approach to the taming of nuclear weapons is the search for truly effective missile defence systems, holding out the hope of cancelling out the enemy's ability to attack or retaliate with nuclear destruction. Some proponents of advanced ballistic missile defence (BMD) technology hold that although no defence can be perfect, any defence is better than none. If the expected damage of a nuclear war can be held to 'acceptable' levels, the credibility of one's deterrent threat remains intact.

Others, including President Reagan and US Secretary of Defense Weinberger, argue that a virtually perfect defence against all forms of large-scale nuclear attack is at least imaginable and certainly worth trying for. The promise they hold out is an escape from the nuclear balance of terror (if not a shifting of the balance unequivocally in favour of the United States).

There is yet another approach to defining the military utility of nuclear weapons: the doctrine of minimum deterrence. In the minimum deterrence school of thought, the possession of nuclear weapons has a single justification: deterrence of nuclear attack on the homeland. The threat of retaliation against high-value targets—cities and industrial sites—should deter any rational potential aggressor from starting a nuclear war. In fact, a relatively small number of weapons ought to be able to inflict enough damage to do the job. Larger numbers of weapons would be superfluous—the point is not how much damage the attacker can do to you, but how much damage he knows he will suffer from your retaliation.[4]

This has been a convenient doctrine for smaller nuclear powers such as France.[5] Although they cannot hope to match the Soviet nuclear arsenal, they can hope to inflict retaliatory damage out of proportion to any possible Soviet gains from attacking the smaller power. The United States, in contrast, has never adopted the minimum deterrence posture, either in doctrine or in weapon deployments. Even so, those who have erroneously characterized US nuclear doctrine of the 1960s and 1970s as one of 'Mutual Assured Destruction', or MAD, have introduced a certain amount of confusion on this point.

A simplistic view of the policies of this era tends to be vogue among those who caricature the MAD doctrine. During his administration of the Defense Department in the 1960s, Robert McNamara decided to stop building additional strategic nuclear weapons when he saw that the USA possessed enough already to inflict unacceptable damage on the population and industries of the Soviet Union. Moreover, McNamara resisted building defence for US cities because he believed that a stable nuclear balance of terror required the USA to remain vulnerable to Soviet weapons. According to the MAD caricaturists, we are still living with the unfortunate consequences of the McNamara legacy:

1. Through unilateral restraint the United States allowed the Soviet Union to acquire strategic nuclear superiority over the United States.
2. Because of slavish adherence to the MAD doctrine, the US government has abdicated its reponsibility to defend its people against foreign attack.
3. The same doctrine has led the United States to rest its security on the threat of 'assured destruction'—or mass slaughter—of millions of relatively innocent men, women, and children.

There are threads of truth in the MAD caricature, but by and large it bears little resemblance to reality. McNamara and his strategic analysts did conclude that, in order to deter Soviet attack, the USA must maintain some minimum level of 'assured destruction' against the Soviet homeland. They calculated that once US forces had delivered the equivalent of about 400 one-megaton bombs on the cities and industrial plants of the Soviet Union, the percentages of additional population and industry destroyed by additional weapons would fall off sharply. Somewhat arbitrarily, they took as an axiom that *at the very least* the United States must maintain the ability to inflict the damage of 400 one-megaton bombs on the Soviet Union. That level of damage would surely deter any rational Soviet leader from attacking the United States.[6]

While the McNamara analysts saw this assured destruction capability as an absolute minimum requirement, the Pentagon under McNamara and his successors by no means limited itself to that minimum. During this period, thousands of strategic warheads were deployed on intercontinental ballistic missiles (ICBMs), submarine-launched ballistic missiles (SLBMs) and bombers. Some 7 000 'theatre' nuclear weapons were deployed in western Europe. Thousands more went to bases around the world and ships at sea. The minimum deterrent was only a baseline: the deployed deterrent was probably 10 or 20 times the 400-megaton level. This is not to say that the Department of Defense deployed as many nuclear weapons as the military services may have asked for, just that it deployed many times more than were necessary for 'assured destruction'.

Early in the McNamara administration of the Pentagon, analysts had studied scenarios of limited or controlled nuclear war, concentrating on damage-limiting targeting schemes. In the spring of 1961 McNamara issued a guidance document to the strategic target planners which called for a set of nuclear war options which ranged from a damage-limiting strike against Soviet strategic weapon bases to the all-out destruction of cities. Within a couple of years, the McNamara analysts concluded that the damage-limiting doctrine was encouraging the Joint Chiefs of Staff to seek an almost unlimited number of new nuclear weapons to use against an almost unlimited number of 'counterforce' military targets. He therefore began to emphasize the assured destruction task as a means of putting some cap on the growth of the strategic arsenal.[7]

Even so, it is obvious that the actual target planners had to do something with all the thousands of weapons which exceeded the needs of the assured destruction task. What they did was continue to follow McNamara's 1961 target planning guidance and aim the weapons at military as well as civilian targets. Whether nuclear war-fighting has been popular in current military doctrine or not, it has long been a major component of *de facto* target *policy*. The question has never been whether or not the United States should have counterforce (ICBM-silo attacking) weapons, but only how many. In fact, McNamara's revised target guidance of 1963, emphasizing assured destruction, called for only 18 per cent of US strategic nuclear weapons to be on alert by 1969 for the task of destroying cities.[8]

Why did McNamara oppose ballistic missile defence of US cities (and why did his successors accept a treaty with the USSR severely limiting BMD)? Given calculations about the likely effectiveness of such weapons, "Secretary McNamara concluded that effective damage-limiting measures against the Soviets were not attainable, regardless of the amount we were willing to spend, as long as the Soviets were determined to maintain their deterrent against us".[9] It was not that the USA had any obligation to remain vulnerable to Soviet weapons, but that the Soviet Union was likely to do whatever was necessary to maintain *its* assured destruction capability against the USA. In short, the assuredness of mutual destruction in a nuclear war is not a military doctrine, but a fact of life in the US–Soviet global competition.

During the Soviet nuclear build-up of the 1970s, and particularly during the

Carter Administration, it was fashionable among the propagators of the MAD mythology to accuse the Soviet Union of attempting to achieve the potential to eliminate the US ability to retaliate against military targets by deploying accurate ICBMs able to knock out a high percentage of US ICBM silos. Once that potential was achieved, the argument went, the USA would face a perilous 'window of vulnerability' during which it would be paralysed by fear of a Soviet counterforce stroke that would leave the USA able only to escalate the war to the destruction of cities. The USA would then be the constant object of Soviet nuclear blackmail.

The Soviet strategic nuclear build-up of the 1970s was no doubt to some extent incited by the US build-up of the 1960s. Even so, there is still no entirely convincing explanation of why the USSR chose to add so many high-yield, high accuracy ICBM warheads to their arsenal. One possibility is that the USSR simply allowed itself to be carried along by the momentum built up while trying to counter the US superiority of the 1960s. Another is that it defines 'parity' or strategic equality with the USA differently than US analysts might: that, for example, Soviet nuclear megatonnage is a compensation for US technological superiority.

The third explanation, that the USSR has sought a usable nuclear superiority centred on a disarming counterforce strike against US land-based missiles, ignores the implausibility of a Soviet attack on missile silos alone. It ignores the massive civilian collateral damage that such an attack would cause anyway. And it ignores the wide variety of military targets besides hardened missile silos available in the Soviet Union for strikes by the US submarine-launched missiles and the bombers that could be expected to survive any Soviet first strike.

Rejecting Carter Administration plans to base the MX missile in an 'invulnerable' mode so as to close the window of vulnerability, the Reagan Administration has closed the window by simply ignoring it. This less costly tactic seems fully effective so far. Nonetheless, other aspects of the Reagan military programme have raised anew the strategic question of the 1960s: can counterforce attacks limit damage in a nuclear war? Will civil defence reduce casualties to 'acceptable' levels? Is it possible to fight a limited nuclear war, with carefully graded options that control escalation? Is it possible to fight and 'win' (or, in Secretary Weinberger's words, "prevail in") a nuclear war? Would a nuclear war be a rapid, 'spasm' event, or could it be protracted over weeks and months? Will new technologies finally make truly effective defence against nuclear delivery vehicles possible? The capabilities of satellites play an increasingly important role in the military responses to most of these questions.

III. Satellites and nuclear war planning

Were it not for satellites, doctrines for limited nuclear war counterforce attacks would not even be conceivable. The repeated scanning of enemy territory by imaging reconnaissance satellites is the only way (at least for the USA) that missile silos and other military targets could have been precisely mapped. Geodetic satellites have contributed the precise gravitational mapping of the Earth necessary for the most accurate working of inertial guidance systems for ballistic missiles. Navigational satellites may, later in this decade, contribute to submarine-based missiles as accurate as today's ICBMs, thus turning them into 'hard-target killers'.

IV. Satellites and the outbreak of nuclear war

Early warning satellites

Because intercontinental ballistic missiles take about 30 minutes to travel between the Soviet Union and the United States, early warning satellites have at least marginally contributed to some crisis stability between the super-powers. In case of actual attack, the target nation would have a few minutes to get its alert bombers off the ground.[10] Thanks to the subsequent, redundant warning provided by ground-based radar systems, the chances of a false warning (by either satellites or radar) leading to war are reduced.

On the other hand, the satellite early warning systems also hold open the possibility of launch-on-warning or launch-under-attack postures for the land-based missile forces. Such a posture could help deter attack by threatening to move the most important counterforce target out of harm's way; it could also contribute to an image of having an 'itchy trigger finger'. It would also leave national decision makers precious little time to make rational choices.

If one or both sides were to place large numbers of highly accurate ballistic missiles on submarines (as the USA plans to put the Trident II on submarines), then the stabilizing effects of early warning satellites would be lost (except for providing redundant information). Bomber bases and missile silos could be attacked simultaneously and with negligible warning times. In a serious military confrontation, the lack of warning would place a premium on launching one's weapons *before* the other side struck. (On the other hand, if both sides had placed their ICBMs in some relatively invulnerable basing mode and kept many SLBMs at sea, the loss of warning time would be less significant.)

Communications satellites

Communications satellites are the central link in the 'hot line' between Moscow and Washington: conceivably they could one day prevent a crisis from escalating into a nuclear war. Satellites are also one means by which the Pentagon would transmit the 'Emergency Action Message' to its strategic nuclear forces. They would be particularly important to highly co-ordinated, highly sophisticated strikes by nuclear weapons based in the continental United States, at sea, and in 'theatres of operation' elsewhere around the globe. On the other hand, the whole communications network is so redundant that the use of satellite transmissions might not be necessary, especially in the case of a relatively unsophisticated retaliatory attack.

V. Satellites and the conduct of nuclear war

A nuclear strategy which calls for a relatively simple set of retaliatory options (against a pre-determined set of hard, soft or hard-and-soft targets) could probably be carried out with relatively little reliance on satellites. A strategy of protracted nuclear war, calling for repeated nuclear strikes over weeks or months, is something else. A protracted nuclear war doctrine calls for enduring 'strategic connectivity' (the ability to receive reports from far-flung forces and to direct them to new targets), for a survivable warning system (one which lasts beyond the first attack) and for continuing target reconnaissance.

With these requirements in mind, US military planners have begun the development or the procurement of several new satellite systems. The officer in charge of its development has identified the new Milstar communications satellite (due later this decade) as a war-fighting system, designed to provide enduring strategic connectivity.[11]

New early warning satellites are designed to identify more precisely which Soviet missiles have been launched and where they are headed, thus providing additional target information for the retaliatory strike. The US Air Force has been purchasing several Mobile Ground Terminals so that it could continue to receive missile warning messages after its fixed ground terminals had been destroyed. According to Pentagon testimony before Congress: "Extended survivability of U.S. tactical warning and attack assessment systems is becoming a matter of increasing importance, arising from the need to provide information for the management of strategic forces during the pre-, trans-, and post-attack periods, including escalation control, orderly and controlled termination of conflict, and management of residual and reserve forces".[12]

The new 18-satellite global positioning system (GPS) will carry nuclear weapon explosion detectors. An Air Force General explained their purpose:

We are able, with the GPS fully deployed, and with so-called IONDS, the NUDET detection capability onboard, to be able [sic] to detect nuclear detonations within 100 meters. So, therefore, when we try to destroy hard targets in the Soviet Union, we are able to demonstrate or to understand our success in destroying those hard targets and, therefore, not have to go back and restrike those targets, and we can retarget in real time.[13]

So, I think in the total sense, it is a war-fighting capability, it is in fact a revolutionary capability as far as navigation and bombing are concerned.[14]

How much is enough?

As impressive as these new satellites sound, would they actually enable the United States to conduct a protracted nuclear war? Given the unprecedented destruction, confusion and sheer horror of nuclear war, one could question whether any amount of money would purchase the ability to fight a controlled and protracted nuclear war. In any case, a strong proponent of trying to do just that has argued that it has not been done yet:

The Reagan Administration has addressed the problems of ensuring a robustly survivable core of C^3I capability to support and direct deliberately sequenced and possible well delayed nuclear strikes, and to support properly the "secure strategic reserve force". However, to address the problem is not the same as to identify timely solutions—let alone to fund them adequately ... [The Reagan modernization plan] ... would contribute very helpfully indeed to the vital mission of ensuring that emergency action messages (EAMs)—nuclear war "go" orders—would be dispatched and received reliably. C^3I for a protracted conflict constitutes a different set of problems and is not addressed persuasively by the capabilities scheduled for purchase thus far.[15]

VI. Implications of anti-satellite weapons for nuclear war-fighting

The varieties of anti-satellite weapons

There are several ways in which an attacker could try to disable enemy military satellites. It is important to note that most of these methods would be more feasible before a strategic nuclear exchange had taken place than during or after. Some actual or potential methods of anti-satellite attack include the following:

1. Disabling the ground stations which either control the satellite or gather and process information from it.
2. Electronically jamming communication links between satellites and ground terminals.
3. Using high-altitude nuclear explosions to jam those links.
4. Taking over electronic command of the satellite from one's own ground stations.
5. Damaging critical sensors or solar panels on the satellite using a ground-based laser weapon.
6. Damaging internal satellite systems using a ground-based particle beam weapon.
7. Launching a nuclear warhead into the vicinity of the target satellite and exploding it there.
8. Destroying the satellite with a ground-based interceptor weapon such as the Soviet killer satellite or the US miniature homing vehicle.
9. Destroying the satellite with an interceptor similar to the above, but based on another satellite instead of on the ground.
10. Exploding a space mine previously 'parked' in orbit near the target satellite.

11. Damaging the satellite with a laser based on another satellite. (In principle, a space-based neutral particle beam weapon would be even more effective, but the necessary technology is too remotely in the the future to take seriously now.)[16]

After the first round of exchange of nuclear weapons, the bases for those weapons launched or aimed from the ground would probably have been destroyed (unless they had sufficient mobility to evade incoming nuclear weapons). What is more, almost all of these anti-satellite methods, ground-based or space-based, would require a global space surveillance network able to track the 4 700 or so objects in Earth orbit so as to locate and identify the target satellite.[17] A nuclear exchange would almost certainly destroy today's networks; a space-based space surveillance network seems far in the future.

Anti-satellite attacks at the outset of nuclear war

The current Soviet anti-satellite weapon and the new US weapon are able to attack only low-altitude satellites (under about 2 000 km for the Soviet system). This means that, for the time being, geosynchronous warning and communications satellites are relatively invulnerable to interception. So are the new US Global Positioning System navigation and nuclear burst-detection satellites and the new Soviet Global Navigation Satellite System satellites. (Whether these satellites will be vulnerable to ground-based laser damage in the future is debatable, but by no means established.) Given current systems, then, only Soviet warning and communications satellites in the highly elliptical 'Molniya' orbit will be clearly vulnerable to attack in the near future.

But as both the USA and the Soviet Union continue development of anti-satellite weapons, it is reasonable to assume that each will seek the ability to disable high-altitude as well as low-altitude satellites. Should these satellites become generally vulnerable, new questions will be raised about the crisis stability of the US–Soviet nuclear confrontation.

The probable loss of most anti-satellite capability after a nuclear exchange has taken place means that an attack on satellites that would be useful during a nuclear war seems practicable only for the side that is planning to strike first. Moreover, that attack would only be attractive if a protracted nuclear war were contemplated. An attack on early warning and communications satellites in advance of the full-scale nuclear attack would constitute a clear warning in itself, and would probably cause the target country to place additional nuclear retaliatory forces on alert. An anti-satellite attack launched simultaneously with a nuclear attack would not substantially reduce the expected nuclear retaliation. What an anti-satellite attack might do is reduce the availability of satellites for communications and intelligence during a long-lasting nuclear war with repeated nuclear strikes.

The fact that attacks on early warning and communications satellites would be most useful to the side which started what it expected would be protracted nuclear war makes for additional crisis instability. For example, if during a conventional or limited nuclear war one side began attacking satellites, those attacks might be perceived as the first step in escalation to strategic nuclear war. Escalation by the side whose satellites were attacked might follow.

Whether violence had broken out or not, large-scale anti-satellite capabilities might still contribute to crisis instability. In a crisis in which each side expected the other to attack at any time, the incentives to pre-emption might be increased. The side which felt most vulnerable to disruption of its command and control facilities through anti-satellite attacks might be tempted to strike before the other side had a chance to use its ASAT weapons. On the other hand, the side which wished to try to control escalation and 'prevail' in a protracted nuclear conflict might be tempted to strike with nuclear weapons and ASAT weapons while its own ASAT systems were still usable. The intended result would be to both weaken the other side's space-based command and control facilities and protect one's own by destroying the enemy ASAT system. Should the other side's command and control system appear particularly vulnerable to disruption by ASAT warfare, the temptation to strike could be even greater.

Assessing these potential instabilities is complicated since the temptation to strike enemy command and control facilities must always be a mixed one. Such strikes may weaken enemy military capabilities. At the same time, they may weaken the enemy's ability to discuss, agree upon and execute any cease-fire arrangements. The war could be protracted out to the last weapon.

In any case, as present satellite systems are constituted, the nuclear attack itself would have much the same effect as attacks on the space segments of the systems. Most military satellites would quickly become useless because the ground control stations which maintain them would be destroyed. Similarly, the many ground stations which send or receive information through satellites or process the information satellites gather would be destroyed. Many electronic circuits both in ground terminals (whether they were stationary or mobile) and aboard satellites would be fatally damaged by the electromagnetic pulse and systems-generated electromagnetic pulse produced by nuclear explosions.[18]

With all these dangers in mind, the US Defense Department has begun to design (and in some instances already to build) satellite systems somewhat less vulnerable either to anti-satellite weapons or to the effects of nuclear warfare. Measures to make satellite systems less vulnerable to attacks on fixed ground stations include: designing mobile ground control stations to keep operating satellites after primary control centres have been destroyed; building mobile read-out stations to receive data from the missile-warning satellites; placing, on Strategic Air Command aircraft, terminals capable of receiving nuclear detonation information directly from GPS satellites; building laser–communication cross-links into the missile-warning satellites so they can by-pass ground-based links; hardening electronic components in satellites and air or ground terminals; designing satellite systems to 'degrade gracefully' after the loss of ground support (this feature is advertised for the Global Positioning

System), and designing greater autonomy—independence from ground control—into satellites.

These measures suggest that the doctrines of protracted nuclear war have actually reached the research and development, and, to some extent, the operational branches of the US armed services. On the other hand, the debate goes on as to whether these measures would be sufficient to assure a real protracted nuclear war-fighting capability—and, indeed, whether such a capability can (or should) be bought at any price.

VII. Space-based ballistic missile defence and nuclear war-fighting

At first glance, a system which would seem to make nuclear war-fighting a much more plausible proposition is the kind of space-based ballistic missile defence implied by President Reagan's 'Star Wars' speech of 23 March 1983. A highly effective anti-ballistic missile and anti-aircraft defence backing up a powerful counterforce capability could make the resort to nuclear war a fairly attractive military proposition. The first strike would eliminate some portion of enemy retaliatory capability and the defensive system would screen out most of its remaining forces, thus reducing the first-striker's damages to 'tolerable' levels.

On the other hand, if the other side possessed a similar defensive capability, then it could protect the retaliatory forces from the initial counterforce attack. If one believes that today's growing vulnerability of ground-based missiles actually invites pre-emptive attacks (and therefore that aircraft and sea-launched missiles are negligible deterrents), then the mutual build-up of defences might make some sense. It would have to be done with the greatest co-ordination, however. In the absence of clear agreements beforehand, the likely response of either side to a defensive build-up by the other would be an offensive compensation. Indeed, both sides are at work today on new penetration aids designed to overcome potential new defensive systems.

It is conceivable, though improbable, that defensive technology could be found for which there was no immediate offensive answer. President Reagan suggested that such technology might be shared at some point. This suggestion implies the political possibility of voluntarily giving up what must look like the opportunity to win overwhelming nuclear superiority over the adversary by, in effect, unilaterally disarming him.

If that sharing did not take place, or if the side developing the technology appeared to be waiting until his superiority was achieved before being willing to share, what would the defenceless side do? Would it suspect the other side of planning nuclear blackmail, at best, or a nuclear attack, at worst? Would it wait to find out, or would it strike pre-emptively, before enemy defences were in place? Such a pre-emptive strike might be especially tempting if the defensive system were being deployed in space, where it could be attacked without hitting the enemy's territory or population.

If highly effective, though imperfect, ballistic missile defence systems could be built more or less simultaneously on both sides, it is clear that they would at least reduce the plausibility of doctrines of limited nuclear options and counterforce attacks. What the defensive build-up would not do is provide any more security to populations if nuclear war actually occurred. On the contrary, heavy defences would place a premium on each side striving to maintain its 'assured destruction capability' against the other. Each side would probably: (a) develop offensive countermeasures against the defence; (b) add more warheads to its arsenal; and (c) aim its weapons at cities, many of which could surely be destroyed, instead of at military targets, since precision attacks would no longer be possible. The end result would be the same old balance of terror we knew before doctrines and technologies of limited nuclear war became fashionable. The price of these results would be vast expenditures on new defensive *and* offensive systems.

President Reagan's dream of a perfect defence which dissolved the nuclear balance of terror might just come true if some new technology can do what now seems impossible (defeat *every* plausible kind of strategic nuclear delivery vehicle) *and* if both sides could agree to deploy such technology in unison. (Alternatively, the two could agree to deploy such defensive systems while drastically reducing all types of offensive systems.) The United States and the Soviet Union would be invulnerable to each other and to attacks from other, lesser nuclear powers.

This scenario leaves some questions unanswered, however. First, how would the rest of the world react to the abilities of the United States and the Soviet Union to wield their power (nuclear or conventional) against third powers? Second, what would the United States substitute for its current doctrine of extended deterrence, according to which the Soviet Union is thought to be deterred from unsavoury actions by the risk of ultimate escalation of any conflict with the United States to nuclear war? Third, if the condition of mutual invulnerability between the United States and the Soviet Union is truly attractive to both, why do not the two simply agree today to a drastic reduction of offensive nuclear forces coupled with a build-up of currently available defensive technologies to handle what is left?

Notes and references

1. Kahn, H., *On Thermonuclear War* (Princeton University Press, Princeton, NJ, 1960), seemed to argue in both directions. On the one hand, he pointed out that, given the destructiveness of nuclear weapons, a variety of nuclear options beyond a simple, spasmic nuclear war was desirable. On the other hand, in arguing for civil defence, he encouraged the squeamish to "think about the unthinkable" and to believe that society could, with proper preparations, survive a nuclear war more or less intact.
2. Reagan Administration Deputy Under Secretary of Defense T. K. Jones as quoted by Scheer, R., *With Enough Shovels: Reagan, Bush & Nuclear War* (Random House, New York, 1982), p. 18.

3. For a history of Pentagon and military think-tank debates about the feasibility of limited war, see Kaplan, F., *The Wizards of Armageddon* (Simon & Schuster, New York, 1983).

4. Cf. Bundy, M., 'To Cap the Volcano', *Foreign Affairs*, Vol. 48, No. 1, October 1969, p. 10.

5. Cf. Gallois, P., *The Balance of Terror* (Houghton–Mifflin, Boston, MA, 1961).

6. The evolution of McNamara-era thinking on assured destruction is related to two of his Systems Analysis office 'whiz kids': Enthoven, A. C. and Smith, K. W., *How Much is Enough? Shaping the Defense Program, 1961–1969* (Harper & Row, New York, 1972), especially pp. 165–210.

7. Cf. Kaplan (note 3), pp. 315–327 and Enthoven and Smith (note 6).

8. Kaplan (note 3), p. 219.

9. Enthoven and Smith (note 6), p. 189.

10. This means, incidentally, that fewer bombers need be maintained in the first place, since more would be expected to survive attack.

11. Hendricks, G. K., 'Electronics and military space systems', Presentation at Air Force Association Wakefield, MA, unpublished, p. 7, reported in Karas, T. H., *The New High Ground* (Simon & Schuster, New York, 1983), pp. 91–92.

12. Testimony of Harry L. Van Trees in US Congress, Senate Committee on Armed Services, *Department of Defense Authorization for Appropriations for Fiscal Year 1982*, Hearings before the Committee on Armed Services on S. 815, 97th Congress, 1st session, 1981, p. 4205.

13. In principle, imaging satellites with near-instantaneous electronic data transmission could be used for wartime tactical reconnaissance. The resulting target damage assessments could guide 're-strike' decisions for bombers and reserve missiles. But, as things stand, even if the satellites were to survive the opening stages of the war, the ground stations needed to control them and receive and process their data would not.

14. Testimony of Brig. Gen. B. P. Randolph, in US Congress, Senate Committee on Armed Services, *Department of Defense Authorization for Appropriations for Fiscal Year 1983*, Hearings before the Committed on Armed Services on S. 815, 97th Congress, 2nd session, 1982, pp. 4624–4625.

15. Gray, C.S., *American Military Space Policy: Information Systems, Weapon Systems and Arms Control* (Abt Books, Cambridge, MA, 1983), pp. 29–30.

16. This list is loosely adapted from a useful reference work: Giffen, R., *US Space System Survivability: Strategic Alternatives for the 1980s*, National Security Affairs Monograph Series 82–84 (National Defense University Press, Washington, DC, 1982), pp. 25–32.

17. The exceptions might be space mines (if their targets had not been manoeuvred out of range) and nuclear weapons exploded in the general vicinity in which the targets *might* be.

18. Cf. Lippert, J., 'The hidden destroyer: EMP—disturbance from space', *NATO's Sixteen Nations*, Vol. 28, April–May 1983, pp. 38–40, 43.

Paper 2. Strategic doctrine, the militarization and the 'semi-militarization' of space

Deborah Shapley*

2236 Q Street NW, Washington, DC 20008, USA

I. Strategic doctrine and space systems

The trend of US strategic thinking in the last decade towards considering seriously the possibility of *fighting out* and winning a nuclear war has prompted concern on both sides of the Atlantic. Critics denounce it as madness and a lowering of the threshold for nuclear war, while advocates argue that it is more 'humane' than earlier doctrines that stopped at massive nuclear retaliation and is, therefore, a more credible deterrent.

One question is whether this new emphasis has been prompted by growing military space capabilities. Besides more accurate intercontinental ballistic missiles (ICBMs), space technology has had the most to do with changing perceptions so that nuclear war-fighting seems possible. This technology already includes improved systems for early warning and tracking of missiles in flight, command and controls 'hardened' against nuclear blast effects and anti-satellite (ASAT) systems. It tempts political leaders to believe that their forces could ride out a nuclear attack and make successive counter-strikes—that they may communicate with and control their own forces throughout a nuclear war.

Which came first, military doctrine that assumed a nuclear war can be fought out or the technology, particularly space technology, that seems to make this possible? The first part of this paper briefly discusses the evolution of nuclear war-fighting doctrine in the United States and concludes that until recently it has evolved independently from technological capabilities in space. The second part takes up the present space technology explosion that is now influencing doctrine and inducing some laymen to believe that nuclear war is

* The author is currently a freelance writer on defence and scientific affairs, and a guest scholar at Resources for the Future, Inc. The views expressed herein are those of the author and not those of RFF, Inc.

practical. The third part of this paper discusses the impact of increasing military research, development and testing in space. It argues that several 'grey areas' are emerging as a result of this new arms race, the effects of which could be destabilizing even in conventional conflicts and crisis situations. It asks: can doctrine, or explicit national policy, stop the erosion of the sanctuary of space?

From massive retaliation to assured destruction

Lawrence Freedman[1] has ably described the US military's early thinking about the atomic bomb. According to Freedman, in the early days there were two schools of thought about how it should be used. What can be termed Doctrine Number One was based on existing doctrine for conventional bombing with long-range aircraft. It stressed "the critical importance of the first blow" as a war-winning event. Such strikes had used massive amounts of conventional bombs in the past but could be more effective with atomic bombs in the future. Their purpose was to break enemy morale; their use was psychological, aimed at civilians and political leaders. This was the strategy behind the choice of Hiroshima and Nagasaki as targets, Freedman writes.

Doctrine Number Two was illustrated in a post-war book by Basil Liddell Hart, quoted by Freedman in his analysis. Liddell Hart predicted that the reach and destructiveness of atomic bombs carried by aircraft, as well as the V-2 weapons, would make warfare 'automatic'; the new systems would reach over the heads of land armies battling one another directly on the ground. They could therefore eliminate some of the grittiness of war, making it precise, remote and automatic.

These two concepts have come down to us today in various forms. Both 'massive retaliation', enunciated by John Foster Dulles in April 1954, and Robert McNamara's 'assured destruction' of the 1960s stressed the psychological shock value of a US nuclear counter-strike against the Soviet Union. The massive retaliation doctrine said that in response to (apparently any) Soviet aggression, the United States would retaliate 'without inhibition' using its nuclear weapons. The assured destruction doctrine stated that the United States would respond to a *nuclear* first strike by the Soviet Union with a nuclear counter-attack certain to destroy 20–33 per cent of the Soviet population and 50–75 per cent of Soviet industrial capacity. The two doctrines evolved in different circumstances and were, of course, very different from one another. But both aimed to influence the thinking of Soviet political leaders and civilians as much as to address the military situation; both sought to use the shock value of a certain, nuclear blow as a deterrent.

Neither doctrine relied on precision bombing or sophisticated command and control. And by today's standards, little such existed in the 1950s and 1960s. Assured destruction's counter-city, counter-industry strategy was especially suited to the relatively inaccurate submarine-launched ballistic missiles (SLBMs) of the 1960s that would survive the first strike to retaliate. The guarantee of 'massive' response in Dulles' doctrine did not require precisely targeted weapons. In another context, Freedman cites a crisp comment from Liddell Hart that might apply to these doctrines: "inaccuracy of weapon-aim fostered inhumanity of war-aim".[2]

It could be concluded, therefore, that technology limited the nuclear war-fighting doctrines of the 1950s and 1960s; that massive retaliation and assured destruction arose *because* of the absence of accurate guidance, terminal homing, or lock-on stellar navigation aids and the like. If all that US forces could do was to lob nuclear bombs more or less blindly into the Soviet Union the way a child lobs stones over a fence, it was best for the United States to have a doctrine that assumed that the resulting destruction would be indiscriminate.

In fact, especially when given new guidances in 1961 by McNamara, who was trying to get away from the rigidity of massive retaliation policy, US targeting commands began including precise military targets in their nuclear war-fighting plans. In effect, they implemented Doctrine Number Two: the use of nuclear weapons as more powerful, long-range conventional bombs. Later, McNamara found that the targeting commands were using his 1961 guidance to add more and more targets, and to argue for very large numbers of nuclear weapons. So he turned to assured destruction to stress the limited requirements for the nuclear arsenal. Nonetheless, 90 per cent of the targets of the US Strategic Air Command's (SAC) nuclear weapons in the 1960s consisted of precise, military locations, although SAC's ability to carry out precision atomic bombing was dubious. In the early days, technological capability and nuclear doctrine did not march in step.

Counterforce and nuclear war-fighting

Space assets, such as photographic and geodetic satellites, made both side's ICBMs more and more accurate in the 1970s. Overall, however, most military uses of space helped maintain peace. Space technology enabled global, high quality communications, reconnaissance to verify arms control agreements, and nuclear-blast detection to monitor compliance with nuclear test bans: on balance, all contributed to stability. In addition, for the last 25 years, neither side has had an efficient, high-confidence way of shooting the other side's satellites down. So space evolved as a 'sanctuary' and an early, important goal of arms control became the continued non-militarization of space.

Meanwhile, counterforce doctrine for nuclear war emerged in the early 1970s. It started with a review of alternative strategic options ordered by Henry Kissinger in 1972, but did not receive much publicity until Secretary of Defense James Schlesinger began discussing it publicly in 1973. The new doctrine stressed US readiness to fight small-scale nuclear exchanges, demonstration 'shots across the bow' with nuclear weapons, or response to a Soviet attack with only part of the US retaliatory force.[3]

Schlesinger's counterforce doctrine resembled Doctrine Number Two mentioned above, in that it aimed to treat nuclear war as a more destructive version of conventional war. It grew out of criticism of assured destruction doctrine and from SAC's long-standing interest in precision bombing. Harold Brown, as Secretary of Defense, echoed Schlesinger's view that counterforce was more realistic than assured destruction: the President needed some other option than flinging all his nuclear stones over the fence at the Soviet Union.

Schlesinger's counterforce doctrine focused on the more likely contingencies, such as a Soviet attack using only one or two nuclear weapons. The idea was to alter targeting plans and political leaders' thinking so that some more restrained form of retaliation could be chosen depending on circumstances. Since 1973 this view has evolved to stress the entire nuclear war-fighting process. Officials now speak of being able to redirect and control successive exchanges and military forces in the 'trans-attack' and post-attack periods.

This refinement of counterforce doctrine, which can be termed nuclear war-fighting doctrine, requires that the military be ready with a range of nuclear responses, and that global military command, control, communications and intelligence (C^3I) systems be hardened against nuclear blast effects. Since many C^3I systems are based in space, and since space is the only 'hill' from which these war-planners can view the nuclear battle, the new war-fighting doctrine has been accompanied by an emphasis on nuclear-hardened space technologies. It could even be said that the new nuclear doctrine proposes to use space technology the way balloons were used in the nineteenth century, to follow the course of the battle from the highest possible ground.

In terms of doctrine, we seem to have come full circle back to Liddell Hart's predictions made after the V-2 campaign, Hiroshima and Nagasaki. The latest press scenarios which talk about fighting a nuclear war entirely up in space make it sound like the ultimate remote-control war, with the 'eyes', 'ears', and perhaps one day the 'brains' of the command authorities, located up in space.

Space technology: a double-edged sword

Technology has had an important role in giving credibility to counterforce and nuclear war-fighting doctrines. Steady upgrading in the accuracy of US land-based ICBMs, for example, has made precision targeting of ICBMs and now SLBMs seem practical. In turn, this engendered doctrinal debates. Should the USA seek the implied ability to carry out a 'first strike'? What would happen when—as was inevitable—the Soviet Union caught up and deployed its own high-accuracy ICBMs, thus making US forces theoretically vulnerable to a Soviet first strike? These debates entailed many issues of doctrine and technology and their interaction.

Space technology has played an important, though ambiguous, role in them. An excellent example is provided by the Defense Support Program (DSP) satellites whose infra-red detectors can sense the heat plumes from missile launches from the Soviet Union and China. Such information is sent to ground stations in Australia and Colorado indicating the number of missiles launched and their trajectories. They are also used for detection of nuclear explosions to verify the 1963 Partial Test Ban Treaty.

These early warning satellites play a double role. On the one hand, they are stabilizing, enabling US leaders to learn of Soviet missile launches as they happen and to compute the trajectories so as to know, ahead of time, which targets are being attacked. With half an hour's warning, there is conceivably time for the President to query Moscow as to whether the launch is an error, to move himself and other leaders to safe locations, and to make critical decisions about a response. The DSP satellites thus eliminate much of the uncertainty about a Soviet attack that prevailed in the days of the ground-based defence early warning (DEW) line, which provided far less warning, no knowledge of which targets were being attacked and could mistake even the rising moon for an incoming Soviet missile.

On the other hand, now that Soviet missiles have a high likelihood of hitting US missiles in their silos, and now that US missile command centres can re-target weapons more rapidly, the DSP satellites could help the United States launch its land-based ICBMs only on *warning* of an attack.

The DSP is a good example of how space technology, which has played a secondary role in nuclear war-fighting doctrine in the past, could entice some people to consider nuclear war a 'practical' proposition.

A great difficulty in space arms control will be the double-edged character of much space technology. The DSP satellites contribute to stability through verification and advance warning. But the same systems enhance war-fighting capabilities (if they survive and work) and thus are inviting targets as well. So they can be considered, for arms control purposes, as both 'stabilizing' and 'destabilizing' at the same time.

II. Current explosion in space technology

Characteristics

So the rather stable situation space has enjoyed for the last 25 years is changing. More and more space systems are acquiring this double-edged character. Moreover, three 'streams' of technological development are accelerating this trend, and eroding the sanctuary of space still further. Most of these developments do not involve revolutionary new technologies, insofar as is publicly known. Rather, they are the application to space of technologies already proved on Earth, or incremental improvements in existing technology which have evolved into significant new capabilities through a process called 'technology creep'.[4]

These developments raise new problems which require resolution by the United States and the Soviet Union, either in the form of explicit agreements, tacit ones or unilateral—but clear—national policy. While it is unclear how much of this technology will find its way into completed systems, and what those systems will be exactly, their development could undermine the old arms control goal of demilitarizing space.

The technologies have three characteristics relevant to policy. First, space is like the oceans, the land and the atmosphere: it can be used by many different users, for different purposes, with different hardware. A given bit of technology can have many uses. A piece of hardware in space—say a weather satellite—in the hands of one user may be of critical importance to civilian life. Yet in the hands of another user, say, SAC, a weather satellite enables US B-52 pilots to have round-the-clock weather information along their flight paths to their targets in the Soviet Union.

A second characteristic is the extreme asymmetry between the Soviet Union's and the United States' space programmes. US military communications depend heavily on satellites; Soviet military communications rely more on overland and airborne communications between its central and peripheral areas. Since arms control agreements are most acceptable when they appear to be symmetrical, arms control agreements for space may be difficult to negotiate because of this problem. This asymmetry also makes especially futile the copy-cat character of a space arms race: a system needed by one side may be fairly useless to the other, which may, nonetheless, feel compelled to copy it.

Third, the United States and the Soviet Union use the same test ground in their military space R&D—unlike their competition in tanks, fighters or even ICBMs. It is easy to see that if the United States and the Soviet Union were to field-test their tanks in the same place, there might be a lot of accidental or mischievous snooping and tampering, and to avoid incidents the two sides might agree to a protocol governing R&D activities. In space, both sides now test anti-satellite systems and are increasing other military R&D; to avoid 'accidents' a protocol governing testing may be needed, even though it would be extremely difficult to make airtight or to verify.

Indeed, this long, intermediate phase—perhaps while arms control negotiations were going on—might be called the 'semi-militarization' of space. Perhaps it is a subject for policy making and arms control in its own right.

C^3I improvements and doctrine

Historically, space-based reconnaissance, electronic intelligence and communications systems have contributed to stability. Existing arms control agreements would be impossible to verify without the benefit of national technical means of verification in space. Since 1960, when the USSR declared its airspace off limits by shooting down Gary Powers' U-2 spy plane, both sides have had a tacit understanding that reconnaissance satellites—which are beyond the range of ordinary anti-air weapons—enjoy sanctuary.

Now, however, both sides are upgrading the capabilities of these C^3I systems. The new KH-11 photographic reconnaissance satellites are hardened against some nuclear effects in the Earth's atmosphere, though not a direct attack by a nuclear-armed ASAT weapon. Nuclear-hardened reconnaissance satellites will not only aid stability in times of crisis but be useful in nuclear war-fighting too.

The capabilities of the DSP satellites in geosynchronous orbit are being upgraded. The DSP system has been upgraded from having 2 000 sensors on board to having 80 000, thus providing a finer 'picture' of the location, number and flight paths of the missiles.[5] Another key modernization is that they will relay their data faster to command authorities. They are being made more independent of their ground stations, so as to operate after the ground stations are destroyed at the outset of war. The US military also enthusiastically supports research in artificial intelligence (AI). AI-aided, space-based command and control aimed at fighting out a nuclear war sounds like the ultimate scenario for remote-control warfare, in which the role of man becomes irrelevant!

Several improvements in military C^3I are blurring the distinction between military and civilian space systems, and making peaceful systems, such as those for weather and navigation, into possible military targets.

One example is the Global Positioning System (GPS) of NAVSTAR satellites, of which some are already in orbit and the complete set is expected to be up by the late 1980s. The GPS offers tempting new capabilities to military users, on the ground, at sea or in the air. When their vehicles are equipped with simple receivers they can take a fix on their position to within a few inches over encrypted channels. Even old-fashioned 'dumb' bombs become precise, 'smart' weapons at little cost once they are equipped with the receivers linking them to the GPS. GPS enables planes and helicopters to land knowing their position exactly, making landings on unfamiliar terrain or beaches, or at night, feasible. Yet over unencrypted, civilian channels, the GPS will offer three-dimensional position information only to within 200 m and so be no more accurate for civilian aircraft, for example, than present air traffic control systems.

Meanwhile, the GPS satellites will also have on board the Integrated Operational Nuclear Detection System (IONDS), the replacement for the older VELA nuclear blast detection satellites. IONDS will be nuclear-hardened as well. The new GPS system could revolutionize commercial transportation world-wide—but it remains only partially a civilian system. Since it could be most useful in the conduct of both conventional and nuclear war, it will be a tempting target for enemy anti-satellite attacks. GPS typifies the ambiguity of the space arms race, for it tempts the US military to depend on GPS, even in wartime, even though there is a good likelihood the GPS could be knocked out of operation.

These improvements in C^3I raise doctrinal problems. On the one hand, they are stabilizing: secure, reliable global communications will help the President to bring a nuclear war to a quicker conclusion. But at the same time, they tempt political leaders (who are not engineeers, and cannot know the system's faults and shortcomings) to believe they will be able to fight out and control nuclear war—a belief which smacks of divine omniscience.[6]

The ASAT programmes and doctrine

As mentioned, one reason for the sanctuarization of space for two decades has been the inability of either side to shoot down, efficiently, the space systems of the other. Now, however, just as the lower-orbit systems for reconnaissance, electronic ferret and other C^3I purposes are becoming more valuable assets, both sides are acquiring the ability to shoot them down. Two destabilizing technologies are converging: the technological improvements that make them more valuable targets, and the technology for attacking satellites with high precision, and high confidence, and in ways that are hard to detect.

The Soviet system, which has been tested from time to time since 1968, caused little alarm in the United States. It entails launching a rocket bearing an attack satellite, placing it in orbit and manoeuvring it to have it approach the orbiting target satellite. Only one of the 20 tests conducted so far has been said by the US media to have been a 'kill', although 13 others, in which the attack satellite passed within a kilometre of the target, have come close enough to have inspected it or to have destroyed it had the attack satellite exploded (see paper 5, page 83). Currently, the Soviet ASAT system is estimated to be able to reach targets up to 2 300 km out, although with a larger booster it could conceivably reach targets in geosynchronous orbit. Despite its clumsy, time consuming mode of operation, the programme's existence—or rather the existence of the Soviet ASAT tests—created strong pressures in the US military to have an ASAT programme of its own. The official rationale for restarting a US ASAT programme was the need to disable Soviet ocean surveillance satellites. But a more basic reason was the copy-cat compulsion; if the Soviets had an ASAT programme—no matter how clumsy—the USA should have one too.

Thus the United States is now testing its own ASAT system, one which, when copied by the Soviet Union, could backfire, becoming a serious threat to US space systems.

Unlike the Soviet system, which requires an easily detectable rocket launch and time-consuming manoeuvre of the satellite into co-orbit with the target, the US system consists of an easy to hide kit that can be mounted on any F-15 aircraft. Almost instantaneously, the non-nuclear ASAT 'bullet' locks onto its target in space and collides with it.[7] The side whose satellite was attacked would not know an attack was contemplated or under way (except in the unlikely case that its radar coverage of all F-15 flights world-wide was so complete that it tracked every flight and picked up the launch of a smaller, faster, upward-moving object from the aircraft).

The flexibility of the US ASAT system is another major advance over the Soviet one. Because the F-15s can be based in many parts of the globe, and can fly around before launch of their ASAT 'bullets', it need not wait for the satellite to pass over the launch site. Further, an ASAT system that can put many ASAT 'bullets' on many launch vehicles could attack many satellites at once, and, conceivably, 'clean out the sky' of a particular group of satellites. At present, both the US and Soviet ASAT systems can only reach targets at low altitudes. The F-15 based ASAT would have to be modified substantially to be able to attack targets in geosynchronous or near-geosynchronous orbit.

The US ASAT system is a major jump in space technological capability because of its flexibility, ability to hide, speed and efficiency of operation.

Moreover, it could stay in the test phase for years and still be viewed by the other side as a significant threat. The US ASAT thus resembles the bomb that a terrorist surreptitiously places under the hood of a car parked on the street: once the attack occurs, he can be far away and have erased all trace of his actions.

The US system may not in itself change the balance of power in space. Indeed, the argument for it is that it is needed to compensate for other Soviet capabilities—their ocean surveillance systems. The arguments for and against proceeding with the US ASAT system, as recent US Congressional debate shows, resemble those over whether to arm US ICBMs with multiple, independently-targetable re-entry vehicles (MIRVs) in the late 1960s—a significant new capability which the Soviet Union did not have at that time. But just as the Soviets proceeded to develop and deploy their own MIRVs after the USA did—thereby making the US land-based ICBM force theoretically vulnerable to a Soviet first strike—the Soviets may proceed with a flexible, high-precision, high-confidence ASAT weapon once the USA proceeds with the F-15 system.

What could change the balance of power in space, therefore, would be the Soviet copy of the US ASAT system or some variant with the same characteristics. As far as is publicly known, the USSR is not developing one, and it would face formidable technological obstacles in doing so. For example, the F-15's 'bullet' relies on a cryogenically cooled lens to detect the faint heat of the target satellite from the background of the sky. The only publicly known Soviet attempt at cryogenically cooled lenses was a telescope aboard one of their manned missions, reported not to have worked well or been much used. Technology aside, however, the USSR has a great incentive to develop such a system in the next few years, if only because of the extreme US reliance on a relatively small number of very important, very expensive satellites (for example, the USA usually has only two or three reconnaissance satellites in orbit).

So, as with MIRVs, the Soviet version of the F-15 ASAT system may come back to haunt US military planners with a problem far larger than the one the F-15 ASAT was originally built to solve. The asymmetries between the two sides' space programmes mean that a flexible, easy to hide, clean-out-the-sky system in the hands of the USSR will be a far greater threat to US military capabilities than the US version is to Soviet capabilities.

The F-15 ASAT system enables a nation having few scruples about protecting itself to shoot down almost any space target at will, even surreptitiously. The Soviet shooting down of the Korean civilian airliner in September 1983 suggests that the USSR may have few inhibitions concerning using such a weapon to knock out US reconnaisance, electronic ferret or even weather satellites, no matter how 'peaceful' the USA claims them to be.

What is doctrine on this point? Would the USA take the position that an attack on one of its reconnaissance satellites was an act of war? Would an attack on a weather satellite be an act of war? And how, especially if the attack were surreptitious, could the USA prove to the world that a 'sniper attack' on one of its satellites had taken place? Clearly, if both sides acquire such 'mischief' weapons, policy on these points will have to be very clear indeed. The need for more exploration of the status of space systems—in the sense of the consequences of shooting them down—should be the subject of national policy making and discussed in any future space arms control negotiations.

The implications of the Soviet copy of the F-15 ASAT system go well beyond mischief making. As stated earlier, one reason that the stabilizing systems, such as reconnaissance satellites, have remained in sanctuary for so long is that neither side has had a practical way to attack them short of detonating a nuclear weapon in space. Buy why should both sides declare reconnaissance satellites off-limits once they have the ability to shoot them down? Developments in ASAT technology are introducing grave new uncertainties into previously successful understandings about space and already eroding its status as a sanctuary.

Space-based lasers and doctrine

Another technological development posing doctrinal problems is the prospect of mounting unmanned battle stations capable of both anti-satellite and anti-ballistic missile (ABM) attacks in space. The most discussed version would use a laser beam, generated on the station, able to hit pin-point targets such as ICBM missiles in flight, and sweep from one target to another. Laser research has been actively pursued by both superpowers for years; and the possibility of charged particle beam weapons was raised when the US aerospace press charged in 1978 that the Soviets had an active programme. These rumours gave rise to stepped-up US charged particle beam efforts, and the US military has also paid greater attention to laser weapons since then too. The technical feasibility of such weapons, both within the atmosphere and in space, has always been in doubt. Nonetheless President Ronald Reagan, in a speech on 23 March 1983, advocated the creation of systems that could provide a shield against nuclear attack and thus relieve the USA of the spectre of nuclear war. The speech (the so-called 'Star Wars' speech) provoked much talk about space-based ABM systems, and whether they indeed offer a realistic hope of future invulnerability. These systems are discussed in paper 7, page 107.[8]

There is a crucial difference between the completed system alluded to by President Reagan in his speech—which would be stabilizing if both sides had equally effective systems *and* renounced their offensive weapons—and the process of getting there; during the 10, 20 or more years of research, development and actual testing in space, whichever side happened to be ahead in its R&D programme would be, *de facto*, destabilizing the balance of power.

The system outlined by the President can be dubbed a 'black box war-stopping machine'. It is up in space, unmanned presumably, and equipped with its own AI, sensors and C^3I systems. Presumably, when it sees a missile attack it sprays its beam on the missiles and hits every single one. Since it can stop *all* the attacking missiles, theoretically it is a shield in the sky, a machine for executing a doctrine of assured survival, the opposite of assured destruction. The latter rested on mutual vulnerability; with perfect ABM systems, both sides could conceivably have mutual invulnerability.

But, however superficially attractive, the black box war-stopping machine and the mutual invulnerability doctrine have many, many problems, so far barely examined in the general debate. For instance, while the space-based laser (SBL) may hit ballistic missiles above the atmosphere, it cannot hit ground-hugging cruise missiles having smaller heat trails and masked from the laser beam by the atmosphere itself. Both sides could still execute attacks by non-ICBM means: for example, if the USSR felt its land-based and long-range sea-based ICBMs could be stopped by the SBL, it would have great incentive to send its missile-carrying submarines close in to US coasts to execute quick nuclear attacks on the USA using missiles with perhaps three or seven minute flight times that provided little warning indeed. Moreover, it would be hard to prevent both sides, as they researched their space-based ABM weapons, from also figuring out ways to penetrate the other sides's SBL. Therefore, SBL *development*—even that which falls far short of deployment—could stimulate a dangerous new race in offensive arms.

Indeed, in the case of this prospective technology, doctrine is at best a mere afterthought. The real advocates of SBL development in the United States appear to be those in the military, in Congress and in the civilian defence community who see space as a new military frontier—and one in which the United States has a clear technological lead. Recent discussions in Congress and elsewhere suggest that the driving force is a longing—not for a new dawn in strategic doctrine—but for clear US military superiority, which, this group feels, has been lost in other theatres. To this group, SBL is an urgent priority.

Obviously, if one side starts developing a 'shield' against nuclear attack, without reducing its offensive forces, it creates an unacceptable threat of a first strike against the other. This is not to say that the US military should not use new technology, or ignore the potential for stabilizing new systems in space. But it should be obvious that a push by the United States to dominate this new high ground with the SBL will only provoke new offensive arms building and deployments by the USSR. To continue the example above, in which the Soviet Union counters by preparing closer-in submarine-launched nuclear strikes against the USA to avoid sending its nuclear weapons above the atmosphere where they are vulnerable to the SBL, one must ask if the US military would prefer to be threatened by nuclear attacks with three to seven minutes' warning time than by attacks with the present warning time of 30 minutes? So before there is any serious effort at SBL development, the consequences should be considered closely.

Finally, the black box is a far cry from what is possible at the moment. There are a number of laser R&D programmes which have had mixed results, and enormous technical obstacles to even building the black box. Tsipis[9] has listed most of these: to operate the battle station would require thousands of space shuttle trips carrying only fuel; a mirror to point such a beam—if it can be built—could just as easily be used by the defending side to deflect it; and aiming and tracking the beam would be extremely difficult. Moreover, a variety of countermeasures are available to make ICBMs invulnerable that might be cheaper than building the SBL in the first place. And, of course, one side's SBL battle station (let alone the 50 or so needed for an effective, global shield) is a prime target to the other side, so the SBL stations would be the objects of ASAT fire, space mines and other measures. In the end, the valuable, big SBL stations might become the aircraft carriers of the sky, requiring an entire fleet of defending satellites to protect them, defensive zones around them and automatic 'launch on warning' systems to get any object that comes too near. What would it do about a Soviet inspection satellite coming into the vicinity for the peaceful purpose of assuring there was not some new gizmo on board? The problems are legion.

The SBL proposal presents the unfortunate dilemma found in so many other space technologies. It has a chance of being stabilizing, under a few, very limited configurations, and if both sides build their respective systems in step. But it requires a long, intermediate stage which would easily become a massive race in offensive and defensive arms. So, however tantalizing the dream of a 'black box war-stopping machine' (let alone an automatic one, remote from the fragile Earth), further study may show it to be a chimera.

New instabilities

In sum, these new technologies raise critical new instabilities. In the field of C^3I, does the nuclear hardening of systems warrant specific policies or doctrines to avoid misinterpretations? In general, the argument that better communications and information will help stop the war—hence that hardening contributes to stability—will be hard to refute, even though it makes C^3I systems inviting targets.

ASAT systems pose other problems. Some ASAT development is identical to ABM development, and either side could undertake ABM developments prohibited by the 1972 ABM Treaty, under the guise of ASAT research. Another problem is the potential of easily concealed, high-confidence ASAT weapons to violate the sanctuary of space. A ban on the F-15 style ASAT and other weapons with these characteristics might not only close the loophole in the rules of research mentioned above, but could prevent the instabilities caused by such mischief weapons.

More important, if R&D makes SBLs seem practical, the pressure will build up to proceed with a 'black box war-stopping machine'. Critically, a decision to build a shield against ICBMs means turning away, for once and for all, from the doctrine of mutual vulnerability, and going towards its opposite. The implications of such a step warrant much study and public discussion.

III. Implications for crises, conventional wars and the 'semi-militarization' phase

Most media and public attention to the new military space technologies has focused on their use in nuclear war. Yet they could be just as destabilizing in conventional wars or in crises. Many of the systems described earlier have tactical uses in more limited theatres of war. Many provide critical information in times of crisis: US satellites, for example, were rumoured to be providing Great Britain with data on the movement of the Argentine fleet and troops during the 1982 Falklands/Malvinas conflict. Arms control measures for space must take account of these important, if less exotic, roles. Perhaps the strongest case for arms control and new attention to doctrine for space systems comes from these far more likely cases (see papers 9, page 131 and 10, page 145).

Some of the technologies discussed earlier could be used in conventional wars or crises. A prime example is the F-15 ASAT system of the USA. This system, or some other hard-to-detect, high-confidence ASAT system, could tempt its owner to use it to knock out a vital reconnaissance or ferret satellite to gain advantage in a crisis. Particularly 'mischief' ASAT activities, such as microwave jamming or laser blinding, could be handy in times of crisis. Such possibilities raise 'grey areas' of national policy and doctrine. Would such an attack be considered an act of war by the side whose satellite had been hit? Would it justify escalation of a low-level conflict already in progress? In war or crisis, what is the understood *quid pro quo* for the loss of an important satellite? An aircraft carrier? A home port? Firing a single nuclear weapon? None of this is, at present, clear.

Another little-publicized grey area is whether conventional wars will spread to space, and whether this will be considered escalation, and, if so, what level of escalation. Does it depend on the kind of space system that is attacked? Certainly, some of the new space technology could make space systems tempting targets in a conventional war. For example, the US space shuttle will fly two experiments: Teal Ruby, a satellite launched from the shuttle which will try to track aircraft flying around below; and Talon Gold, which will test pointing and tracking of lasers in space, aimed at the ground, presumably to track targets for ground or space-based weapons.[10] Future capabilities could include the ability to distinguish, from space, between foliage and camouflage, and possibly to 'see' vehicle engine signatures on the ground, through infrared, even at night. These capabilities could help US commanders execute the new US army doctrine for fighting a conventional war in Europe, which emphasizes moves deep behind enemy lines and surprise actions. Remote sensing, through satellites, aircraft and drones, will be critical for this kind of war fighting.[11] There are doubtless some Soviet space systems that US commanders likewise would find tempting targets during a conventional war. So, as F-15 ASAT style technology is developed, and as the Soviets develop their own version in the future, it invites the spread of a conventional war to space.

How could the spread be prevented? One approach would be for either or both sides to declare all their space systems, including those useful in a conventional war, as effectively part of their home territory, so that an attack on a space object becomes tantamount to an attack on Washington, or Baltimore, for example. Thus, if satellites became the 'vital interests' of the United States, the USSR would understand that term to mean that in attacking one, it risked a US nuclear response. Such a unilateral declared policy would be stronger, of course, if it were also reinforced by bilateral agreement. This is one way to amplify existing law, such as the UN Charter and the SALT I accord's ban on interference with 'national technical means of verification', and make clear the risks on both sides. One problem would be, however, that an attack would have to be unambiguous; it would be hard for a US President to justify lobbing a nuclear bomb on the Soviet Union in response to a satellite 'malfunction'.

Other scenarios suggest other grey areas. The US·F-15 ASAT system is justified on the grounds that the USA needs to be able to destroy Soviet ocean radar satellites. Yet under what circumstances would it be used? When would the USSR be threatening the US carrier fleet, which would be, for example, steaming towards some trouble spot or pre-existing conflict, so much that an attack on a Soviet satellite would be justified? What would be the risk of escalation? What value does the USSR place on its space systems, particularly its ocean radar satellites? What response would it consider justified?

These few examples show how the evolution of space technology is posing new problems in both conventional and nuclear war, and to the roles of satellites in crisis periods. The sanctuary of space is being eroded. It would seem urgent, therefore, not only to explore arms control for space but also to explore ways in which doctrine and declared policy could clarify the value of the different space systems. Arms control and doctrine, working together, could help check the militarization of space.

Notes and references

1. Freedman, L., *The Evolution of Nuclear Strategy*, Studies in International Security, No. 20 (Macmillan, London, 1981).
2. See Freedman (note 1), p. 12.
3. See Freedman (note 1), pp. 359, 340, 377–382.
4. Shapley, D., 'Arms control as a regulator of military technology', *Daedalus*, Vol. 109, No. 1, Winter 1980, p. 145 ff; 'Technology creep and the arms race: ICBM problem a sleeper', *Science*, Vol. 201, No. 4361, 22 September 1978, pp. 1102–1105; 'Technology and the arms race: a world of absolute accuracy', *Science*, Vol. 201, No. 4362, 29 September 1978, pp. 1192–1196; 'Technology creep and the arms race: two future arms control problems', *Science*, Vol. 202, No. 4365, 20 October 1978, pp. 289–291. The first and last item specifically predict the impact of improved technology in militarizing space.
5. Karas, T., *The New High Ground* (Simon & Schuster, New York, 1983), p. 114.
6. See Karas (note 5), pp. 114, 122, 130–140.
7. See Karas, T. (note 5), pp. 148–154.
    Broad, J., 'Weapon against satellite ready for test', *New York Times*, 23 August 1983, p. C1.
8. See also Holloway, D. and Tyler, P.E., 'War in space: hardware and politics of an idea that's no joke', *Washington Post*, 3 April 1983, p. D1.
9. Tsipis, K., 'Laser weapons', *Scientific American*, Vol. 245, No. 6, December 1981, p. 51 ff.
10. See Karas, T. (note 5), pp. 120, 121, 185.
11. Shapley, D., 'The army's new fighting doctrine', *New York Times Sunday Magazine*, 28 November 1982, p. 35 ff.

Paper 3. Advantages and disadvantages of an eventual ban on deployment of military satellites

Carlo Trezza*

Ministry of Foreign Affairs, Piazza Farnecina, 00100 Rome, Italy

I. Introduction

In examining the issue of whether the deployment of military satellites should be banned, it is necessary to establish what kinds of satellite should be considered as belonging to such a category. At such an early stage of political research in this field a broad approach is advisable; one should therefore take into consideration all satellites the activities of which can have effects in the military field, regardless of whether they are directly owned or manned by the armed forces of a particular country. A military satellite need not necessarily be, and is usually not, a weapon, either offensive or defensive. The capacity to deliberately cause damage to another party is not a main criterion for attributing a military character to a satellite. Most of the ones performing military functions are, in fact, incapable of directly destroying or damaging another country's property.

In most cases military satellites accomplish a task which can be defined as auxiliary or instrumental to other more direct military activities. In a number of instances satellites can have a dual purpose: both military and civilian.

The categorization most widely used in today's literature on the subject, which defines as military satellites the broad range of reconnaissance and surveillance satellites, the auxiliary satellites (communication, meteorological and geodetic) and the anti-satellite (ASAT) satellites, is most suitable for the purposes of this study.

The destruction of any kind of satellite, civilian as well as military, would have, without any doubt, a destabilizing effect and should therefore be prevented. But the issue whether military satellites should be banned requires

---

*The views expressed in this study are the author's own and do not necessarily reflect official Italian positions.

a more articulate answer and more accurate distinctions must be made relating to different types of satellite.

II. *Reconnaissance and surveillance satellites*

The reconnaissance and surveillance satellites which perform an ever increasing role as 'national technical means of verification' (NTM) in arms control and disarmament agreements have a highly stabilizing function. They are also the most complex and the most important satellites carrying out military activities.

Although there is a certain official reluctance to identify satellites as national means of verification, the importance of such monitoring systems for arms control will grow in view of the increasing emphasis being given to transparency and to the verification of any commitment to arms reduction. The trust which each side places upon the means of verification has been an essential element in obtaining results, especially in strategic negotiations, and it remains a prerequisite for achieving progress in the future. Therefore satellites which have a direct use in the field of arms control provide a positive contribution to international stability: their banning is certainly not advisable as there is no question that it would entail destabilizing effects. The provision of non-interference with the national means of verification contemplated by many of the recent arms control texts indicates the importance that is attached to these devices and to their survival.

The same argument which was made for NTM can be repeated for satellites that perform reconnaissance and surveillance functions not related to a specific agreement and whose purpose lies in monitoring and collecting intelligence on the military activities of an adversary. The extensive use, especially by the USA and USSR, and the relative invulnerability, until now, of such devices, have established a certain degree of acceptability or legitimacy for such systems. These satellites can have an indirect defensive as well as deterrent purpose (monitoring a possible hostile act such as a military build-up on the part of the adversary, but also identifying new targets). Even if such observations are unrelated to a particular arms control agreement they accomplish an important task in the field of verification generally and create confidence through transparency.

Early warning satellites also belong to the broad category of satellites performing a task of surveillance. A system capable of detecting from great distance the launching of any kind of missile is to be considered as stabilizing since it makes a surprise attack less probable and less rewarding. The possibility of being alerted at the earliest moment to any missile take-off not only enhances stability but constitutes, together with appropriate measures of notification and a reliable communication system between adversaries, an important and effective confidence-building measure, especially in the nuclear field.

A reliable warning system based on satellites should also provide crisis stability in the event of the launch of a missile or the explosion of a nuclear weapon through accident or error.

Banning these satellites through an international agreement would not be advisable since it could lead to increasing uncertainty and mistrust.

III. 'Auxiliary' satellites

The other large category of military satellites comprises the so-called auxiliary satellites, which are instrumental to other military activities. Among these, communication satellites are the most important. They are mainly employed for long-distance command, control and communications (C^3) activities.

Their use has continuously expanded, especially in the USA, to the extent that it is calculated that about three-quarters of US military communications are now routed through space. These devices as such are not offensive; they cannot create any direct damage to the adversary and their role is auxiliary with respect to the whole framework of a military system. Especially during a crisis, stable and predictable behaviour is likely to be encouraged by an efficient network of communications.

Even if banned or destroyed, communications satellites could well be substituted by other forms, either more sophisticated or more rudimentary, of military communications. In view of their greater reliability and rapidity, communications via satellites can also prevent lack of information, false alarms and autonomous decisions by military commanders. Viewed from this angle they can be considered as having a stabilizing effect, given that continuous and precise knowledge of a situation should also imply the prevention of errors and useless bloodshed.

The benefits of greater efficiency should also be taken into account when considering other kinds of satellite that perform auxiliary and instrumental functions in the military field. Navigation satellites are used to accurately guide missiles to targets as well as to navigate warships and aircraft. Such devices can also be employed on land, for example in order to enable a tank to precisely determine where it is located at any given moment.

Weather satellites are used to monitor meteorological conditions during the flight over a target. They are primarily instrumental in determining the most appropriate moment for an attack. In this sense they promote efficiency. Their non-existence does not imply that an act of war might not take place; by enhancing the effectiveness of such an act, they might sometimes even reduce in time and space the damage inflicted; their prohibition would create great practical problems in view of the large and increasing use which is being made of this type of satellite in the non-military field.

Geodetic satellites are used to determine the precise shape of the world, the exact position of a target as well as the gravitational field which controls the path of a missile. These satellites are particularly important for the accuracy of cruise missiles, the guidance systems of which depend on detailed maps of surface contours. As such they increase the counterforce capabilities of an army and can render an attack more effective. In their absence, however, such an attack would probably still take place; it would be less accurate and could therefore be more damaging. On the whole it can be said that the prohibition of what have been defined as auxiliary satellites, integrated into a weapon system of which they are the orbital appendix, would only make sense if coupled with the general ban of such systems in their entirety. Moreover, practically in all cases, these satellites have a dual civilian and military purpose. Their prohibition would create considerable practical problems in view of the large use which is at present being made of these types of satellite and of the great difficulties involved in verification.

IV. ASAT satellites

The issue of whether to ban the third major category of military satellite, the ones capable of destroying and damaging other satellites in orbit, is a totally different one.

The importance of civilian as well as military satellites (whether reconnaissance or auxiliary), their potential vulnerability due to the present lack of protection or defence and the ease with which they can be tracked, make them tempting targets.

Both the USA and the USSR have contemplated the option of damaging, destroying or interfering with the activities of satellites. Among the devices which have actually been developed for such a purpose, the simplest system is an ASAT satellite carrying a warhead made to explode in the vicinity of an enemy satellite in order to destroy it. Another tested device is an unarmed satellite capable of destroying or damaging a second satellite by way of ramming. Since the late 1960s the Soviet Union has developed and tested—apparently with some success—this type of ASAT weapon. It has also developed a fractional orbital nuclear weapon capable of delivering a nuclear device onto a target after performing an incomplete orbit around the Earth. It is doubtful, however, that such a device could be considered a satellite in view of its partial orbit.

The US programme in the field of ASAT warfare appears to be more heterogeneous; it is focused particularly on developing a system involving a high speed aircraft equipped with a missile and a miniature homing vehicle and less on satellites with ASAT capabilities. The latter, the classical form of anti-satellite system, has not totally been excluded by the USA, although priority is apparently being given, at present, to more sophisticated devices. An issue which remains controversial is that of a possible future use of the space shuttle as an ASAT system. Its cost and vulnerability, the fact that it is a manned vehicle, and the uncertainties about its capabilities at high altitudes make it inappropriate to define it as an ASAT system. It is in any case debatable whether the shuttle can be considered a satellite.

It is more difficult within the context of this study, which is restricted to military satellites, to foresee limitations or bans on the future, more sophisticated directed-energy weapons which might or might not be placed on board satellites. The space environment seems to be particularly important for laser weapons which—at least theoretically—are capable of hitting a target with precision and speed from great distance. The effect of such a weapon would be more conspicuous in outer space where it would not encounter the interference of the atmosphere.

It seems needless to demonstrate the advisability of banning anti-satellite satellites which, in view of their potential destructive capacity, could generate an arms race in outer space. Although these weapons appear mainly as counterforce systems aimed at neutralizing other satellites, and although they are in principle directed at 'surgical' military operations, their potentially destabilizing and therefore spiralling effect has been amply dealt with in the literature. The issue of whether these satellites will effectively become operational depends mainly on the convenience of their deployment, seen from a cost-effectiveness point of view, and also on the possiblity of concluding suitable arms control agreements capable of preventing their deployment. The question of how costly an operational system of ASAT weapons would be still remains open. It is true that costs have rarely constituted a real hindrance to the development of even the more expensive and sophisticated weapon systems, and it is also true that in selected cases they actually should not constitute a hindrance when security and balance are at stake. A rudimentary anti-satellite satellite would probably not be too expensive to produce and to deploy. Yet it remains to be proven that the development and launching of a powerful missile along with a satellite (both of which could only be used once) is worth the destruction of another, easily replaceable satellite. And it is very doubtful that the costly, though re-usable, space shuttle might constitute, even in the future, an effective device for such missions. It is moreover almost certain that, if ASAT systems were to be further developed and became standard equipment, additional devices would be introduced to protect satellites from such a danger—for example, the thickening of their 'skin' or orbiting of decoy satellites. Moreover, a greater number of satellites might easily be sent into orbit, making it practically impossible for a potential aggressor to hit them all.

In this case as well as in the case of more sophisticated anti-satellite devices (eventually including directed-energy weapons) the costs would probably be enormous.

High costs as well as technical obstacles and questionable effectiveness have seldom constituted a sufficient brake to the development of new sophisticated weapons. Suffice it to recall how complex and costly the process of 'MIRVing' US ballistic missiles was, and how rapidly the Soviet Union made up for its initial disadvantage in those sophisticated systems (MIRV = multiple independently targetable re-entry vehicle). It is hard to imagine, at this stage, the superpowers spontaneously abandoning the programmes they have under way. Public opinion—principally in the West, of course—could play a certain role in this field, as its attention is being more and more focused on this issue. Although not much is known as yet by the public about the prospects of an arms race in outer space, and priority is given, understandably, to mass destruction as well as to conventional weapons, it is a fact that a number of recent developments in this field have attracted the interest of the mass media and of the public to the issue of outer space, and to the possibility of reaching an agreement which would ban the development of weapons in such an environment.

In order to enhance the effectiveness and credibility of such a ban, a vast network of verification measures would be necessary, especially since it is very difficult to establish *a priori* whether a given satellite is a weapon or just a civilian device. The issue of verification in this field is extremely complex. These are not classical weapons for which a technique of control and verification has already been established by negotiations and agreements already in force: the 'dual use' of satellites makes this task even more complicated but all the more important. In view of the relatively limited number of satellites in orbit and of their vital importance for the defence systems of the major powers, even if only a small number of ASAT satellites were in the possession of the superpowers, dissimulation of these could have very important implications for the military equilibrium.

There is a certain amount of consensus in the international community around the fact that ASAT satellites should be banned: a number of resolutions have been passed on this issue by the UN General Assembly in the last few years. The work of the Committee on Disarmament in the field of outer space will have to focus primarily on this issue if substantial results are to be achieved.

Paper 4. Why anti-satellite warfare should be prohibited

Non-nuclear Disarmament Section, International Organizations Department, Ministry of Foreign Affairs, Casuariestraat 16, 2511 VB The Hague, The Netherlands

I. Introduction

Any approach to an anti-satellite (ASAT) treaty presupposes that satellites should be protected. This means that satellites which fulfil vital military functions in waging war on Earth (e.g., communications and navigation satellites) would also enjoy protection, in principle, from attack or other hostile interference.

To make this point quite clear: the protection of satellites according to an ASAT treaty means an undertaking not to damage, destroy or remove satellites and not to interfere with their functioning. Such an undertaking could only be considered effective if it were supplemented by a prohibition of at least the testing, deployment and use of anti-satellite weapon systems. Otherwise no credible assurance could be given that such a rule of warfare would be observed in times of conflict or war. Any ASAT treaty should therefore consist of these two interrelated elements. As will emerge below, such a treaty does not concern a total prohibition of ASAT weapon systems, but in fact a prohibition of anti-satellite warfare. Furthermore, it deals with ASAT weapon systems regardless of whether they are Earth- or space-based.

At first sight it may seem somewhat strange to provide for the protection of satellites that are vital for waging war on Earth as they constitute valid military targets. The disabling of such satellites might even end a conflict before it could start on Earth, although it is argued—and quite rightly so—that such an act would be more likely to precede a conflict on Earth than confine it to the

---

*The opinions expressed in this paper are those of the author and should not therefore be considered as a statement of Netherlands policy.

realms of outer space. This paper therefore argues that strictly military considerations underlie an ASAT treaty, and these will now be closely examined.

To begin with, we should bear in mind that the development of ASAT weapon systems has attracted much attention because of the increasing importance of the use of outer space for military purposes. This role can be conceived in at least the following five ways:

1. The use of outer space as a base for attacks against targets on Earth by means of nuclear or non-nuclear weapons.
2. The use of outer space as a passage for intercontinental ballistic missiles (ICBMs).
3. The use of satellites in outer space to support, both actively and passively, military operations on Earth.
4. The use of ASAT weapon systems in outer space to disable other satellites.
5. The use of outer space as a base for ballistic missile defence (BMD).

This paper deals with the fourth of these possibilities, which would be prohibited by an ASAT treaty. The unavoidable result of such a treaty would be unimpeded military use (point 3). It is precisely that particular use which has made the development of an ASAT weapon system militarily attractive, for both major space powers have become increasingly dependent on satellites, which have been called the eyes, ears and commanding voices of modern armed forces. Their elimination by ASAT weapon systems would have serious consequences for the ability of a country to take effective military action or to control a crisis or a conflict which had already broken out.

Before examining the pros and cons of an ASAT treaty it is important to recall once more the active and passive role of military satellites in supporting military activities on Earth. First of all, it should be pointed out that the primary purpose of arms control measures with respect to the military use of outer space should be their contribution to maintaining the stability of current nuclear deterrence. As was rightly stated in the report by the Union of Concerned Scientists "any threat to satellites, whether real or potential, will undermine confidence in the ability to deter attack".[1]

A Canadian working document, submitted to the Committee on Disarmament in August 1982, examined the stabilizing and destabilizing effects of the various types of military satellite and concluded that military satellites tend on balance to stabilize deterrence, from which it follows that anti-satellite measures tend to be destabilizing.[2] It is of little comfort to us that, in practice, certain types of military satellite—navigation, meteorological, photoreconnaissance and electronic intelligence—in specific cases constitute a formidable threat to the effectiveness of other armed forces on Earth. Military planners would therefore be reluctant simply to give up the option of disabling such enemy satellites. On the other hand, an ASAT capacity also implies an ability to disable military satellites that have mainly stabilizing effects, such as those for communications, arms control verification and crisis monitoring.

It should duly be taken into account that, where an ASAT capacity exists, these satellites will be seen to run the risk of being disabled with all the attendant escalating consequences, including pre-emptive attacks. Military planners and politicians would therefore be eager to ensure that these mainly stabilizing satellites enjoy the protection of an ASAT treaty.

Given that technological developments could seriously undermine the stability of the current nuclear deterrence, three possible ways of maintaining or improving this stability will be more closely examined here. The starting point of this paper is the ASAT weapon systems which could become operational within the next few years. The situation would become significantly more complicated if current research and development in the field of directed-energy weapons (high-energy laser and particle beam weapons) were to lead to a new, feasible anti-ballistic missile (ABM) technology. The development and deployment of such BMD systems in outer space would not only undermine nuclear deterrence, but would also make it impossible to conclude an ASAT treaty, as space-based BMD systems are considered to be well suited to anti-satellite warfare.

II. Options

No ban on ASAT

If a ban is not imposed on ASAT weapon systems, current efforts by both the USA and the USSR to develop an ASAT weapon system will undoubtedly be continued and even accelerated. The course of the resulting traditional arms race could hardly be considered as a contribution to the maintenance of a stable nuclear balance, quite apart from the enormous investment in human and financial resources.

The most favourable possible outcome of an unbridled ASAT arms race would be that the ASAT capacity of one side might deter the other side from using its own capacity. However, it must be assumed that the disabling of even a single satellite by one side would be considered as a *casus belli* for the other side to start a war in space. A space war could easily be a prelude to an armed conflict on Earth. A dangerous state of escalation could be produced even by an unsuccessful attempt to disable a satellite or by a technical malfunction which could not be immediately explained, particularly in periods of tension.

Apart from developing an ASAT capacity both sides would apply themselves to the physical protection of their satellites, in the following ways:

1. The use of armour and other protective materials.
2. Hardening to prevent interference with the activities of the satellite.
3. Increasing manoeuvrability to allow satellites to avoid ASAT weapon systems (evasion).
4. The use of sub-satellites (decoys) to distract attention from the main satellite.

5. Stationing reserve satellites on the ground or in very high orbits to enable damaged satellites to be replaced immediately.

6. Active defence, for example, equipping satellites with miniature homing vehicles to provide a shoot-back capability.

No ban on ASAT weapons combined with agreed protection for specific military satellites

If this approach were adopted, the major space powers would agree to grant certain types of military satellite protection from attack or other hostile interference. Such an approach would allow ASAT weapon systems to disable only those satellites which are vital for waging war on Earth. Although at first sight attractive to military planners, this option has important disadvantages. As the Canadian working document stated, it is not possible to distinguish clearly the active or passive military supporting role of all types of military satellite. Certain types of military satellite, such as those for command, control and communications (C^3) and reconnaissance, can be used both actively and passively. Moreover, it would be impossible to ensure that civilian satellites for communications, navigation, weather forecasting and remote sensing were not also used for military purposes. This applies even more to the Soviet space programme, where, unlike the US programme, it is difficult if not impossible to distinguish between civilian and military satellites.

On the other hand, protection might be offered to specific satellites, instead of to certain types of satellite. In this way, both sides could build on what the USA and the Soviet Union have agreed in the context of SALT. Both the Interim Agreement and ABM Treaty of SALT I (1972) and the unratified SALT II Treaty provide for non-interference with national technical means of verification. Although it is generally understood that these include reconnaissance satellites it is not clear whether other types of military satellite are also included. Therefore, further negotiations are required to establish which satellites already enjoy a degree of protection. The next question to be dealt with is whether this protection is broad enough to counter all hostile interference, as would an ASAT treaty, and how this protection should be extended to include other specific military satellites. In sum, this approach seems more attractive than the first option which rules out any ban on ASAT systems, but it entails many of the same disadvantages such as a costly and still destabilizing arms race.

An ASAT ban

The greatest advantage of an ASAT ban, that is, a ban on at least the testing, deployment and use of ASAT weapon systems, is that both sides would be assured of their satellites' safety and thereby of the military effectiveness of their armed forces. This knowledge alone could contribute to controlling a conflict or to bringing it to an end at an early stage. However, no absolute assurance could be given that satellites would not be disabled in periods of tension or conflict. Certain complementary measures would therefore seem to be required both to strengthen confidence in an ASAT treaty and to make its violation as unattractive as possible from a military point of view. This is connected with the assumption that observance of any ASAT treaty has to be adequately verifiable if it is to have any chance of being acceptable. As has been pointed out before, an effective ASAT treaty should in any case prohibit testing, deployment and use of ASAT weapon systems. These three essential elements, particularly testing, can be adequately verified by national technical means.

This does not, however, apply to research and development and the possession of ASAT weapon systems, although generally speaking the safe approach from the arms control point of view would be simply to ban these elements as well in order to make an ASAT treaty comprehensive. At present, however, they do not seem to be adequately verifiable, at least not enough to reassure the two major space powers, taking into account the closed character of Soviet society. Of course, this does not preclude subsequent negotiations to make an ASAT treaty comprehensive, if both sides are satisfied with an initial ASAT treaty and the anticipated gradual improvement in monitoring capabilities is taken into account.

Attention should also be paid to residual ASAT capacity. Common satellites of one side could, for example, be used to disable the satellites of the other by a simple collision or self-explosion near the target. (The present Soviet capacity is based on self-explosion.) Furthermore, ballistic missiles not specifically designed for anti-satellite purposes could be used against satellites. However, as these possibilities could not be adequately tested under the terms of an ASAT treaty, they can hardly be considered as a reliable military option and they would certainly not be able to give decisive military advantages. Moreover, the knowledge that both sides have this capacity at their disposal might keep them from using it.

A ban on anti-satellite warfare would also be significantly strengthened if protective measures such as those mentioned earlier were permitted. The extent to which they would be allowed should be the subject of negotiations. However, satellites should not be permitted miniature homing vehicles for defence against anti-satellite systems, as satellites equipped in this way could also be used for offensive missions. In any event, leaving other protective measures aside, it seems advisable to keep some vital satellites in reserve.

Any prohibition of anti-satellite warfare would be strengthened by the adoption of confidence-building measures, such as prior notification of the characteristics of space missions, and the adoption of co-operative measures to remove any suspicions that might be aroused by certain manoeuvres during space missions.[3] In this connection, it should be recalled that such complementary measures would cost much less than the unconstrained development and deployment of ASAT weapon systems. The fact that neither of the two major space powers will tolerate any technical lead or superiority on the part of the other for any length of time will certainly contribute to enormous and ever rising costs. This will also lead to resources being diverted from other defence programmes which are likely to be more essential for the security of both sides.

To sum up: although much could be said in favour of an ASAT treaty, the fact that military satellites, vital for waging war on Earth, will also enjoy protection remains a major disadvantage. This aspect of an ASAT treaty should, however, be weighed against the hazards for stability and security of unbridled ASAT competition. In particular the opponent's ocean surveillance satellites are considered to be a special military risk because of their ability to detect, track and identify surface ships and, in the future, possibly even submarines. However, the development of countermeasures to deceive or confuse those satellites, such as radio silence, decoys, camouflage or electronic countermeasures, would be a more adequate response than the development of an ASAT capacity. More generally, it has to be said that effort should be devoted to developing measures of a clearly defensive character rather than to developing an ASAT capacity which also has a clear potential for offensive use and could be perceived as a prelude to a first-strike capacity. This could only lead to an unrestrained arms race which would be a tremendous drain on financial and human resources without offering any prospect of greater stability and security. At best a precarious balance at a high level of armaments might be maintained.

III. Conclusion

Looking again at the three options discussed above, it will be clear that an ASAT treaty as an instrument for negotiated constraints would be greatly preferable to totally unrestrained competition in space weaponry. There is no need to invoke moral or ethical considerations in favour of arms control and disarmament, in general, or safeguarding outer space, in particular, from an arms race which has already reached dangerous proportions on Earth. An ASAT treaty can be advocated on strictly military grounds alone, because by stabilizing nuclear deterrence it will do more to ensure the security interests of both major space powers than would an arms race in ASAT weapon systems. The technical complexities involved as well as the question of adequate verification of an ASAT treaty are not insoluble if an actual prohibition of anti-satellite warfare, strengthened by a number of complementary measures, is considered to be in the mutual long-term security interest.

References

1. *Anti-Satellite Weapons: Arms Control or Arms Race?* (Union of Concerned Scientists, Cambridge, MA, 11 May 1983), p. 2.
2. 'Arms control and outer space', a working document submitted by Canada to the Committee on Disarmament CD/320, 26 August 1982, p. 12.
3. 'Prevention of an arms race in outer space', a working document submitted by France to the Committee on Disarmament CD/375, 14 April 1983, p. 6.

Paper 5. Satellite and missile ASAT systems and potential verification problems associated with the existing Soviet systems

Marcia Smith*

The Library of Congress, Science Policy Research Service, 10 First Street SE, Washington, DC 10540, USA

I. Introduction

The term 'anti-satellite' (ASAT) is generically used to describe any device that can be used to destroy the operational capability of satellites in Earth orbit. These devices can be based on the ground, on aircraft, or in outer space and can involve: (*a*) the direct ascent of a missile carrying either a nuclear or non-nuclear warhead; (*b*) co-orbital devices with explosive devices; or (*c*) use of directed-energy weapons. The latter is not discussed in this paper.

The Soviet Union has a co-orbital interceptor, and may have a direct ascent system using nuclear warheads launched via a Galosh anti-ballistic missile (ABM) missile. There was a report in the Western trade press that a Soviet spacecraft attached to a space station in 1981 carried miniature homing vehicles, but there is no evidence that this was accurate. The United States had a direct ascent system with nuclear warheads based in the Pacific, but it was deactivated in 1975. A new US ASAT system, using a direct ascent impact vehicle launched from an F-15 aircraft, is now in development. A private group in the United States, High Frontier, has proposed a ballistic missile defence system based on conventional technology that, if deployed, might also serve an ASAT function.

This paper is partially based on CRS Issue Brief 81123, 'Antisatellites (killer satellites)', prepared by this author for use by the US Congress. The issue brief is appropriately referenced. The references given in this paper have been added

*Views presented in this paper are those of the author and do not necessarily represent those of the US Congressional Research Service, any Member or Committee of the US Congress or staff thereof.

only for information which is not included in the issue brief and seems to require such citations. Since the Soviet Union does not publicly admit to having an ASAT capability, information on its ASAT systems necessarily comes from non-Soviet sources. In the United States, the existence of an ASAT development effort and many of its capabilities are publicly documented, although certain information is classified. For this report, only unclassified material has been used.

II. Soviet ASAT systems

Possible direct ascent system using the Galosh missile

On 16 July 1962, in an interview with US newspaper editors, Soviet Premier Nikita Khrushchev stated that the Soviet Union had a missile that could "hit a fly in outer space". Some Western experts speculated that this was a reference to the use of a nuclear warhead launched by a Galosh ABM missile, a system which is still deployed around Moscow. Whether or not the USSR ever intended to use the Galosh in an ASAT capacity, or if it still has such plans, is unknown, but the statement prompted development of a comparable system by the United States (see below).

SS-9 co-orbital ASAT system

Since October 1968, the Soviet Union has conducted 20 tests of an interceptor launched by the SS-9 missile (also known in the West as the F-1-m launch vehicle or the SL-11). In this type of system, the interceptor manoeuvres close to the target satellite and explodes, destroying the operational capability of the target. The ASAT system uses a chemical explosive, not a nuclear one. Since the explosion takes place only in the vicinity of the target, the targeting system does not have to be as precise as for a device which would have a direct impact on the target. It has been reported that radar was used on the tests conducted through the first part of 1977, after which optical sensors were introduced,[1] although other analysts have concluded that the optical sensors were used for a test at the end of 1976, and have been used intermittently since then.[2] The interceptor's orbit can be elliptical, so that it intercepts the target either at apogee or perigee; co-planar with the target; or variable (popping up from a lower orbit using onboard propulsion).

In some of the tests, the interceptor moves away from the target before exploding, while in others no explosion takes place and the interceptor is commanded to re-enter. In the first type, the explosion might take place away from the target so that the target can be re-used; it is not unusual for two interceptors to be flown against the same target. In the second type, where the interceptor re-enters, it could indicate that the interception failed, or that the device was meant only to inspect the target.

From October 1968 to December 1971, seven tests were made. A long hiatus followed, until tests were finally resumed in February 1976. What prompted the resumption in ASAT testing is unknown, although there has been speculation that it might have been meant as a warning to the Chinese, who launched their first prototype reconnaissance satellite in September 1975. Another possibility is that the test signalled the introduction of a second-generation system.

Nine more Soviet ASAT tests were made from 1976 to 1978, at which time testing was again suspended during the three rounds of ASAT limitation talks initiated by the United States. In April 1980, after further ASAT negotiations did not materialize and it became clear that the United States would postpone ratification of the SALT II Treaty, testing was resumed. One test was conducted that month, and two more were made in 1981.

The most recent test was made on 6 June 1982, the day before the opening of the UN Second Special Session on Disarmament. This test was made as part of what was described in the West as a simulation of a nuclear first strike against the United States—concurrently with the ASAT test, the Soviets launched a reconnaissance and a navigation satellite, and made live missile firings. This was seen by some US observers as a demonstration of how space fits into Soviet strategic war doctrine.

Assessing the percentage of the ASAT tests which have been successful is difficult since the Soviet intentions are not known. According to the Western media, only one target (Cosmos 1241) has actually been destroyed by an ASAT weapon, but this has been disputed by other experts who point out that the target is still in orbit intact. As noted earlier, in other cases the interceptor has exploded after moving away from the target or has re-entered, prompting speculation that there may be one programme for inspecting satellites and another for destroying them.

One possible method of measuring success is to consider a test in which the interceptor manoeuvres to within 1 km of the target as being sufficient to have inspected the target, or to have destroyed it if that action has been desired. Using this measure and media accounts of the tests, one can conclude that 13 of the 20 Soviet ASAT tests have been successful.

The SS-9 system is limited to altitudes and orbital inclinations achievable with the SS-9 rocket and its associated launch pads. According to the Federation of American Scientists, there are three SS-9 pads at Tyuratam and four at Plesetsk.[3] All ASAT tests so far have been launched from one of the pads at Tyuratam and have occurred at orbital inclinations between 62° and 66°. The highest altitude reached in a Soviet ASAT test is approximately 2300 km, within the range used by US reconnaissance, weather and Transit navigation satellites, as well as by the space shuttle. NAVSTAR navigation satellites at 20000 km and communications and early warning satellites at geosynchronous altitude (35800 km) are out of reach of the current Soviet system.

The possibility exists that the Soviets may place the ASAT device on a more capable launch vehicle, perhaps the D or D-1 (also known as the SL-9 or SL-13) vehicles or the new 'super booster' rumoured to be in development, to increase its range.

Cosmos 1267/Salyut 6

Aviation Week and Space Technology reported that the "Soviet Union is operating in low earth orbit an antisatellite battle station equipped with clusters of infrared-homing guided interceptors that could destroy multiple US spacecraft".[4] In subsequent issues, the magazine claimed that the battle station was Cosmos 1267 which had docked with the space station Salyut 6 on 19 June 1981. The Soviet Union had previously identified this satellite as a test vehicle related to constructing modular space stations. The US Department of Defense publicly rejected the magazine's assertion.[5]

The Cosmos 1267/Salyut 6 combination was de-orbited on 29 July 1982, with no known test firings of any projectiles. The subsequent launch of Cosmos 1443 in March 1983, which the Soviet Union announced as being an operational version of Cosmos 1267, and the docking of that satellite with Salyut 7 for use as a space tug/re-supply vehicle, leads to the conclusion that the *Aviation Week and Space Technology* charges were incorrect.

III. US ASAT systems

Deactivated direct ascent system using Thor missiles

In response to fears generated by Khrushchev's 1962 comments mentioned above, the United States developed a direct ascent ASAT system using nuclear warheads launched by Air Force Thor missiles from Johnston Island in the Pacific. This system was termed operational by President Johnson in 1964 and was deactivated in 1975. At least 13 tests were made from 1964 to 1968. The Army conducted tests of a similar system using Nike-Zeus missiles based on Kwajalein Atoll in the Pacific, beginning in May 1963, but in 1964 the programme was terminated.

F-15 system in development

The United States is currently developing a direct ascent ASAT device which will be launched from an F-15 aircraft. Basing on the F-15 provides greater flexibility in attacking satellites than is possible with a ground-launched system. The ASAT device involves a miniature vehicle on top of a two-stage rocket (a short-range attack missile—SRAM—and an Altair stage). An inertial guidance system located in the Altair stage would guide the device to the proper location in space. Using infra-red sensors, the miniature homing vehicle (MHV) would locate the target, after which it would separate from the Altair, track the target and then ram into it with destructive force. No explosive device is involved. Targeting accuracy is obviously critical with this type of system.

According to the head of the Defense Advanced Research Projects Agency (DARPA), six captive tests of this device had been conducted by April 1983.[6]

The first test of the missile (without the actual warhead) was conducted against a point in space in January 1984—see Part I, page 13. The first test against an object in space is expected in 1985.

The US system is thought to have the same altitude limitations as the Soviet ASAT, although its basing on an aircraft removes limitations associated with orbital inclinations. Thus, Soviet satellite systems within the range of the US ASAT system would include reconnaissance, weather and Tsikada navigation satellites (similar to Transit), Salyut space stations and associated manned and unmanned ferry and re-supply craft. In addition, Molniya communications satellites and early warning satellites would be vulnerable at perigee in the southern hemisphere. Satellites in geostationary orbit and the GLONASS navigation satellites (similar to NAVSTAR) would not be within range. The United States, like the Soviet Union, could use a more capable launch vehicle (such as Minuteman) to reach higher altitudes, although this would negatively affect the flexibility of the system.

High Frontier proposal

In March 1982, a private group in the United States called High Frontier proposed a new national defence strategy that included an orbiting ballistic missile defence system based on the same technology as that used for the F-15 ASAT system. Although the focus of the High Frontier proposal is on BMD, which is outside the purview of this paper, it should be mentioned that such a system, comprising 432 orbiting satellites, each equipped with 40–50 homing interceptors, could also serve an ASAT function. The High Frontier proposal has not been adopted as US government policy.

IV. Space mines

There has been considerable discussion of the possibility of placing mines in space where they could remain hidden until activated for use against a target. There have been no reports of either side deploying such devices so far.

The launch of a space mine would probably be detected in the normal manner by either side, but if it were manoeuvred into a new position while out of range of the opposing country's detection systems, its precise location might be difficult or impossible to determine until re-activated. This would be especially true if the mine were stored in a remote place, such as at an altitude higher than geosynchronous orbit, for later activation when needed.

V. Potential verification problems associated with Soviet ASAT systems

Verification issues have already arisen as a major potential obstacle to achieving a treaty to ban ASAT weapons either on a bilateral or multilateral basis.

This section addresses verification problems with respect to Soviet systems only; similar issues related to US ASAT weapons are outside the scope of the report, but in general it can be assumed that US compliance with a treaty would also be difficult to verify. Problems with verification will depend, of course, on exactly what is being prohibited—research, development, testing, deployment, possession or use.

Galosh direct ascent system

The R&D, testing and possession of the Galosh system have already been completed, so need not be considered here other than to point out that there have been no known tests of the system against space targets. The question then arises as to how much, if any, testing would be required to make the Galosh a useful ASAT system. If the assumption is made that testing would be needed, then verifying that such tests do not occur would involve considerations similar to those for the SS-9 system discussed below. If it is assumed that no testing is required, verifying whether a particular missile's intended target is in space or on Earth would obviously be impossible without access to Soviet war plans. If an ASAT treaty required the dismantling of existing ASAT systems, the question of whether to include the Galosh as part of the Soviet ASAT programme would have to be considered.

SS-9 co-orbital ASAT system

Banning research and development of this system is moot since the United States considers it operational. As for testing, verifying such a ban would be difficult. For example, the SS-9 used to launch the ASAT interceptor is also used for launches of radar ocean reconnaissance satellites (RORSATs) and electronic ocean reconnaissance satellites (EORSATs). Whether or not US national technical means of verification can determine if a payload on top of an SS-9 is an ASAT, RORSAT or EORSAT cannot be determined from the open literature, so suffice it to say that some measures may have to be taken to ensure that an ASAT is not being carried by the SS-9 (perhaps by "functionally related observable differences" as suggested for cruise missiles in the SALT II agreed statement).

Other difficulties would arise if changes were made to the now well recognized pattern in which ASAT tests are conducted. At the present time the tests have a distinctive signature: a target is launched from Plesetsk with an SS-5 missile (also known as a C-1 vehicle or an SL-8) into an orbit with an inclination near 65°; some time later (days, weeks or even months) an interceptor is launched by an SS-9 from Tyuratam with a similar inclination; after one or two orbits the target is intercepted and the interceptor either explodes or is deorbited. Changes that might occur include launching against a point in space instead of an object, so the target's launch, which currently provides the first clue that an ASAT test is imminent, could be avoided. Also, a different launch vehicle could be used, for example, a larger vehicle for testing an improved

ASAT. A different SS-9 pad at Tyuratam or Plesetsk could be used. Also, although it has been reported that the telemetry stream from an ASAT can be monitored,[3] the transmissions could be altered so that it could not be monitored in a useful manner. Thus, verifying that ASAT tests are not being made is not as simple a matter as had been portrayed by some advocates of an ASAT ban.

Concerning prohibitions against deployment and/or possession of the SS-9 ASAT system, many of the above considerations would apply. In addition, assurances that the existing system was dismantled and could not be quickly reconstituted would probably require on-site inspection, but even that might not be sufficient. The SS-9 would probably continue in production for its use as a launcher for other satellites, and a small number of ASAT payloads could conceivably be hidden from on-site investigators or simply moved off-base until they had left.

Lasers

A ban on R&D associated with laser ASAT systems would be extremely difficult to verify simply because lasers, even powerful ones, have so many applications other than space warfare.

Ground-based lasers for use against satellites in low or high Earth orbit would be large, but since they would be housed in large buildings, their exact nature probably could not be determined by national technical means. The size would depend on required power output, which in turn would depend on the intended missions: blinding a satellite in low Earth orbit would obviously not require as much power as destroying a satellite in geosynchronous orbit. A ground-based laser intended only to blind low-orbit satellites might go undetected until it was tested, and even then, there might be some doubt as to whether an attempt had been made to blind or destroy a satellite.

In 1983, *Aviation Week and Space Technology* reported that a US reconnaissance satellite had ceased functioning while over the Soviet Union and that some analysts suspected a laser had been used against it.[7] Similar reports had been made as early as 1975. Since satellites currently have no way of signalling that they have been attacked, the actual cause of any failure is difficult to determine. In addition, it has been widely discussed that lasers are used for tracking satellites, and it is always possible that a laser pointed at a satellite for tracking purposes could unintentionally damage the satellite's sensors. This possibility, in fact, has been raised in connection with several of the incidents that have occurred since 1975.[8]

The testing, deployment and use of space-based lasers would probably involve large structures in space whose existence would be readily observable. Thus, for this type of system, the problem would be in the R&D phase. For example, the United States reportedly plans to fly an experiment on the space shuttle called Talon Gold, for testing an aiming and tracking device for potential application to space-based lasers.[9] There is no realistic way to verify whether such activities are taking place on orbiting space vehicles without on-site inspection of the vehicle itself. It seems unlikely that US astronauts would be allowed to fly on Soviet space stations for verification purposes any more than cosmonauts would be flown on the space shuttle for such a reason.

Space mines

Verifying the existence of space mines would be extremely difficult if they were camouflaged as failed satellites which had been launched for another purpose and which showed no signs of activity (such as station-keeping) until needed. The disadvantages would be that the satellite would slowly drift away from its location and might not be in a good position for attacking a target satellite when the time for such action arrived. The advantage would be that by having a space mine in geosynchronous orbit, for example, there would be less warning time that an attack was imminent since the space mine could approach the target more quickly than if launched from the ground. Its movement across the geostationary arc would be detected, however, so some warning would be inevitable. Nevertheless, such a device might be considered useful and its existence would be difficult to verify if it were not tested.

Summary of verification issues

The ultimate concern with the verification problems associated with an ASAT treaty is that relatively few US satellites would have to be neutralized in order to have an impact on the US strategic posture. Thus, if even a few of the existing SS-9 ASAT interceptors escape the verification process, a severe impact on US national security could result. This is not the case for ballistic missiles, where thousands are permitted by treaty; if a few were missed, it would barely make a difference. Thus fool-proof verification measures are more critical in the case of ASAT systems.

VI. Conclusion

The USSR currently has an operational ASAT capability and the USA is expected to have such a capability by 1987. Attempts to reach an agreement banning ASAT systems will almost certainly encounter problems in terms of how to verify that each side is fulfilling its treaty obligations, which could well include a prohibition on testing, deployment and use of ASAT systems, plus the dismantling of existing systems.

Verification problems associated with the US system are not within the scope of this paper. For the Soviet system, methods for determining that the existing system has been dismantled and that it can not easily be reconstituted will form one issue area. Other issues could involve ensuring that tests are not taking place under circumstances different from previous tests and are therefore not as easily identifiable. On-site inspection will almost certainly have to be accepted.

If conventional systems other than the existing Soviet co-orbital ASAT and the US F-15 ASAT systems are included in an agreement, verification problems will probably grow. For example, with the Galosh ABM missile it would be virtually impossible to know whether the missile's target was on Earth or in space. The existence of space mines would further complicate the process since they would be difficult to detect, particularly if they are stored at higher than geosynchronous altitudes.

The verification problems associated with ASAT systems are numerous. Whether or not an agreement can be concluded despite these difficulties will depend on the determination of both sides to ban these weapons.

References

1. Berman, P. and Baker, J. C., *Soviet Strategic Forces: Requirements and Responses* (Brookings Institution, Washington, DC, 1983), p. 152.
2. Johnson, N., *Soviet Year in Space—1982* (Teledyne-Brown Engineering, Colorado Springs, CO, 1983), p. 26.
3. Pike, J., 'Verification of limits on the Soviet anti-satellite weapons—A safety study', *Congressional Record*, 21 July 1983, pp. H5414–H5415
4. *Aviation Week and Space Technology*, 26 October 1981, p. 15.
5. *Flight International*, 7 November 1981, p. 1363.
6. 'Cooper emphasizes ACM range gains, says ASAT is on schedule', *Aerospace Daily*, 11 April 1983, p. 234.
7. *Aviation Week and Space Technology*, 21 February 1983, p. 13.
8. 'Soviet LADAR may be taking the measure of US spacecraft', *Aerospace Daily*, 12 September 1983, p. 51.
9. *Aviation Week and Space Technology*, 27 April 1981, p. 23.

Paper 6. Space-based directed-energy beam weapons

Paul Nahin

Department of Electrical and Computer Engineering, Kingsbury Hall/EE, University of New Hampshire, Durham, NH 03824, USA

I. Introduction

The use of directed-energy weapons (DEWs)—lasers and particle beam accelerators—has been debated by academics for some years now.[1] More recently, the so-called 'Star Wars' speech by President Reagan on 23 March 1983 has dramatically brought the DEW issue to the attention of the layman. The public reaction to the speech has generally evolved through two stages. First came astonishment, usually expressed something like: "They've got to be joking! That's just Buck Rogers, Flash Gordon, Darth Vader nonsense". Then, noticing that the President of the United States seemed not to be laughing, and that the Soviet reaction, after some initial blustering, was equally serious, came the next stage: "Can it *really* be done? Is it actually possible to build and use such seemingly fantastic weapons?'

This paper will comment on these two responses.[2] That is, is the DEW debate a mere academic squabble over a technological absurdity, or is it something more substantial?; and, supposing the DEW concept is a valid one, then what are some of the concerns with which arms control negotiators might eventually find themselves confronted?

II. Are space-based DEWs feasible?

The answer to this question is almost certainly a solid 'yes'.[3]

The arguments of space-based DEW opponents tend to be based on economic, arms control or moral considerations.[4] These are concerns not lightly dismissed, naturally, but they have precisely nothing to do with the

Plate 1. The advanced test accelerator, upper floor[a]

[a]The most advanced US work on charged particle beams (Project 'Chair Heritage', sponsored by DARPA and the Navy) is the advanced test accelerator (ATA) at the Lawrence Livermore National Laboratory, California. Charged beams are not useful for space-based weapons (but are representative of the massive commitment to particle beam research in the USA), and are most likely to appear as a close-in defence against sea-skimming anti-ship missiles. This massive, two-floor structure is 165 m long and will accelerate electrons to an energy of 50 MeV with a beam current of 10 kA. The above photograph shows the upper floor of the ATA, at ground level, containing its pulse-forming system of spark gap, resonant transformer, and Blumlein transmission line energy compression/discharging networks. This system dumps energy into the near light-speed electron pulse as it propogates through a sequence of accelerator cells in a tunnel below.

Source: Photo courtesy of Lawrence Livermore National Laboratory, CA.

Plate 2. The underground floor of the ATA[a]

[a]The picture shows a block of 10 accelerator cells, through which the electron beam passes. There are a total of 190 individual accelerator cells, each providing 0.25 MeV of energy to an initially injected 2.5 MeV beam. The final conditioned beam has a pulse duration (at peak current) of at least 50 ns, and a diameter of about 50 mm. For an actual weapon the parameters will be 10 kA (equal to that of the ATA) and 500 MeV (10 times that of the ATA). The ATA is located at site 300, a remote experimental facility at the Lawrence Livermore National Laboratory suitable for the potentially hazardous open-air testing of such an energetic beam.

Source: Photo courtesy of Lawrence Livermore National Laboratory, CA.

Plate 3. Damage caused by an electron beam in an aluminium disc[a]

[a]A space-based ABM ASAT particle beam weapon will use neutral beams to avoid aiming errors caused by the Earth's magnetic field, and beam blooming from self-repulsion. The US programme on such beams (Project 'White Horse', sponsored by DARPA and the Army) is being conducted at the Los Alamos National Laboratory, New Mexico. Los Alamos declined to provide pictures, or to discuss their work. The above indicates, however, the damage produced by a charged particle (electron) beam in an aluminium disc (16 cm in diameter, 1 cm thick), which may be representative of what a neutral beam could do. The particle energies were one-fifth that of the ATA, with a beam energy equal to that of the ATA. Even though the disc was completely penetrated, the beam itself melted only about two-thirds of the way in. The second damage mechanism involved was a shock wave that, when it reached the backside (shown) of the disc, caused the remaining metal to detach. This effect is called 'scabbing' and is well-known. It occurs for example, inside tanks hit by HESH (high explosive squash head) ammunition.

Source: Photo courtesy of *Military Electronic/Countermeasures* magazine. Original source: Air Force Weapons Laboratory, Kirtland AFB, NM.

question of technical credibility for space-based DEWs. The issue of credibility is, itself, a two-part concern, which may be called the *single shot* and the *many shot* questions.

The single shot question

Given unlimited technical and financial support, is it possible for a space-based DEW to destroy a *single*, *unprotected* intercontinental ballistic missile (ICBM) after its launch and before the release of its warhead(s)? This is something like the 'shooting a bullet with a bullet' question from the old missile-based anti-ballistic missile (ABM) debates. As already said, it appears this is definitely possible (or eventually will be) with beams. Those who deny this support their arguments by reciting limits of present-day engineering (e.g., the beam spreads too much, the reflecting mirror will get too hot, the laser requires too much fuel, the accelerator will be too long, and so on). Such 'limits' are, in fact, nothing but limits of imagination. Unable to see beyond their own extrapolation of current engineering capability, these critics make the fatal error of believing the limits they perceive are nature's limits. Vannevar Bush, one of the USA's most honoured and inventive men of science, made the famous error of stating (in 1945) that the intercontinental ballistic missile was "impossible". He even went so far as to declare himself "annoyed" with those who insisted it wasn't. Bush was in good company, of course, as it was the eminent Ernest Rutherford who, in 1933, warned nuclear energy proponents that their hopes were "the merest moonshine".[5]

The many shot question

This question raises the stakes considerably. Now we ask: given unlimited technical and financial support, is it possible for a space-based DEW system to destroy *multiple*, *protected* ICBM missiles after their launch and before the release of their warhead(s)? This is a much harder question to answer, but some of the proposed DEW systems do seem to be easily countered, particularly the chain of orbital laser battle stations supported by US Senator Malcolm Wallop,[6] and implicitly endorsed in President Reagan's speech.

There has been much talk about how the fire-power of these battle stations could be drained by subjecting them to heavy attack; and only *then* would the ICBMs be launched, unmolested by the energy-exhausted, or even demolished, DEWs. An orbital system could be defeated even more easily than that, of course, as has been often pointed out, by just inserting clouds of junk into the same orbits as the battle stations (but moving in the opposite direction). The kinetic energies of impact would shred the battle stations into even bigger clouds of 'high-tech' junk. Sophisticated satellites might be able to manoeuvre to avoid this form of attack, but this may require much extra cost for an object the size of a battle station.

A more sophisticated and less vulnerable ABM DEW system would take advantage of the total invulnerability of the deep-diving nuclear missile submarine. These submarines, so goes the proposed scenario, would launch warheads containing nuclear bomb-pumped X-ray lasers in response to the enemy's ICBM first-strike launch.[7] These bomb-lasers would quickly climb to altitude, somehow lock on to all the targets, perform some sort of aiming function, and then detonate, thus generating incredibly intense directed beams of X-ray energy which would instantly destroy the targets (the same kill mechanism, in a more highly refined way, as proposed for the old Spartan ABM missile). There are a lot of 'ifs' in all of this, but the major attraction for ABM DEW proponents is that it solves the 'cloud of junk' attack problem. *There is nothing in orbit to be attacked.* Edward Teller, who still carries a great deal of influence in the US Department of Defense and in Congress, is a vocal supporter of this concept.[8] However, the nuclear bomb-pumped laser would also generate an electromagnetic pulse (EMP), a potentially long-range, indiscriminate phenomenon that may be as large a threat to one's own electronic resources as to the adversary's.[9]

The ABM X-ray laser also seems to suffer from another flaw: it may possibly be 'underwhelmed'. Suppose the perpetrator of a first strike launches his missiles slowly, one after the other. To destroy the first missile, the defender must expend a complete bomb, grossly under-utilizing its multiple ICBM engagement capability. The attacker continues this process until there are no more X-ray bombs. If, when that occurs, the attacker still possesses ICBMs, then the X-ray laser ABM shield will have failed.

Those who believe banning *all* weapons from space will automatically make the world safer ought to think about these points. Such a total ban may merely *increase* the incentive for building submarine-launched bomb-pumped X-ray lasers. That would be a development we can all agree would be terrifying, particularly since there is reason to believe such a weapon would be most effective as part of a first-strike attack.

The X-ray laser form of DEW is, of course, an idea with disquieting arms control implications. How, for example, could orbital tests (particularly of the aiming mechanisms) be conducted without violating the Partial Test Ban Treaty of 1963?[10] Just orbiting the nuclear bomb, with no testing, would clearly violate the Outer Space Treaty of 1967. What is equally clear, however, is that the orbiting of other, non-nuclear forms of DEW for use as anti-satellite (ASAT) weapons is *not* forbidden at present.

III. Space-based DEWs and the ABM Treaty

The obvious military uses for DEWs in space are for ASAT and ABM purposes. So far, no weapons have been placed in permanent orbit; the USSR has done so only on a temporary basis while testing its 'hunter-killer satellites'. ASAT capability is generally perceived as hostile in intent and destabilizing, as its use could deny vital intelligence information during a period of escalating tension. Below, in section VI, some elementary calculations are presented on the energy requirements for such a weapon. Any space-based

DEW deployment suitable for ABM use would almost surely satisfy the technical requirements for an ASAT system. Therefore, banning ASAT DEWs would automatically ban ABM DEWs. To many, this would be a desirable side effect. Indeed, since 1972 we have had the ABM Treaty[11] which, apparently, both the USA and USSR have honoured with reasonable care.

A careful reading of the ABM Treaty shows, however, that space-based DEWs are *not* explicitly forbidden. This is an issue still subject to negotiation. Article II of the Treaty clearly defines an ABM system as one utilizing interceptor missiles, missile launchers and radars. Then we find, in the initialled attached agreed statements, common understandings, and unilateral statements to the Treaty (in Statement D), a proviso that should ABM systems based on other physical principles and including components capable of substituting for ABM interceptor missiles, ABM launchers or ABM radars be created in the future, specific limitations on such systems and their components would be subject to discussion. Space-based (or ground-based, too, for that matter) DEWs certainly fall under the category of "other physical principles". The legal disposition of an ABM/ASAT DEW has yet to be determined.[12]

The ABM Treaty was pragmatically signed because it was patently clear to both sides that a terminal defence against re-entry vehicles (RVs) would be up against enormous difficulties. As long as the difficulties still looked severe, and as long as neither side had even a moderate chance of deploying a system that could work, it was agreed it was best for both sides to stop pursuing it. These difficulties include distinguishing decoys from armed RVs (a problem made even worse with the deployment of missiles with multiple re-entry vehicles— MRVs), radar degradation from fireballs and beta blackout due to atmospheric nuclear explosions, and the ability of the offence to saturate even a perfect ABM defence by the obvious expedient of just attacking with more armed RVs than there are ABM missiles.[13]

Terminal ABM defence advocates are still active, however. One proposal that avoids conflict with the ABM Treaty's definition of an ABM system, for example, suggests the use of a 30 mm Gatling gun that would provide, in the words of one supporter, a "withering hail of small explosive projectiles".[14] This would be used for the point defence of missile silos and be dependent on radars. It would obviously suffer from the same technical difficulties as the original ABM systems, and as such does not seem a credible idea.

Space-based ABM DEWs would not be a terminal defence. All proposals tend to call for the engagement of ICBMs either during the boost phase (the preferable time, as that is when missiles are hot and easy to track, and full of fuel and easiest to destroy), or, less desirably, during the intermediate phase of the ballistic arc through space before multiple RVs are released. A space-based ABM DEW would be an *initial* defence. This avoids the MRV decoy problem, unless the adversary launches decoy *missiles* (which seems an unlikely proposition), as well as the radar blackout problem; beam weapons do not need the range of information provided to missile interceptors, but would rather utilize the detection and angle-rate signals generated by passive infra-red and optical sensors. The ABM DEW target acquisition system could probably be impaired by high altitude nuclear explosions, but this could also subject the nation below to devastating EMP effects.

IV. Space-based DEWs and MAD

The claim is often made that space-based DEWs would be a destabilizing development because they would weaken the credibility of the mutual assured destruction (MAD) theory that now forms the cornerstone of nuclear strategy.[15] The DEW, it is feared, seems to be the long-sought technology that could give reason to believe a nation might survive retaliation for its surprise first-strike. Therefore, goes the reasoning, if one side sees the other on the verge of achieving such an advantage it will be tempted to launch an attack before it can be thwarted.

Enthusiastic supporters of space-based DEW, such as Senator Wallop, reject this and ask their critics how they can morally deny nations the right to self-defence.

Back and forth goes this debate, until after a while the DEW opponents bring out what they consider their most powerful technological argument; the assertion that to be worthwhile space-based DEWs must be perfect. That is, as an ABM system it must operate with zero 'leakage'. This argument is illogical, as *none* of the armaments of MAD currently in place operate with perfection. Indeed, if you believe in MAD, it is this very feature of uncertainty that bedevils war planners, making their calculations sufficiently cloudy that no sensible leadership would place the fate of the world at their mercy. Proponents of MAD have even quantified the uncertainty of their ICBMs by inventing the concepts of 'circular error probable' and 'bias'. Indeed, to *reduce* these uncertainties is said to be provocative. MAD *depends*, in large part, on a fog of uncertainty for much of whatever credibility it can lay claim to.

The original 'race-track' or 'shell game' basing mode for the US MX missiles was specifically designed, for example, in an attempt to generate doubt and uncertainty. The enormous uncertainty in the location of nuclear missile submarines is precisely what makes them such fearsome weapons. To summarize, what we have now are offensive weapons that kill horrific numbers of people but are considered desirable because both sides have doubts about their location (the adversary's) and/or their effectiveness (their own *and* the adversary's).

We thus seem to be faced with a paradox because space-based DEW is declared to be undesirable for two reasons: first, it threatens the precept of MAD (presuming a highly reliable DEW); and second, it is not perfect (i.e., it is *not* reliable). This is a preposterous situation and, as any good logician would tell you, if your conclusion is absurd then maybe so is your premise. And the premise, I suggest, is MAD.

MAD is a flawed concept, one that attempts to make legitimate the mass suicide of the world (most of it without ever being asked) as national policy.

Never, as has been pointed out many times before, has an acronym been more self-defining. MAD has created war machines of such near incomprehensible complexity it is impossible for anyone who knows the most elementary probability theory to believe these war machines aren't doomed (and we with them) to eventual self-destruction. The US MAD hardware has experienced many well-publicized failures.[16] One can only wonder at what other near-horrors have been kept hidden from the public (and will be, as they are sure to continue to occur), or what potential disasters the Soviet nuclear missile commands have suffered.

MAD, the theory that the world's best chance for survival is on a see-saw grotesquely call the 'balance of terror', has succeeded only in arming both the USA and the USSR with thousands of strategic nuclear warheads, as well as something like quadruple that number of theatre atomic bombs in Europe. MAD is a positive-feedback, unstable system that *stimulates* the acquisition of nuclear weapons. As one writer has put it, MAD has led us to our present situation and shown us ". . . the bankruptcy of stockpiling pellets of destruction till Hell won't hold them".[17] Furthermore, a MAD war must be judged as immoral; it could never be a 'just war'.[18]

Well then, one might ask, suppose all the people who have said this for years are right? How can we begin to undo the frightful nuclear armaments mess the world is in? And what does space-based DEW have to do with it? Without claiming a superior insight into this question of ultimate survival, a suggestion is presented below that may promote some discussion.

V. A revised ABM Treaty

The present ABM Treaty now bans what is effectively ground-based, terminal defence. This should not be changed. However, the Treaty could be amended, as provided for in article XIV, to *allow* space-based, initial defences using non-nuclear technology (that is, DEW). Further, each new deployment of, and/or enhancement to, a nation's space-based ABM DEW systems could be coupled with a removal of some silo-based ICBMs. The formula to be used to determine this number would be negotiated, but might include a provision to maintain the current relative strengths of each nation. The meaning of the word 'strength', as measured by some combination of numbers of warheads, total throw-weight, numbers of missiles, and so on, would be negotiated. A nation's sea-based nuclear missiles, and nuclear weapons carried by aircraft, would not be affected.

This proposal will now be discussed in more detail.

From a realistic point of view, world disarmament is probably not going to happen soon. Anything that encourages the *removal* of some of the present over-abundance of nuclear bombs is, however, clearly a step in the right direction. Sea-based missiles are, for any reasonable time into the future, invulnerable. They represent a country's most reliable nuclear forces, and as such are not likely candidates for removal. Further, the verification of such a reduction would be very difficult, probably impossible to perform.

Weapons carried on aircraft are much less of an immediate threat (but a no less appalling one) than missiles, as their delivery time is measured in hours, not minutes. They can probably survive a first strike in some strength as they can be launched on warning and then recalled. The aircraft are also much less reliable (i.e., less threatening) than missiles, in that no country can know with any precision just how well it can penetrate the air defences of the adversary. And again, verification of a reduction of aircraft-carried weapons would be essentially impossible.

This leaves us with the land-based missile forces. These ICBMs are the ones that can be reduced, even eliminated, as space-based DEWs are deployed. They are now the most vulnerable of weapons. The silo locations are yearly more precisely known through satellite surveillance, while at the same time each side's missile accuracy is increasing to the point that even silo super-hardening is in danger of being insufficient for survival. And finally, the removal of these weapons would be relatively easy to verify in number, again by satellite surveillance. To remove these weapons would be to remove targets presently in danger of becoming so vulnerable (and tempting) that their only hope for survival would be to launch on warning, a policy that increases tension and further puts the world at the mercy of some malfunctioning $1.39 computer chip. Unlike aircraft, there is no recalling ICBMs.

The deployment of *initial* space-based ABM DEW systems by the Soviet Union and the United States, if coupled with ICBM reductions, would not be a destabilizing development, for the following reasons.

1. As each side puts up more ABM DEWs, the other side sees fewer missiles pointed its way. These two factors can be interpreted as simultaneously increasing the ability of each side to survive a first strike, as well as making a first strike less attractive; both results are stabilizing influences. And the rest of the world can enjoy watching the superpowers actually reducing offensive inventories, something they promised to do in the 1970 Treaty on the Non-Proliferation of Nuclear Weapons.

2. Space-based initial ABM DEW defences make multiple-warhead missiles unattractive. Single-warhead missiles (e.g., the US Midgetman) become more attractive, as does the 'de-MIRVing' of existing missiles.[19] In particular, the case becomes weaker for the multi-warhead MX with the existence of Soviet initial ABM DEW systems.

3. Space-based ABM DEW systems address the two nightmare questions of the single missile attack by a terrorist organization and the 'accidental' launch of missiles.

4. Ground-based ABM systems suffered from the internal political problem of *where* to put them, that is, some portions of the defended homelands would be more protected than others. Space-based systems engaging ICBMs at launch time defend everyone equally well.

5. Space-based DEWs would transform part of the arms race from one of

the acquisition of ever more bombs, into a technological research competition. This is less likely to suddenly and catastrophically kill millions of people than are Minuteman, MX and SS-18 missiles.

There are at least two potential problems with space-based ABM DEW systems: the ASAT issue; and the question of allowed testing of the systems. However, perhaps the ability of an ABM DEW system to serve as an ASAT DEW may not be perceived as a major threat if both sides have equivalent systems in orbit, and if ASAT tests are forbidden. (This should be reasonably open to verification, as the systems are on clear display.) ABM testing should be possible in a non-tension producing way by requiring that each side provide the other with advance notice of all such tests. These are topics certain to be on the agenda of any negotiations along the lines proposed in this paper.

VI. Space-based laser ASAT damage mechanisms

Calculations on the performance of directed-energy weapons have been published.[20] Estimates of the capability of such weapons depend, for example, on the target-weapon range and on properties of the type of target assumed. The author presents his calculations below, asssuming aluminium as a satellite material and a range of 500 km. It must be emphasized that these are 'back of the envelope' calculations that fail to account for many of the realities of laser radiation/target coupling.[21] But they are most useful for suggesting possibilities.

To begin, assume a beam angular divergence (σ) of one microradian. This is the diffraction limit of a mirror about 3 m in diameter, used with a hydrogen fluoride chemical laser (2.7 μm wavelength). At range R (metres) this gives a beam diameter of $R\sigma$ and area $(\pi R^2 \sigma^2)/4$ m^2.

If we denote the specific heat of the target by c, the temperature elevation of the target caused by the beam by T (°C), and the target depth as ϱ(g/cm^2), then the energy density of the incident beam works out to be 4.2 $\varrho c T$ joules/cm^2.

To do the calculations for an ASAT laser, let us use $R = 500$ km, $T = 600$°C (appropriate for melting the aluminum skin of a satellite), $\varrho = 0.54$ g/cm^2 (minimum appropriate for penetrating a skin 0.2 cm thick), and $c = 0.24$ (the specific heat of aluminium). Then we obtain a beam energy density of 326 J/cm^2 and a total beam energy of 640 kJ. This energy could be delivered, by definition, in *one second* by a 640 kW (kilowatt) laser. Not all the incident energy will be absorbed by the skin, however, so we can use another factor of 10 to account for reflection (polished aluminium has an absorption coefficient of about 0.01, so 0.1 seems reasonable for a real satellite that has an oxide film on its surface, and has been in space long enough to be 'broken in' by the environment, for example, by micro-meteorites and the solar wind). In that case, a 6.4 MW laser could kill a satellite at a range of 500 km in one second.

How much fuel would it take to operate such an ASAT weapon? The hydrogen/fluorine reaction can theoretically release about 6 MJ per pound of *pure* reactants. Because of the vigorous chemical activity of fluorine (which has been known to result in fuel storage tanks spontaneously exploding) it is likely the hydrogen and fluorine will be obtained from normally less reactive compounds and a more reasonable value might be around 500 kJ per pound of fuel. Thus, for a 6.4 MJ shot, and assuming a 10 per cent conversion efficiency, the requirement is 60 kg of fuel for a one-second melt-through kill of a satellite at 500 km. If the ASAT laser carried just one tonne of fuel, that would suffice for about 16 such engagements.

An alternative laser damage mechanism is impulsive loading. This effect is the result of intensely heating, very quickly, a thin layer of satellite skin, producing an explosive vapourization of surface material. The explosive blow-off of this surface mass produces a shock wave in the remaining skin, that is, the momentum of the suddenly ejected mass can produce an effect similar to hitting the satellite with a sledgehammer, possibly rupturing the skin.

To be specific, let Δt denote the duration of the laser pulse (seconds), K the thermal conductivity of the skin (calories/cm/s/°C), c the specific heat of the skin, δ the density of the skin (g/cm^3), W the total absorbed beam pulse energy (joules), R the target range (metres), and σ the beam divergence angle. Then the momentum density delivered to the satellite works out to be

$$\frac{50.5}{R\sigma}\sqrt{W\sqrt{(K\Delta t\delta)/c}} \text{ dyne s/cm}^2 \text{ (this unit is also called a 'tap')}$$

For an aluminium skin, $K = 0.5$, $\delta = 2.7$, and $c = 0.24$. Then, the delivered momentum density is

$$\frac{77.8}{R\sigma}\sqrt{W\sqrt{\Delta}} \text{ taps}$$

Δt must not be too long, or else the absorbed energy will diffuse too deeply into the skin to cause sufficient heating for thin layer vaporization. For example, if $\Delta t = 1$ μs then it can be shown that the layer depth is 0.001 cm, which is fairly thin, that is, 0.5 per cent of a 0.2 cm thick skin.

According to Ferriter et al.,[22] the minimum impulse required to rupture an aluminium plate 0.2 cm thick is 64 000 taps (this value varies linearly with thickness). If, for example, a laser can switch 100 kJ in 1 μs and if the skin absorption coefficient is 0.1, and if σ is 1 μrad, then the maximum range for an impulsive kill is 3.8 km.

Notes and references

1. McDougall, W. A., 'How *not* to think about space lasers, *National Review*, 13 May 1983, pp. 550–556, 580–581.
   Tsipis, K., 'Laser weapons', *Scientific American*, December 1981, pp. 51–57.
   Barletta, W. A., 'The advanced test accelerator', *Military Electronics/ Countermeasures*, August 1981, pp. 21–26.
2. Several conversations with Mr Jeff Hecht aided preparation of this paper. Mr

Hecht also allowed the author to read a pre-publication manuscript draft of his book *Beam Weapons: New Round of the Arms Race*, published by Plenum Press, New York, 1984. This book discusses many of the issues touched on in this paper (and much else).

3. This is not to say that space-based DEW devices *should* be constructed (nor that they shouldn't be). It is merely being asserted that they eventually *could* be made.

4. One of the most often expressed fears of those who heard President Reagan's speech was that he was speaking of orbiting 'Death Star' or planet-busting weapons. A much more realistic concern would be whether it might be possible for space-based DEW to become a weapon of mass terror (e.g., one able to cause fires below on a vast scale). Because of the difficulties in propagating a high-energy beam through the atmosphere over great distances, this is not an immediate concern.

5. *Nature*, 16 September 1933, pp. 432–433.

6. Wallop, M., 'Opportunities and imperatives of ballistic missile defence', *Strategic Review*, Fall 1979, pp. 13–21.

7. Browne, W. W., 'Stopping missiles with energy beams', *Discover*, June 1983, pp. 28–32.

8. *Aviation Week and Space Technology*, 20 September 1982, p. 15.

9. Ironically, Teller is also a prolific writer on the dangers of EMP. See Teller, E., 'Electromagnetic pulses from nuclear explosions', *IEEE Spectrum*, October 1982, p. 65.

10. Some tests could conceivably be possible if done via *sub-orbital* flights, e.g., as the Soviets did with their fractional orbit bombardment system (FOBS) in the early 1960s.

11. US Arms Control and Disarmament Agency, *Arms Control and Disarmament Agreements*, 1982 edition, pp. 137–147.

12. For a discussion on different interpretations of the Treaty, see paper 8, page 127.

13. Garwin, R. L. and Bethe, H. A., 'Anti-ballistic-missile systems', *Scientific American*, March 1968, pp. 21–31.

14. Graham, D., *High Frontier* (Tor, New York, 1983), p.145.

15. It is not clear that the USSR believes in MAD—it certainly views deterrence from a different angle than the USA; see Scott, H. and Scott, W. F., *The Armed Forces of the USSR* (Westview Press, Boulder, CO, 1981), pp. 89, 382. And China, with its vast subterranean civil defence tunnels beneath cities, apparently believes nuclear war between the superpowers is inevitable. It must surely consider MAD irrelevant to its decision making.

16. Cunningham, A. M. and Fitzpatrick, M., *Future Fire* (Warner, New York, 1983), pp. 205–241.

17. McDougall (note 1).

18. Walzer, M., *Just and Unjust Wars* (Basic Books, New York, 1977).
Sider, R. J. and Taylor, R. K., *Nuclear Holocaust and Christian Hope* (Inter-Varsity Press, Downers Grove, IL, 1982), pp. 59–81.

19. MIRV = multiple independently targetable re-entry vehicle.

20. See, for example, Garwin, R. L., 'Are we on the verge of an arms race in space?', *The Bulletin of the Atomic Scientists*, May 1981, pp. 48–53.

21. Schriempf, J. T., *NRL Report* 7728, July 1974.

22. Ferriter, N., Maiden, D. E., Winslow, A. M. and Fleck, J. A., 'Analysis of efficient impulse delivery and plate rupture by laser supported detonation waves', *Lawrence Livermore Laboratory Report* UCRL-51836, 2 June 1975.

Paper 7. Implications of anti-satellite weapons for ABM issues*

Donald Kerr

Director, Los Alamos National Laboratory, Los Alamos, NM 87545, USA

I. Introduction

Recent trends and events have focused attention in the West on anti-satellite (ASAT) weapons and their relationship to anti-ballistic missile (ABM) defence and the ABM Treaty. Attracting most attention has been the imminent testing by the United States of its new, developmental ASAT system.[1] But the US Administration's decision to go ahead with testing and deploying an ASAT weapon is based on the belief that the USA must possess a counter to a significant Soviet ASAT capability in order to deter its use. The Soviet Union has extensively tested its operational ASAT system. Now the USSR is apparently integrating it into its total strategic force infrastructure and operational doctrine. The most recent evidence of this comes from the 18 June 1982 ASAT test involving the Cosmos 1379 interceptor spacecraft against the Cosmos 1375 target launched 12 days earlier. Within a six-hour period of the ASAT attack, the USSR also conducted two intercontinental ballistic missile (ICBM) tests, two anti-ballistic missile tests, one submarine-launched ballistic missile (SLBM) test and one SS-20 intermediate-range ballistic missile test.[2] This integration of ASAT and ABM operational capabilities is an ominous development. It raises a question of immediate concern: should the present asymmetry in ASAT capabilities be eliminated, and, if so, would a US deployment as a deterrent to the Soviet ASAT system seriously affect ABM issues?

Beyond this immediate problem, long-term trends in ASAT weapon technology and military strategic thinking pose much deeper and more complex questions for the strategic regime underwritten by the ABM Treaty. Many of the more advanced technologies that are now being considered for

*This paper was written under the auspices of the US Department of Energy.

anti-satellite use are virtually indistinguishable from ABM technologies. Accordingly, a serious commitment to develop these advanced ASAT weapons, particularly space-based directed-energy weapons, might undermine the ABM Treaty's restrictions on development and testing of such weapons for ABM purposes. (The ABM Treaty currently prevents development of space-based ABM weapons beyond the laboratory stage.) Conversely, an early and effective ban on ASAT development and deployment might reinforce the ABM Treaty prohibitions against development of these technologies for ABM purposes as well.

If there were universal agreement that the indefinite continuation of the present strategic regime is desirable, based as it is on retaliation by offensive nuclear forces, then closing this potential loophole in the ban on ABM weapon development would appear to be desirable. However, in an important speech on 23 March 1983, President Reagan called for a research and development programme which would allow the USA to move beyond a strategic nuclear policy based on offensive retaliation to one based on the active defence of the people and territory of the United States and its allies and friends. If such a defensive policy is feasible and desirable, the development of those weapons that would make it possible might be seriously impeded by the reinforcement of the ban on advanced space weapons in the ASAT context.

Decisions made over the next year or two—particularly decisions regarding ASAT and ABM systems—will strongly influence the character of future space activity. The further militarization or demilitarization of space is sure to have a profound influence on the military-strategic relationship between the superpowers, and may affect centrally the prospects for and the character of arms control henceforth. Many of the more detailed consequences of the militarization or demilitarization of space are not, however, well understood. This is particularly significant when the additional complicating factor of a possible change of strategic policy, in the direction of defence dominance, is added. This paper examines some of the implications of ASAT weapons for ABM issues, relating to both the development of more effective ABM defences and to the ABM Treaty. These relationships to ballistic missile defence are, to some observers, among the most troubling aspects of ASAT technology development and ASAT system deployment.[3]

II. Current ABM issues

Two sets of issues related to ballistic missile defences are currently in a state of change, or at least under scrutiny which may lead to change. The first is military policy, particularly within the United States, concerning the role of strategic defence; the second is the improving state of ballistic missile defence technology in both the USA and the USSR. While the US government remains firmly committed to the ABM Treaty, these trends are leading to more frequent questioning in unofficial circles about the wisdom of unlimited commitment to the ABM Treaty.

Military policy

The ratification of the ABM Treaty strongly influenced strategic nuclear doctrine. It ensured that the majority of the civilian population or military assets of the USA or USSR could not be protected via active defensive measures. Secretary of State Rogers, explaining the ABM Treaty to the US Senate in 1972, stated that "without a nationwide ABM defense, there can be no shield against retaliation". He continued, "Both great nuclear powers have recognized, and in effect agreed to maintain mutual deterrence".[4] A single US ABM site was subsequently completed to protect one ICBM wing in North Dakota, and immediately decommissioned. The Soviet ABM deployment was limited to a single field near Moscow, where the 64 old interceptors have recently been augmented or replaced by modern ones.

While ABM technology development has continued in both countries, no nation-wide ABM systems have been deployed and the strategic doctrines of the two sides have come to rest primarily on offensive missile capacities and whatever passive defences they choose to employ. At the time of the signing of the ABM Treaty and the Interim Offensive Agreement, deployed offensive missile technologies were such that the ban on ABM systems ensured that neither side could hope in any way to limit damage to itself if a massive nuclear exchange occurred, whoever started it. With subsequent improvements in accuracy, however, the missile silos and all other military assets which can be located have become vulnerable to an offensive missile strike. That is, a time is foreseeable when damage to one's homeland might be limited to a considerable degree by pre-emptive offensive use of ballistic missiles. The Soviet Union began to acquire large numbers of offensive forces with such capabilities subsequent to the SALT I Treaty, and the USA for a time planned to acquire 200 MX ICBMs with 2 000 accurate warheads. Such programmes have led to concern that the survivability of the retaliatory forces (especially land-based forces) is declining, and therefore that the strategic stability supposedly assured by the ABM Treaty regime is disintegrating.

This concern led in the late 1970s and early 1980s to a regeneration of interest in ABM defence in the United States. While some interest was expressed in defence systems to protect US cities, interest centred on ABM systems as a means to protect ICBM sites and therefore ensure that enough ICBMs would survive a surprise first strike to retaliate effectively. That is, particular interest was given to ballistic missile defence (BMD) as a way to reinforce the very strategic regime that the ABM Treaty had sought to codify.

It has never been clear in the United States that the Soviet Union ever really espoused mutual vulnerability as a desirable strategic regime. The Soviet Union steadily added to its strong ABM research and development programme after the ABM treaty was signed. As the US Director of Defense Research and Engineering said in 1976, "Their [Soviet] activity continues monotonically steadily to go up. So they have an intensive activity in ABM research and development from which they could react at some time in the future".[5] And Soviet writings on military doctrine, despite public endorsements of the mutual assured destruction doctrine, continue to emphasize all forms of defence and damage limitation as necessary elements of national strategy, even in nuclear war.[6] Whatever the Soviet investment in ABM research and deployment of hard-target capable ICBMs may portend, the United States remained unquestionably attached to the concept of strategic stability based on the threat of nuclear retaliation. Interest in active defence as a means of moving away from this strategy never faded altogether in the USA, and by 1980 was being revived and presented to a more receptive audience. The High Frontier proposal for a spaced-based constellation of BMD satellites employing conventional weapons was widely discussed publicly, in Congress and within the Administration. As the difficulty in restoring the US offensive nuclear force to its former level of survivability became fully appreciated, and the public discomfort with the moral basis of mutual assured destruction became better understood, active defence was once again seriously considered. On 23 March 1983, President Reagan endorsed the objective of developing defensive weapons that one day might render offensive ballistic missiles "impotent and obsolete". First, he cited the moral irresponsibility of relying on a strategy of assured destruction if it were no longer imposed by technological imperatives: "I have become more and more deeply convinced that the human spirit must be capable of rising above dealing with other nations and human beings by threatening their existence". Then, he indicated that it is time to initiate such a programme because "current technology has attained a level of sophistication where it is reasonable for us to begin this effort".[7] The US government then initiated a major study to evaluate defensive system candidates and define a long term research programme for defence against ballistic missiles.

ABM systems and technologies

The US Safeguard ABM system deployed briefly in 1975 was a two-layered system employing exo-atmospheric and endo-atmospheric nuclear ballistic missile interceptors. One reason for abandoning the US ABM system in 1975 was that the technologies represented in the Safeguard system were judged to be incapable of coping with a massive ICBM attack.

Safeguard was a layered defence that used ground-based radars for detection, assessment, tracking, discrimination and interceptor guidance for both midcourse and terminal defences. Long-range perimeter acquisition radars provided early warning and determined the size of the attack and its targets. As attackers neared the intercept range, battle management and engagement were taken over by smaller missile site radars, coupled to central computers, with one radar—computer assembly for each wing of the Minuteman force. For the exo-atmospheric layer, multistage Spartan interceptors, guided by the radars, operated out to several hundred kilometres. The Spartan carried a single high-yield nuclear warhead. Those warheads leaking past the Spartan's defence layer would be intercepted by fast-reacting Sprint low-yield nuclear interceptors at altitudes of 3–30 km also guided to intercept by radar. Each interceptor would engage one warhead.

The large ground-based radars were Safeguard's weakest point. It was soon recognized that the first Spartan nuclear explosions would render large regions of the atmosphere opaque to radar propagation, thereby blinding the radars and making them vulnerable to attack. Other problems existed as well: (a) the computers needed were beyond the state of the art; (b) discrimination by radar signatures was only marginally effective; and (c) the system was easily defeatable by a cost-effective increase in the threat size.[8]

Many of the same considerations lead US Defense Department officials today to believe that the Moscow ABM defence "cannot presently cope with a massive attack". "However," they add, "the Soviets have continued to pursue extensive ABM research and development programs, including a rapidly deployable ABM system and improvements for the Moscow defenses".[9] These improvements are reportedly the addition of an endo-atmospheric, nuclear-armed, Sprint-like interceptor which became operational in 1980, and a replacement exo-atmospheric interceptor along with newly developed phased array radars to work in conjunction with upgraded battle management and engagement radars from the earlier Galosh nuclear deployment and perhaps the Ablakova phased array radar.[10]

As long as ABM systems remain relatively ineffective against a large and sophisticated attack, neither the USA nor the Soviet Union have much incentive to consider ABM deployment beyond the 100 allowable launchers and challenge the ABM Treaty. However, advances in all of the technologies noted above have made an ABM system appear feasible which, though leaky, is thought by some officials to be sufficient to ensure the survival of enough hardened ICBM and command, control and communications (C^3) facilities to meet retaliatory requirements. Pursuing the development of technologies for such a system, and for early development of even more capable ABM technologies, the US Department of Defense requested over \$700 million for ballistic missile defense R&D for FY 1984, and proposed an authorization of more than twice as much for FY 1985.

For the past 10 years the main US ABM research and development effort has been the Army's missile programme. Until recently it focused on the development of a site defence system that could overcome the deficiencies noted in the Safeguard ABM of the early 1970s. Distributed, netted radars and associated data processors, discrimination of re-entry vehicles from decoys, and radars and data processors that are both cheap enough and have enough capacity to function in the ABM system have been developed and tested. The programme manager claimed in 1982 that, while the technology represented in the site defence system could only limit to some degree the damage to cities, "the kind of work we did with Site Defense falls in the right effectiveness ballpark for the defense of hard targets".[11]

The current Army programme emphasizes the development of exo-atmospheric intercept technology programmes. If perfected, they could lead to a non-nuclear 'overlay' system that would be able to destroy a large number of the incoming weapons before they reached the area protected by the endo-atmospheric missiles of the site defence. Several specific technologies are being developed which are thought to be the keys to accomplishing this mission. They are: the homing overlay experiment, which is designed to demonstrate exo-atmospheric homing and non-nuclear kill; the forward acquisition system, to demonstrate the use of the long-range missile-borne acquisition sensors which would be required for BMD and early warning applications; and the designating optical tracker to demonstrate the feasibility of optical systems for BMD detection, discrimination and designation.

An important new direction for the US Army ballistic missile defence programme is the attempt to develop a non-nuclear intercept capacity for the endo-atmospheric missile as well. Separate programmes are being pursued to develop the warhead, seeker, and guidance and control capabilities to conduct non-nuclear kill within the atmosphere.[12] Many of these technologies are already proven, or thought to be low- to medium-risk R&D efforts. Together they offer the possibility of developing a reasonably effective, two-layered missile-borne BMD system over the next 5–15 years which would provide an effective though leaky hard target defence system.

In addition to these ABM missile programmes, the United States has for many years been conducting research and development on laser and particle beam technologies which eventually may have application as ballistic missile defence weapons. Most of these programmes are designed to explore the technologies and potential of directed-energy weapons. The purpose of the High Energy Laser Program, which is among the most advanced technically, is to continue developing the technology for laser beam generators, laser beam pointing and tracking, and fire control systems, and to demonstrate that high-energy lasers are feasible as weapons.

Research and development programmes are also proceeding in the USA on a variety of other beam weapons with possible BMD applications which might be placed in orbit or stationed on the ground. These include short-wavelength lasers and pulsed lasers, free electron lasers and both charged and neutral particle beams. In addition to these specific directed-energy weapon technology development programmes, several supporting technologies are being developed which may be applicable to most directed-energy weapons. Since most are equally applicable to ASAT and BMD, they will be considered in the section of the paper dealing with ASAT technology.

If directed-energy weapons are added as boost phase or mid-course intercept layers to missile-borne ABM systems, the overall ballistic missile defence system might offer leakage rates which are low enough to suggest consideration of not just defence of retaliatory assets, but of the civilian population itself. It is this possibility that was addressed by President Reagan in his speech on 23 March 1983.

Status of ABM arms control

So far these ABM technology developments and possibilities have not led either superpower to withdraw from the ABM Treaty, to suggest renegotiation, or to deploy systems admitted to be in violation of the Treaty. In fact, the Treaty was reconfirmed perfunctorily in 1982 during its mandatory five yearly review. But in light of new technological possibilities for ABM defence and the strong technical promise and momentum of these R&D efforts, and because of the current US Administration's desire to explore the possibility of a defence-dominated strategy and technology, and because of concern over Soviet intentions with regard to BMD, the ABM Treaty may receive closer scrutiny in the 1987 or 1992 reviews.

III. Implications of ASAT weapons for ABM defence

So far this paper has looked at the status of ballistic missile defence in relative isolation. For reasons both of military policy and technological progress, the permanence of the ban on ABM systems and particularly on space-based ABM systems is now an open question. But thinking about the future of ABM must also take into account other issues, prominent among them the increasing weaponization of space with ASAT and other non-ABM weapons. For the development of these weapons and their deployment will strongly influence the decision to move towards or refrain from a commitment to space-based defence against ballistic missiles.

Technological implications

Former US ASAT systems and the operational Soviet ASAT systems have been missile and satellite weapons. The US systems, now decommissioned, were the interim ASAT system based on the Nike-Zeus ABM missile, and the US Program 437, based on Thor rocket boosters, which was deployed at Johnston Island until 1975. The US ASAT system relied on direct ascent, nuclear attack of target satellites. The Soviet one is based on a modified SS-9 ICBM booster, and uses a conventional warhead to attack targets after partial or full orbits, most recently employing a 'pop-up' manoeuvre.[13] In the June 1982 test, the ASAT booster reportedly was launched 90 minutes after rolling the launcher out of its shelter. Sufficient launch sites are said to exist at the Tyuratam centre to threaten all US reconnaissance satellites.

The new ASAT weapon consists of a small, non-explosive interceptor called the miniature homing vehicle (MHV), which is mounted on a two-stage rocket designed to be launched into space from a high-flying F-15 fighter aircraft. The MHV is equipped with a combination of infra-red sensors, a laser gyroscope and an array of small rockets that will enable it to seek its target and destroy it by direct impact at very high velocity. Currently, both the Soviet ASAT satellite and the US MHV are capable of only low-altitude intercepts, because of the limited capacity of their boost vehicles. However, if mounted on larger boosters, the inherent capabilities of the weapons would probably allow them to attack synchronous satellites as well, after the long flight to 36 000 km. In addition to these current ASAT programmes, both the USA and the USSR are conducting research and development programmes which might allow anti-satellite operations to be carried out with directed-energy weapons or by other exotic approaches.

Many additional approaches to anti-satellite weapons are possible. Present and potential anti-satellite weapons can be grouped into the categories of satellites, missiles, beam weapons and weapons using nuclear effects. Diverse physical principles and weapon system concepts are represented in these categories. Most of these ASAT weapons have quite direct links to ballistic missile defence weapon developments: in fact, many potential ASAT technologies are being pursued actively as possible BMD candidates.

US developments

Satellites and missiles

Direct-ascent and orbital satellite and missile ASAT systems do not offer much potential as ABM systems, since they are generally designed to destroy much more fragile targets, and can only be deployed in relatively small numbers if they are to be justified as ASAT systems. It should be noted, however, that the Nike-Zeus interim ASAT system was initially developed as an ABM system, and that the warhead for the miniature homing vehicle evolved from the US non-nuclear kill ABM development programme. (Development of this technology was allowed under the ABM Treaty, as long as it was not a multiple-warhead ABM system.) So while missile and satellite ASAT weapon systems themselves should be only marginally useful for ballistic missile defence, certain of the technologies for this ASAT form are common to ABM systems. It has also been suggested that satellites could be used as ASAT weapons by placing them (perhaps surreptitiously) in a common or slightly displaced orbit with target satellites, silent until receiving the order to attack.[14]

Laser weapons

Many of the laser weapon technologies being developed for ASAT weapons are identical to BMD technologies, although since satellites are generally 'softer' than ballistic missile boosters, post-boost vehicles or warheads, ASAT technology requirements are usually thought to be less demanding. As a result of their technological similarity, many of the US directed-energy programmes are generic, and do not distinguish at their early R&D stage between possible ballistic missile defence and anti-satellite applications. The *Fiscal Year 1983 Arms Control Impact Statement* notes that,

While high energy lasers and particle beams differ in state of development and in the technology required to realize them, they have potential for weapon systems of similar operational characteristics. Moreover, if they can be developed as weapons, they could have similar implications for the future of the Anti-Ballistic Missile (ABM) Treaty, possible anti-satellite (ASAT) negotiations, and space defense issues generally.[15]

Two major laser programmes in the USA are the visible laser programme and the Space Laser triad of programmes for a space-based laser. The visible

114

laser programme aims to show the feasibility of "using long-range, ground-based, and eventually space-based visible lasers for strategic applications. The earliest application would utilize visible lasers directly to negate satellites at long ranges from ground-based visible lasers ... and, in the longer term, to provide ballistic missile defense (BMD)". The 1983 plan for the programme indicated that development and experiments were proceeding to demonstrate the capability of the laser to produce higher power levels (but not ABM weapon levels yet) and to demonstrate the integration of all the technologies.[16]

The Space Laser triad of programmes comprises three major technology development efforts which, while intended to develop relatively near-term system concepts, also are designed to provide technology scalable to more capable laser weapon systems.[17] The first, Talon Gold, is developing the fire control and precision laser beam direction capabilities, including target acquisition, tracking and precision pointing, necessary for a laser weapon to be able to operate in space. The Alpha laser programme aims to develop an efficient chemical laser scalable to high power levels. The near-term applications of this programme would be to demonstrate the laser technology required for a long-range space-based ASAT weapon. Other applications of the technology include ballistic missile defence.[18] The third element of the triad is the Large Optics Demonstration Experiment (LODE). It aims to develop and demonstrate the beam control and optics technologies needed for the space-based weapon, particularly design and construction of large diameter mirrors.

Several other R&D programmes are being pursued in the USA which aim to identify and develop laser, particle beam and directed-microwave approaches that will provide greater power output than current techniques. Several are exploring the feasibility and characteristics of various short-wavelength lasers. They include the chemical laser technology programme for both near-term and far-term chemical lasers, and programmes to develop free electron and excimer lasers which may offer higher frequency radiation that has some potential gain in wavelength scaling and impulse delivery, features useful for ballistic missile defence. The free electron laser has the added advantage of selectable frequencies from the infra-red through the visible to the ultraviolet.

Particle beams

The Defense Advanced Research Projects Agency (DARPA) 1958 Seesaw programme, which continued until 1972, considered the use of particle beam weapons, specifically electron beams, as a defence against ballistic missiles. The programme was discontinued because of anticipated difficulties in propagating an electron beam through the atmosphere to the ranges necessary in ballistic missile engagements and the prohibitively high costs projected for a deployed e-beam system. In 1974 electron beam feasibility was reconsidered for shorter range anti-ship missile defence as part of the Navy's Chair Heritage programme.[19] Transferred to DARPA sponsorship as a technology base programme in 1979, this approach uses a linear induction electron accelerator with chosen operating parameters (50 MeV, 10 kA) to explore beam control and propagation.

The Army began a second type of particle beam programme in 1976, charged with studying the feasibility of using neutral particle beams in space. This programme, called White Horse, does not face the atmospheric propagation problems of Chair Heritage, but still must contend with the stringent beam quality requirements associated with engagements at the very long ranges inherent in ballistic missile defence outside the atmosphere.[20] However, neutral particle beams are not deflected by the Earth's magnetic field, simplifying the pointing and tracking problem.

It is well known that high-energy particle beams tend to deposit their energy within the target rather than on the surface, as do laser beams. This suggests that laser weapons may be countered more readily than particle beam weapons if targets are coated with material designed to absorb or reflect the laser energy.

Other approaches

The notion of nuclear weapon-driven beams has been discussed in the public press. One such concept would use a nuclear explosive to pump an X-ray laser. Applications against missiles have been suggested. Notwithstanding political restraints, collateral effects from the detonation of the nuclear weapon power source might destroy other friendly satellites and create radar blackout zones and other conditions that might reduce the feasibility or military utility of weapons based on either approach.

Microwave generating systems have been considered as the basis for weapons which might attack and kill electronic sub-systems, thereby paralysing military forces and their supporting infrastructure. Microwave-generating systems have improved immensely over the past decade or two, particularly in delivering high power at short wavelengths. Short wavelengths are important because the required antenna size is smaller and thus more practical for military purposes. In spite of these improvements, reasonable demands on system size, weight and cost will probably require still higher microwave generator power at appropriate wavelengths for many direct weapon applications. Significant improvements in current technology, or novel generation concepts, are needed, although considerable potential for tactical weapons may exist with lower performance levels.

Because of the early stage of development and the many similar sub-system technologies of most directed-energy weapons, whether for ASAT use, space defence, ballistic missile defence or other applications, a number of more basic R&D efforts are being pursued to develop basic or common technologies which are required for many systems. These include, for example, programmes to develop advanced laser optics, improved (beyond Talon Gold) acquisition and tracking, spaceborne detection targets, and advanced on-board signal processing.[21]

116

Soviet developments

No Soviet publications provide information on Soviet ASAT and ABM technologies equivalent to that in, say, *Aviation Week and Space Technology* for the USA, so the discussion thus far has emphasized US developments. There are some indications that a prototype stationary particle beam weapon (PBW) and/or an extremely powerful laser system has been constructed at the Soviet ABM test centre at Sary Shagan, Kazakhstan. In either case, the multiple high-energy explosive magnetic generators reportedly on the site could be used for testing the energy technology necessary for building a PBW. The picture is still rather hazy.[22] Other reports have suggested a co-ordinated Soviet space weapon programme involving the operational anti-satellite weapon and development of an anti-satellite laser that could either be ground-based, placed on an unmanned spacecraft or placed on the next generation of Soviet manned space stations.[23]

Military-strategic implications

First, there is the question of the consequences of ASAT development and deployment for the military strategies of the superpowers. Within a strategic environment where ABM defence is prohibited and security ultimately rests upon mutual deterrence via second-strike retaliation, satellites play an important role. An ASAT threat to satellites might be very troublesome.

Anti-satellite weapons in an offensive force dominated world

The minimum essential military capability in this strategic environment is the ability to endure the most powerful surprise attack an enemy can deliver, and still retaliate with an unacceptably devastating and highly credible nuclear response. For second-strike retaliation, current strategic nuclear forces depend on early warning satellites for initial detection of ballistic missile launches. Without this warning, insufficient time might be left to decide upon a response, execute an emergency action message, and launch vulnerable retaliatory forces before they are destroyed, or to move critical trans-attack command, control and communications facilities from exposed locations, so that they could transmit the action message to surviving forces.

Since early warning satellites are typically stationed in geosynchronous orbits, ASAT systems capable only of low-altitude intercepts may not pose too great a threat to the survival of the retaliatory capability. Development and deployment of ASAT weapons capable of high-altitude intercepts, or of space-based or ground-based directed-energy ASAT weapons with sufficient power to damage a satellite in synchronous orbit, pose a grave threat. For in the absence of a BMD capable of defending retaliatory ICBMs and C^3I facilities, or of other means for protecting retaliatory forces, an ASAT attack on early warning satellites could open the way for a reasonably effective surprise first strike against targetable nuclear weapon systems and command and control capabilities. Direct ascent or pop-up satellites appear to be marginally effective for this mission, since they would have a long flight to synchronous orbit, which should be visible to the other side. This would itself be a warning of attack. The greater danger to the eyes of the retaliatory force, then, would seem to be posed by directed-energy ASAT weapons, by missile attacks (e.g., SLBM attacks) on the ground links of early warning satellites and on undeployed C^3 facilities such as airborne command posts, or perhaps by surreptitious placement of dormant ASAT weapons (e.g., space mines) in orbits near to early warning assets.

A situation which provides for mutual deterrence of massive attacks on the civil and military assets of the superpowers may not be adequate to deter either conventional war or even limited nuclear war. Should such conflicts arise, the military satellites of the superpowers would be expected to play many roles, both strategic and tactical. The side that could utilize its own satellites and nullify those of its adversary might enjoy decisive advantages. In this realm, therefore, where a wide spectrum of military satellites almost certainly would be used, ASAT capabilities might be viewed as especially valuable to military plans and outcomes. In conventional war, satellites would be called upon to provide tactical and strategic C^3, navigation, meteorology, electronic and photographic reconnaissance, ocean surveillance and targeting, and post-strike assessment, as well as maintaining early warning of escalation to nuclear weapon use. A recent US assessment noted that "The United States' ability to utilize its military power continues to be increasingly dependent on the effective and reliable operation of various satellite systems. ... Space systems provide critical strategic and tactical support to military forces and political leaders in the area of attack warning navigation, surveillance, communications, intelligence and meteorology".[24]

Tactical satellites—electronic and photographic reconnaissance and ocean surveillance satellites—tend to be placed in low Earth orbits.[25] Attack of these satellites would be most significant during a conventional war, or during a limited nuclear war which the combatants wanted to remain limited. Because of the heavy dependence of the superpowers on tactical satellites, the employment of ASAT weapons against the tactical military space assets of the other side would be very tempting during a major conventional war. This fact has led to increasing attention to both satellite defence and to ASAT weapons as either a deterrent to attacks on satellites or as an offensive tool.

While in such a war all of the satellites on both sides could be attacked, there might be strong incentives to withhold attack or to limit ASAT warfare to tactical satellites. An attack on satellites almost certainly would result in attacks on one's own satellites, and the loss of capabilities might be thought to outweigh the advantages of denying the enemy the use of his satellites. Even if ASAT weapons were used, attacks might intentionally be limited to tactical satellites. For the destruction during a conventional or limited nuclear war of those military space assets which are essential to assess central and massive nuclear strikes "would make attack assessment and associated communications more difficult, and therefore might raise the risk of a massive, rather than a limited retaliation. Such an attack could also complicate post-attack communications between the two sides".[26] If one or both sides desired to try to prevent the escalation of the war, and if satellites were sufficiently differentiated by mission, the belligerents might try consciously to spare the satellites of the other side which are essential for warning, escalation control and post-attack communications.

Since conventional or limited nuclear wars are usually thought to be more likely than a nuclear 'bolt out of the blue', and current generation ASAT weapons are designed to operate in the regime where tactical support satellites are stationed, special attention might be given to the strategic and arms control aspects of low-altitude ASAT systems. It might be desirable to develop ASAT limitations to enforce a 'firebreak' between high- and low-altitude ASAT systems, and as far as possible between tactical and strategic ASAT. (Unfortunately for this idea, tactical satellites may increasingly be placed in the more secure sanctuary of the synchronous orbit.) On the other hand, the use of these satellites in a conventional or limited nuclear war might be considered so crucial that one side or both will neither forfeit their use, nor concede it to the other side. The result could very well be an all-out ASAT war, with ominous consequences for subsequent escalation limitation.

In peace-time, satellites provide a variety of military services such as electronic and photographic reconnaissance for military planning, for reassurance about the actions and plans of potential enemies, and for arms control verification, as well as many non-military services. Satellites, especially satellites used for arms control verification, are at present protected by the terms of the Outer Space Treaty and the SALT I and SALT II Treaties. The existence of any ASAT weapons poses a real and a symbolic threat to these guarantees. Secret use of ASAT means in peace-time could result in the destruction or degradation of space military assets in a pre-war period, and cast doubt on the cause of any satellite failures in peace-time (e.g., the suspicions that the USSR may have blinded US reconnaissance satellites on at least two occasions). The threat posed by ASAT weapon use could provide uncertainty and lack of confidence in the viability of national technical means of verification, and cast doubts on the wisdom of investment in satellites on the part of peaceful users of space.

Anti-satellite weapons in a defence dominated world

An entirely different set of ASAT military-strategic considerations arises if the prohibition on ballistic missile defence is lifted. Within a strategic environment where ballistic missile defence is accepted, anti-satellite capabilities almost certainly would be implicit, and space-based weapon systems a near certainty.

The introduction of conventional, missile-borne ABM systems probably would not significantly alter the present situation, where satellites in low-altitude orbits already are vulnerable to conventional warhead ASAT weapons and nuclear weapon effects. The deployment of ground-based or orbiting directed-energy ABM weapons would pose a new order of threat to satellites.

They could be killed more easily than ballistic missiles or warheads, and with directed-energy weapons they could be destroyed almost instantaneously.

In a strategic war where defensive weapons are deployed by both sides, the first priority for the attacker, if he could not simply overwhelm the defence, would be to neutralize or penetrate the defences of the other side, to provide access for offensive operations. With this in mind, a peace-time competition of satellite measures and counter-measures would probably ensue (e.g., the protection of warning or communications space assets within directed-energy weapon platforms has been suggested).

Tactical support satellites and perhaps even strategic warning and communication satellite assets would probably be fair game in a war between the superpowers. The survival of these assets in a world where anti-ballistic missile and therefore anti-satellite weaponry is permitted would depend on the prevailing state of ASAT and satellite defence technology. Even if a ban is placed on ASAT weapons the technical capability to attack satellites will exist and thus compliance with such a ban will be difficult to verify.

Arms control implications of ASAT weapons for the ABM Treaty

Some critics of the US MHV programme argue that since it represents a higher level of ASAT technology than the Soviet system, it will stimulate an ASAT arms race. Moreover, they believe that the US weapon will offer unique arms control difficulties. As a result, there have been resolutions offered in the US Senate and House of Representatives calling on the President to reopen and accelerate negotiations to ban the development, deployment or use of anti-satellite weapons.[27] Generally these concerns relate to the potentially destabilizing effect of ASAT systems on the strategic military situation and on commercial satellite uses. For, given the prevailing US interpretation of the ABM Treaty, the development and deployment of improved missile and satellite ASAT weapons would offer few if any avenues for ABM development that are not already open. The ABM Treaty does not preclude R&D and testing of improved ABM interceptors or components, unless they are sea-based, air-based, space-based or mobile land-launched, or unless they have multiple kill vehicles per launcher or are rapidly reloadable.[28] Indeed, much improvement of defensive missile systems has gone forward under the constraints of the Treaty, including the development of the homing vehicle similar to the one used on the new US ASAT system. It should be noted that fixed, land-based, non-reloadable directed-energy ABM weapons could be developed and tested (but not unilaterally deployed) within the confines of the ABM Treaty.

Development of new forms of ASAT weapon, however, might have direct and powerful consequences for the ABM Treaty and ABM issues generally, because development and deployment of directed-energy and nuclear-effects ASAT weapons could provide a vehicle for the development and testing of similar weapons for ballistic missile defence. Countries successfully conducting these programmes would certainly move closer to the capability for BMD weapon systems. Work on ASAT would help to evaluate the prospects of candidate directed-energy and nuclear-effects weapons for upgrading to ballistic missile defence. Many of the supporting technologies needed for several BMD systems based on these physical principles, and for integrated testing of a variety of components which might be incorporated into BMD systems, could be done under the guise of ASAT development and testing. It should be remembered that the ABM Treaty precludes development beyond the 'breadboard' stage of space-based ABM weapons, including directed-energy weapons. For that reason, ASAT weapon development could offer an avenue for ABM directed-energy weapon development that is not available within the strictures of the ABM Treaty.

IV. Conclusions

Intermingled technologies

As the discussion of ABM and ASAT technology developments has shown, many ASAT and ABM weapon technologies are not discrete. This is particularly true of directed-energy weapons. Lower power levels are needed for any ASAT weapon, but at least in the major US R&D programmes the directed-energy technologies are usually pursued without reference to an ultimate distinction between ASAT and ABM applications. Consequently, it is probable that the development and deployment of directed-energy ASAT weapons would be intermediary to the development of power levels needed for boost-phase or mid-course BMD intercepts. However, it may be that many of the current directed-energy weapon programmes now being pursued will not have the power levels required to carry out ballistic missile defence, especially in light of possible responsive threats including counter-measures. And directed-energy weapons potentially scalable to higher power levels and less sensitive to countermeasures, such as neutral particle beams, may not be feasible as weapons. The other weapon system components, such as surveillance, acquisition, tracking, pointing, damage assessment and attack assessment technologies, which are being developed for space-based ASAT systems and many ground-based systems are either directly applicable to BMD systems or contribute to the technologies necessary to make space-based BMD possible.

Satellite- and missile-based ASAT weapon system technologies, on the other hand, are more distinct from ballistic missile defence systems. Some non-nuclear kill vehicle technologies may be applicable to both ABM and ASAT purposes, but the ABM Treaty does not prevent their development, testing, and deployment in any case, as long as they are ground-based and do not use multiple or reloadable launchers. Thus, the development, testing and deployment of non-nuclear kill ASAT weapons would offer limited additional opportunities for development of weapons for possible ABM uses.

121

Arms control choices

Are there types of deployment which might profitably be constrained, apart from restrictions on the weapons themselves? Efforts to answer questions such as these are complicated by the variety of ways in which space weapons could be categorized. For example, the future possibilities for weapons in space could be categorized in terms of their targets (ground attacks, attacks on objects in orbit, attacks on ballistic missiles in boost phase and mid-course, defence of high-value objects in orbit); they could be categorized in terms of their location (ground-based, endo-atmospheric, low orbit, high orbit); they could be characterized in terms of the technologies used for the weapon (lasers, particle beams, nuclear explosions, kinetic impact, etc.); they could be characterized in terms related to issues of stability (prompt effects, delayed effects, constant deployment, surge deployment, etc.); or they could be grouped in terms of their missions (strategic warning and assessment, escalation limitation, strategic or tactical communications, targeting and retargeting, etc.). While these different categories do not immediately suggest the distinctions that should be made between satellites and uses that should be prohibited, regulated or unconstrained, categorization by mission does suggest one important distinction that might profitably be made between those satellites protected from attack (strategic warning and escalation limitation assets) and those not protected (tactical support assets) in the event ASAT weapons are deployed.

These potentially protected and unprotected satellites are stationed largely in high- and low-altitude orbit, respectively. While trends in technology may make it difficult, it might be desirable to attempt to constrain development of high-altitude ASAT systems but allow low-altitude ASAT systems (while attempting to maintain this division between low- and high-altitude missions). Current and planned US and Soviet ASAT weapons do not have high-altitude intercept capabilities, although both the US MHV and the Soviet killer satellite could probably operate against high-altitude satellites with no more than extrapolation from the lesser technology, and a larger boost vehicle.

The more common arms control approach to the ASAT threat is to seek a ban on the testing, deployment or use of such weapons altogether. This has been the Soviet negotiating position for several years, and it was reiterated by President Andropov in his offer of 18 August 1983. Such a proposal is complicated by the fact that the USSR already has tested and deployed an ASAT system. A moratorium on testing and deployment would forestall US tests of its own system, while leaving the elimination of the Soviet capability to most difficult (and yet-to-be-devised) verification measures.

Without an ASAT Treaty, the development and deployment of directed-energy ASAT technology would offer a severe challenge to the present ABM Treaty regime, as well as posing potentially serious new realms for military competition and threatening one of the key stabilizing and limiting mechanisms between the superpowers. On the other hand, the negotiation of a restrictive ASAT treaty, because of the substantial intermingling of ASAT and ABM technologies, might pose insurmountable obstacles to the development of many of the most promising BMD technologies. The consequence might be to preclude substantial movement away from a strategy based on offensive forces towards defence dominance.

If, over the long term, it is thought to be desirable to maintain strategic deterrence based on the threat of retaliation with offensive nuclear forces, then an ASAT treaty, however difficult it might be to form a satisfactory, verifiable one, should be considered seriously. An ASAT treaty that successfully precluded research, development, testing and deployment of weapons that have ASAT capabilities would not only preclude ASAT weapons, but would reaffirm the prohibition on development of a new generation of ballistic missile defence weaponry.

Tradeoffs and strategy choices

The implications of ASAT development and a possible ASAT ban for ABM issues are, then, much more important than is commonly recognized. The negotiation of an ASAT ban would bring with it strategic and military benefits within the confines of a strategic framework dominated by offensive nuclear retaliation. It would at the same time impede and probably preclude any effort to escape from that strategic framework to one dominated by defensive weapons, the world of 'assured survival rather than assured destruction'.

The security of early warning assets in space is critical to confidence in a retaliatory strategic regime. A premium might be placed by a belligerent on destroying early warning assets in order to accomplish a damage-limiting first strike, and ASAT weapons could be useful in this situation (although destruction of satellite ground links might be quicker, easier and more difficult to defend against). If strategies in this environment are to include possible conventional war and limited nuclear conflicts, the military utility of satellite assets rises dramatically. But in these circumstances, if escalation limitation is viewed as desirable by both sides, they might voluntarily choose to leave operational the satellite assets required for assessing attacks and communicating with the other side. However, a premium would be placed on destroying satellite assets needed for tactical support of military operations.

On the other hand, if defence domination is desired, ASAT technologies almost certainly will be developed within the ABM programme, and deployed at least when the ABM system is deployed. That would mean that whatever declarations might be made about the sanctity of satellite assets, they would increasingly become vulnerable to the new weapons, and this eventually would apply to the synchronous orbit as well as the low-orbit satellites. Prohibitions of ASAT systems might pose serious or insurmountable obstacles to many types of ABM development, and the desirability of an ASAT prohibition must be judged in the light of the choice to remain with offence dominance or to go towards defence dominance.

In any case, the realization of most BMD concepts is at least a decade away. Meanwhile, much of the R&D to create weapons based on those concepts can be accomplished within the constraints of the ABM Treaty. As a practical matter, it is far from clear that the superpowers would choose to further constrain research on directed-energy weapons, even if this is essential as part of a treaty that would protect satellites, because of the great risk that would be implied if a breakthrough were made by the other side. Nor is it clear that an ASAT treaty would be verifiable (e.g., consider the problem of ground-based lasers). But in light of the necessity to rely on offensive retaliatory forces for many years, even if defensive weapons are pursued, a limited and perhaps temporary ban on the production and deployment of ASAT weapons might be desirable—if it could be achieved and verified. This might apply most specifically to ASAT weapons capable of attacking geosynchronous orbit satellites. Such a ban ought to be designed to allow the same degree of freedom to develop and evaluate BMD systems based on directed-energy and other novel concepts as currently exists under the ABM Treaty. That would mean that, at some point in the relatively near future, the maturation of research on these weapons would either indicate that BMD weapon possibilities are very unpromising, or that research on such technologies is too promising to be ignored or constrained. At that time it would be necessary to re-evaluate any and all bans on defensive and ASAT weapons, to see if the promise of defence is sufficiently attractive to run the risk of a transition away from offensive retaliation and life under the sword of Damocles.[29]

Notes and references

1. Covault, C., 'Space defense organization advances', *Aviation Week and Space Technology*, Vol. 116, No. 6, 8 February 1982, pp. 20–22, and 'Antisatellite weapon test planned this year', *Aviation Week and Space Technology*, Vol. 116, No. 18, 3 May 1982, p. 14.
2. 'Soviets stage integrated test of weapons', *Aviation Week and Space Technology*, Vol. 116, No. 26, 28 June 1982, pp. 20–21.
3. See, for example, Hafnet, D. L., 'Averting a Brobdingnagian skeet shoot: arms control measures for anti-satellite weapons', *International Security*, Vol. 5, No. 3, Winter 1980/81, pp. 41–60.
4. *Strategic Arms Limitation Agreements*, Hearings before the Committee on Foreign Relations, United States Senate, June 19–July 20, 1972, p. 5.
5. Malcom Currie, New Conference, 20 February 1978, quoted in Graybeal, S. and Goure, D., 'Soviet ballistic missile defense (BMD) objectives—past, present, and future', Paper presented at Harvard University Symposium, 1–2 November 1979, p. 12.
6. See, for example, Foster, R. B., *The Soviet Concept of National Entity Survival*, SRI International Technical Note SSC-TN-7167-1, March 1978, pp. 32–43.
   Scott, H. F. and Scott, W. F. *The Armed Forces of the USSR* (Westview Press, Boulder, CO, 1981), pp. 47–56.
   Kaplan, F. M., *Dubious Specter: A Skeptical Look at the Soviet Nuclear Threat* (Institute for Policy Studies, Washington, DC, 1980), pp. 18–24.
7. 'The President's speech on military spending and a new defense', *New York Times*, 24 March 1983, p. 8.
8. Barasch, G. *et al.*, 'Ballistic missile defense', *Los Alamos National Laboratory Report* LA-8632, January 1981.

9. US Department of Defense, *Soviet Military Power, 1983* (US Government Printing Office, Washington, DC, 1983), p. 28.

10. *Aviation Week and Space Technology*, Vol. 119, No. 9, 29 August 1983, p.19

11. Major General Grayson Tate, Jr, 'Ballistic missile defense program', *Hearings on Military Posture*, Department of Defense Authorization for Appropriations for Fiscal Year 1984 before the Committee on Armed Forces, House of Representatives, 2–30 March 1982, p. 969.

12. *Hearings on Military Posture* (note 11), pp. 964–990.

13. Karas, T., *The New High Ground: Strategies and Weapons of Space-Age War* (Simon & Schuster, New York, 1983), pp. 148–151.

14. Hansen, R.E., 'Freedom of Passage on the High Seas of Space', *Strategic Review*, Fall 1977, p. 88.

15. *Fiscal Year 1983 Arms Control Impact Statements*, Statements submitted to the Congress (US Government Printing Office, Washington, DC, 1982), p. 299.

16. Defense Advanced Research Projects Agency (DARPA), *FY 1983 Research and Development Program*, 30 March 1982, pp. III-46–III-47.

17. DARPA (note 16), p. III-50.

18. DARPA (note 16), pp. III-18–III-49.

19. See 'Neutral particle programs draw focus', *Aviation Week and Space Technology*, Vol. 114, No. 61, 25 May 1981, pp. 55-60, and Vol. 109, No. 14, 2 October 1978, pp. 14-22.

20. Los Alamos National Laboratory, *Annual Report, 1982*, LALP 82-30, February 1983, pp. 44–46.

21. See Los Alamos National Laboratory (note 20), pp. III-44–III-54, and *Fiscal Year 1983 Arms Control Impact Statements* (note 15), pp. 92–104.

22. Knoth, A., *Particle Beam Weapons* (Fraunhofer-Institut für naturwissenschaftlich-technische Trendanalysen (INT)), November 1982.

23. 'Soviet effects point to antisatellite laser', *Aviation Week and Space Technology*, Vol. 118, No. 12, 21 March 1983, p. 19.

24. *Fiscal Year 1983 Arms Control Impact Statements* (note 15), p. 104.

25. SIPRI, *Outer Space—Battlefield of the Future?* (Taylor & Francis, London, 1978), pp. 12–139.

26. See *Arms Control and the Militarization of Space*, Hearings before the Subcommittee on Arms Control, Oceans, International Operations and Environment, Committee on Foreign Relations, US Senate, 20 September 1982, pp. 1-3.

27. A number of House and Senate resolutions have been proposed calling for a ban on ASAT systems, or all weapons in space, or for beginning negotiations to this end. These include House Joint Resolution 87 (Kastenmeier); House Joint Resolution 120 (Moakley *et al.*); Senate Joint Resolution 28 (Tsongas *et al.*); Senate Joint Resolution 43 (Pressler *et al.*); and Senate Joint Resolution 129. In the same vein, other resolutions called for efforts to foster international co-operation in space as an alternative to an arms race in space. On the other hand, there is some congressional interest in accelerating the weaponization of space, in the context of rapidly deploying a BMD system (i.e., Senate Joint Resolution 100 (Wallop and Laxalt)).

28. See paper 8, page 127, for a discussion on ambiguous provisions of the ABM Treaty.

29. Several Los Alamos National Laboratory colleagues assisted in the preparation of this paper. Noteworthy among them is Steven Maaranen who substantially contributed to several drafts. Robert Selden, Dan Stillman and John Hopkins read the final draft and provided a very useful critique.

Paper 8. New means of ballistic missile defence: the question of legality and arms control implications

Jozef Goldblat

Stockholm International Peace Research Institute, Bergshamra, 171 73 Solna, Sweden

On 23 March 1983, President Reagan announced (in what has been called the 'Star Wars' speech) that the USA would embark upon research to develop a capability of intercepting and destroying strategic ballistic missiles before they reach US soil or that of its allies. The programme was formally set in motion in January 1984. This effort was described as the ultimate salvation from the nuclear threat, because in neutralizing incoming missiles the envisaged defences are supposed to render nuclear weapons "impotent and obsolete" and thereby facilitate nuclear disarmament. Many scientists expressed serious doubts as to whether such a goal was at all achievable. Others, irrespective of its feasibility, characterized this new US endeavour as a measure fuelling the nuclear arms race, and as a step towards transforming outer space into an arena of direct military confrontation.

It is generally assumed that new weapons for protection against nuclear missiles might best be stationed in outer space. It is therefore important to point out that several international agreements restrict the activities of states in that environment. In particular, the 1967 Outer Space Treaty has established rules for the peaceful uses of outer space. It prohibits the placing in orbit around the Earth of nuclear or other weapons of mass destruction, but it can be understood as allowing the placing of other weapons there. Of most direct relevance is the 1972 US–Soviet treaty limiting anti-ballistic missile (ABM) systems, defined as systems to counter strategic ballistic missiles or their elements in flight trajectory.

Under the ABM Treaty (as modified by a 1974 Protocol) each side is permitted only one geographically, quantitatively and qualitatively constrained fixed land-based ABM deployment either at its national capital or at a complex of intercontinental ballistic missiles (ICBMs). Development and testing of fixed land-based ABM systems and components is allowed at the agreed test ranges. Technological innovation is inhibited by provisions banning the development, testing and deployment of ABM systems or components which are sea-based, air-based, space-based or mobile land-based, but these provisions are ambiguous. They can be understood to refer to anti-missile systems only in the form in which they existed at the time that the ABM Treaty was signed. Indeed, for the purposes of the Treaty the ABM system was defined as a system "currently" consisting of ABM interceptor missiles, ABM launchers and ABM radars (article II). Since the systems which are now contemplated by the USA are of a different nature, they might be considered as not covered by the Treaty limitations. A proviso attached to the Treaty as an 'agreed interpretation' permits the creation of ABM systems based on other physical principles. (This may include lasers or particle beams, which travel at or near the speed of light.) Specific limitations on these systems and their components (including their deployment) would be open to discussion. The exact wording of the agreed interpretation is as follows:

In order to insure fulfillment of the obligation not to deploy ABM systems and their components except as provided in Article III of the Treaty, the Parties agree that in the event ABM systems based on other physical principles and including components capable of substituting for ABM interceptor missiles, ABM launchers, or ABM radars are created in the future, specific limitations on such systems and their components would be subject to discussion ... and agreement ...[1]

Another, stricter, interpretation is that the Treaty prohibits *any type* of sea-based, air-based, space-based or mobile land-based ballistic missile defence system. Consequently, the proviso referred to above, which allows for the development of ABM systems based on physical principles other than those of the "current" ABMs, would apply only to fixed land-based systems. It may appear strange that technological innovations in fixed land-based systems should be considered more tolerable than in mobile land-, air- or space-based systems, but this interpretation has been adopted in the arms control impact statements related to ballistic missile defence that were submitted to the US Congress by the US Arms Control and Disarmament Agency.[2] It implies that the creation of space-based means of anti-missile protection would be a breach of the contracted obligations, whereas the creation of a new fixed land-based anti-missile technology would not. (With such an understanding, one wonders what would be the status of a ground-based laser BMD using space-based mirrors.)

However, research alone into 'exotic' space-based weapons is not unlawful *per se*. And while there is no generally accepted definition of the term 'development', the official US position is that development of space-based ABM beam weapons, for example, would not contravene the letter of the ABM Treaty until that point in the development process where field testing is initiated.[3] Nevertheless, such activities are hard to reconcile with the purpose of the ABM Treaty, which is to deny a defence of the territory or of an individual region (except as specifically allowed) of each party against ballistic missiles. Planning for such a defence with whatever means, current or 'futuristic', contradicts the spirit of the ABM Treaty. It may undermine the very philosophy which 12 years ago led the negotiators to recognize that ballistic missile defence was destabilizing and therefore dangerous. In agreeing to leave their countries hostage, the superpowers in essence agreed on no strategic first use. Protection would upset that agreement.

Another disquieting aspect of the possible new means of ballistic missile defence is that they include X-ray lasers powered by nuclear detonations in space, that is, in the environment where the conduct of nuclear explosions is prohibited under the 1963 Partial Test Ban Treaty, and where even the placing of nuclear explosives is banned under the 1967 Outer Space Treaty (see also Part I, page 37). Moreover, the systems envisaged to counter offensive missiles are the same as, or very similar to, anti-satellite systems which are, themselves, basically offensive (see paper 7, page 107).

From the point of view of arms control, it is irrelevant whether or not an effective defence against ballistic missiles can be devised and made operative. What matters is the very pursuit of this goal. For such pursuit is bound to stimulate the development of countermeasures, and to provoke an accelerated build-up of offensive systems capable of overwhelming the defences of the opponent. In the course of such a competition in arms, a superpower which believes it has acquired a defensive potential enabling it to escape retaliation, or to get away with an 'acceptable' damage from non-intercepted missiles, may be tempted to strike first. But even before this happens, another super-power, the one lagging behind in this race for superiority, may be tempted to strike first in order to pre-empt the acquisition of the defensive potential by the adversary. 'Gaps' are unavoidable in a competitive development of nuclear armoury, and the power more advanced is unlikely to share its advances with the potential enemy. Thus, instead of preventing nuclear war, as they are committed to do under several UN resolutions and international agreements (more specifically under the 1968 Non-Proliferation Treaty), the superpowers searching for a ballistic missile defence may render war more probable by creating a new source of strategic instability. Ironically enough, it is the USA, once the most ardent proponent of a ban on ABMs, that now seems to be backing out.

Notes and references

1. For the full text of the ABM Treaty, see Goldblat, J. (ed.), *Agreements for Arms Control* (Taylor & Francis, London, 1982) [a SIPRI book].
2. *Fiscal Year 1983 Arms Control Impact Statements* (US Government Printing Office, Washington, DC, 1982).
3. For the US interpretation of the term 'development' as used in the ABM Treaty, see note 2.

Paper 9. An ASAT test ban treaty

Kurt Gottfried

Laboratory of Nuclear Studies, Cornell University, Ithaca, NY 14853, USA

I. Introduction

On 18 May 1983, Dr Richard Garwin, Admiral Noel Gayler and the author presented a Draft Treaty Limiting Anti-Satellite Weapons at a hearing of the United States Senate Foreign Relations Committee.[1] This proposal emerged from a study undertaken by a panel convened under the auspices of the Union of Concerned Scientists.[2] An explicit treaty text was formulated in an effort to focus attention on issues that are likely to arise in actual negotiations. It is the purpose of this paper to present the rationale for this Draft Treaty and, in doing so, to describe its scope and limitations.*

The text of the Draft Treaty is reproduced in Annex 9.1, but a summary of its essential features is in order here. The Treaty is a bilateral agreement between the United States and the Soviet Union. It would obligate the signatories not to destroy, damage or change the flight trajectory of any space object, no matter to whom it may belong. Fundamentally, the Draft is a test ban, in that the parties would not be permitted to test in space, or against space objects, weapons that could destroy, damage or change the flight trajectory of space objects, or space weapons that can damage objects on the ground or in the atmosphere. Verification would be by national technical means, supplemented by co-operative measures which would take advantage of the SALT Standing Consultative Commission (SCC). In addition, the treaty would obligate the parties to begin negotiations towards a prohibition on possession as soon as the test ban is in place.

The focus on a test ban, and the postponement of negotiations towards a prohibition on possession, are motivated by our assessment that existing anti-satellite (ASAT) capabilities do not yet present a serious threat to either super-

---

*The author wishes to emphasize that he is solely responsible for any statement that is not to be found in reference 2.

131

power, by the implications of imminent developments in ASAT technology and by the different verification problems posed by a ban on ASAT testing as compared to a prohibition on possession.

II. Underlying assumptions

In constructing an arms control proposal, it is essential to understand what is, and what is not, the objective. The objective, in turn, emerges from a set of explicit and implicit assumptions, and it is best to identify these as clearly as possible, so that the foundations of the whole edifice can be properly examined. The set of assumptions[3] that underlie the Draft Treaty under discussion may be characterized by the following assertions:

1. The risk that a severe crisis or low-level conflict would escalate disastrously would be considerably enhanced were either or both superpowers to acquire the ability to destroy a militarily significant portion of the adversary's space-based command, control, communications and intelligence (C^3I) system without resorting to nuclear weapons.

2. A breakthrough in strategic weapon technology, no matter how innovative or sophisticated, is soon negated by the other side if it represents a real military threat, and thereby results in diminished security for all.

3. Ballistic missile defence (BMD), no matter what its basing mode or technology, offers no prospect of escape from our mutual hostage dilemma as long as strategic arsenals anywhere near their present size are maintained.

These assertions will now be examined.

Crisis stability

If present trends in ASAT development continue, all satellites in low Earth orbits (LEO) will be at risk before long. The same remark applies to satellites in highly elliptical orbits, though obviously with somewhat less force. Satellites in geosynchronous orbits (GEO) or other high orbits appear to be relatively safe for the time being, unless and until space mines are deployed.

In the midst of a general nuclear war, space-based C^3I systems would be seriously threatened whether ASAT systems existed or not, because the ground-based communication links and control centres on which these systems rely are themselves highly vulnerable.[4] Furthermore, the utility of surviving satellites could be severely diminished by transmission barriers in large portions of the electromagnetic spectrum created by nuclear explosions. Finally, the early warning, communications and navigation satellites that are of critical importance to the strategic forces in wartime are all in GEO or other high orbits, and relatively secure against ASAT attacks. It would therefore appear that the ASAT capabilities that already exist, or that are likely to be operational in this decade, will have little impact on the ability of the superpowers to prosecute general nuclear war, no matter what one may mean by that term.

On the other hand, these same ASAT capabilities are of great potential import for the prospects of containing low-level conflicts, up to and including hostilities involving small numbers of nuclear weapons.[5]

The bulk of the existing military LEO satellites are devoted to photoreconnaissance, meteorology, ocean surveillance and electronic intelligence. In the foreseeable future, LEO satellites carrying large synthetic aperture radars should provide all-weather night-and-day surveillance of vast areas and, in conjunction with more sophisticated photoreconnaissance satellites, will provide real-time intelligence of unprecedented quality to all military operations. By the same token, the ability to remove such satellites from the sky, coupled with the fear that the opponent may at any moment strike one's own satellites, could well be an irresistible temptation, even in the face of the grave risks that would accompany the ensuing confusion.

In consequence, if both sides can 'sweep the skies' of LEO satellites—and by our second assumption one side could not long retain an ASAT monopoly—a crisis or relatively minor skirmish could become unhinged even though it might have been resolved by diplomacy in the absence of ASAT weapons.

It is widely believed that a relatively restrained conflict, initiated by misperceptions and miscalculations, provides the most likely path towards general nuclear war. If that belief is valid, it follows that a potent and prompt ASAT capability against LEO satellites poses a grave threat to crisis stability, with all that that implies. The current generation of ASAT weapons is therefore much more than just another hazard in an already very dangerous world.

Lead times in strategic weapon technology

The invention of nuclear weapons was the most remarkable breakthrough in military technology in modern history. Only six years separated the discovery of fission from Hiroshima. In a time span that many require to earn a doctorate, the most brilliant scientific team ever assembled, supported by expenditures at an unprecedented scale, transformed a table-top experiment at the very frontier of pure research into a weapon of demonic power. In 1945 it was widely (though not unanimously) believed in knowledgeable circles that the Soviet Union would take at least a decade to develop nuclear explosives. We know now that Soviet scientists recognized the military implications of fission from the very beginning and that the Soviet Union would have embarked on a nuclear weapon programme before 1945 had Klaus Fuchs never existed.[6] While espionage was surely important in the Soviet development of a fission weapon, everything points to the conclusion that Andrei Sakharov and his co-workers independently discovered the Teller–Ulam mechanism for thermonuclear explosions.

In short, though devastated by war, and operating from a scientific and technological base far weaker than that of the West, the Soviet Union was able to respond effectively to an enormous challenge in an astonishingly short time.

That does not mean that the Soviet Union soon achieved strategic parity, but it did acquire the means to retaliate at a level that, under almost all circumstances, provided a viable deterrent. This point was emphasized recently by Robert McNamara[7] in describing the deterrent value of a small number of primitive Soviet submarine-based missiles at a time when the United States enjoyed a very large edge in intercontinental ballistic missiles (ICBM). And to belabour the obvious, there is the infamous history of multiple independently targetable re-entry vehicles (MIRVs) which, it is said, now threaten the very security of the nation that first introduced these weapons.

What is the relevance of all this to military space systems? Here one must distinguish weapons from C^3I facilities, because a relatively crude weapon may wreak havoc, whereas technological sophistication is at a premium in the gathering and dissemination of information.

Virtually all appraisals of the two military space systems reveal that the United States enjoys a very considerable advantage in the sophistication, versatility, longevity and reliability of its space-based C^3I systems.[8] This is likely to be a persistent asymmetry, because the evolution of micro-electronics, computing and optics is significantly more rapid in the West.[9] Turning to ASAT weapons, the Soviet Union has the only operational system, but its level of technological sophistication is certainly inferior to that of the US F-15-based ASAT system if the latter performs according to specifications in forthcoming flight tests.[2] This disparity is such that the US system, once it is operational, could threaten all Soviet LEO satellites if enough ASAT-bearing F-15s are suitably based, whereas the *current* Soviet system represents a much more limited threat, as we shall argue below. In view of the growing importance of LEO satellites to military operations, the Soviet Union cannot be expected to tolerate such a situation for long. While it may not choose to field a weapon that does not even have a warhead, like the US miniature homing vehicle (MHV), there are less sophisticated but quite lethal options open to it. After a few years the net result would be that not only Soviet but also US LEO satellites would be threatened with prompt destruction. ASAT systems capable of attacking GEO satellites would also be under vigorous development in such an era of unconstrained competition, and one would have to anticipate that the safety of the strategic C^3I systems would erode as well.

ASAT–BMD coupling

It would take us too far afield to present the arguments in support of our assertion that one should not expect BMD, no matter how sophisticated, to free us from the intolerable mutual-hostage situation which now threatens our existence. But it is in order to say that if one disagrees with the assertion, and believes that futuristic BMD can provide protection (or strategic superiority),[10] one should resist negotiated constraints on the deployment of ASAT systems. There are two reasons for this: ASAT and BMD technology have much in common, and ASAT systems would be needed to attack an adversary's BMD space platforms.

The commonality of ASAT and BMD technology is explained by Donald Kerr[11] (paper 7, page 107) with an authority and knowledge that this author cannot match. Suffice it to say that the MHV exploits a technology that the US Army is developing for mid-course interception of ICBMs,[10] and that high-powered lasers with an ultimate role in BMD would initially be developed for attacking satellites (see paper 7, page 107). That ASAT systems would of necessity be an integral part of a space-based BMD system needs no elaboration, since such BMD components would be satellites for at least a part of their life.

Because of this commonality, ASAT systems constitute a serious loophole in the 1972 SALT ABM Treaty. A nascent BMD system could be tested legitimately in an ASAT mode since at such a stage it would only have an ASAT capability. In view of the technical obstacles, it could well be that too enthusiastic a BMD programme would only produce an ASAT capability bought at the price of an abrogated ABM Treaty, since even an unsuccessful BMD programme is likely to be misperceived as an unacceptable threat by the other side. The collapse of the ABM Treaty would spawn a rapid growth of offensive strategic forces, and completely undo the modest constraints that now exist.

III. The scope of the test ban

Objectives

The primary objective of the Draft Treaty has been identified by the preceding argument: the creation of the most severe hurdle to further development of ASAT capability that negotiation would permit. The shape and dimensions of this hurdle are determined by the ability to verify compliance, by the time-scale set by the developing US system and by the military significance of the deployed Soviet system. As already indicated, it is our contention that the Soviet system, in its *present* stage of development, constitutes a threat that can be kept at an acceptable level by suitable improvements in US satellite systems, whereas the US ASAT system, if and when deployed, would present an unacceptable threat to the Soviet Union. Hence the hurdle must be put in place as promptly as possible. The monitoring of the agreement is to be by national technical means so as to avert the protracted negotiations that intrusive verification would require.

For these reasons the Draft Treaty is a comprehensive ban on the testing of ASAT weapons in modes that could be subject to surveillance by means of techniques already in existence or devices soon to be deployed, or which could be designed for the purpose of observing objects in space. To be more specific, by 'comprehensive' we mean that weapon tests against any and all objects in space are not permitted, no matter what the basing mode may be; furthermore, tests of space-based weapons against objects in the atmosphere or on the Earth's surface are also prohibited so as to hinder the disguise of ASAT tests.

The Draft Treaty places no restrictions on countermeasures or spoofing, so long as these activities do not damage satellites and are in accord with existing SALT obligations. Above all, the Draft Treaty does not prohibit possession.

Threats posed by current ASAT systems

It has been the position of many, including numerous members of the House and Senate[12] and the panel that prepared the Draft Treaty,[1] that an immediate bilateral moratorium on ASAT flight tests should be agreed upon while negotiations proceed. On the other hand, the existing asymmetry between Soviet and US ASAT capabilities leads a more powerful body of opinion to the conclusion that the moratorium and test ban treaty would permanently freeze the United States into a position of unacceptable inferiority. Hence the threat posed by the current generation of ASAT systems must be assessed.

The Soviet ASAT system is placed into orbit by a modified SS-9 booster. At launch the entire configuration is some 45 m long; the ASAT satellite itself is nearly 10 m long and weighs about three tonnes. All tests have been from Tyuratam and used orbits in the narrow angular interval of 62–65° inclination. The highest altitude reached thus far is reported to be about 2 500 km. Interception takes place after one or two orbits, and the target is destroyed by means of conventional explosives. The earliest test series (1968–71), which used radar homing, reportedly achieved a 70 per cent success rate, but subsequent series that explored more sophisticated homing techniques and quick approach manoeuvres are reported to have been almost uniformly unsuccessful.[13]

A particular satellite is only vulnerable to the Soviet ASAT system when the launch site is under the satellite's orbit. Hence as many as 24 hours may be needed before it can be attacked by a given ASAT interceptor. One must ask whether other Soviet facilities could be used to launch the ASAT interceptor. The SS-9s have been phased out and replaced by SS-18s. If the Soviet Union sought to put an ASAT interceptor on a silo-based SS-18, the silo would have to be modified to accommodate the extra length and the special launch preparation required by the interceptor. Such alterations would be monitored by US surveillance systems. It would therefore appear that in the absence of visible modifications to Soviet launch facilities, the only means of placing the ASAT weapon into orbit are launch sites which have already been used for ASAT purposes, or other pads used to launch satellites and other large space vehicles. This would therefore restrict the Soviet launch sites to a rather small geographical region, and only expose a correspondingly limited set of US satellites to attack at any given time. Furthermore, all the boosters in question are liquid-fuelled; the task of transporting, storing and loading the highly volatile liquid fuel required by such massive boosters is very time-consuming. In consequence we claim that the Soviet ASAT system, as presently configured, constitutes a very ponderous and inflexible threat to US LEO satellites in that many days, at the least, would be required to destroy this portion of the US satellite fleet.

In a limited engagement certain LEO satellites may be of very considerable tactical value to specific military units. Their residual vulnerability can be reduced provided, of course, that a treaty regime prevents further evolution of Soviet ASAT capabilities. The space shuttle will permit refuelling and servicing of satellites, and this is expected to lead to a new generation of US photoreconnaissance satellites that have considerable ability to manoeuvre. Given the approximately one-hour warning time that would be provided by early warning satellites and radar tracking, this would allow manoeuvrable LEO satellites to evade the *existing* Soviet ASAT interceptor.

The US ASAT system is fundamentally different from the one just described. It is launched at very high altitude from an F-15 aircraft, and hunts its quarry by direct ascent. Any F-15 could be carrying the ASAT interceptor, so firm warning would only be available when the aircraft launches its rocket. The very large relative velocity between the MHV and its target implies that evasion would be exceedingly difficult if the MHV's homing mechanism meets specifications in tests that remain to be carried out. But above all, by suitably basing enough F-15s the USA could, at least in principle, launch a simultaneous attack lasting possibly as little as an hour on all Soviet LEO satellites. Even Soviet early warning and communications satellites in highly elliptical (Molniya) orbits might be destroyed in less than a day by air-launched MHVs based in the southern hemisphere (although homing on such satellites at perigee is far more demanding than homing on LEO targets).

ASAT possession

While a more comprehensive agreement that bans ASAT possession would be desirable, it presents verification problems that are formidable.

It would be possible to monitor the dismantling of Soviet launch sites that have been used in ASAT tests, and such a step by the Soviet Union would be welcome as a confidence-building measure. But that could still leave the Soviet Union with a remnant ASAT capability. As we have seen, certain pads used in the Soviet space programme may be able to launch the ASAT interceptor, and the dismantling of interceptors themselves cannot be verified without highly intrusive on-site inspection. As for the US system, its small size and mobile basing mode render it virtually unverifiable.

It is possible that an enforceable agreement on possession could be arrived at in lengthy negotiations if further development of these systems were brought to a halt. However, the formulation of such an agreement would require a knowledge of detailed specifications of weapon systems and of intelligence-gathering capabilities that is not available to a private group working with information in the open literature.

IV. Verification and protective measures

It will now be argued (*a*) that the proposed test ban, when suppplemented by detailed negotiated measures not in the Draft text, would keep the Soviet threat at a level that would, at the worst, be equivalent to the existing threat; and (b) that adequate protection against this risk can be attained by improvements in the US satellite fleet.

Monitoring of ASAT tests

Clandestine tests of the current Soviet ASAT system would be risky because of the extensive US experience in observing such tests. It would seem that the only tests that would stand a good chance of evasion would have to attack a point in space, leave the interceptor intact, and avoid 'pop-up' or other deft approach manoeuvres characteristic of ASAT activities. However, such constrained tests would be of limited value. They could confirm that the ASAT interceptor performs as in the past. Perhaps they could even demonstrate that improvements have made it less unreliable. But the Soviet Union could not rely on such tests to evaluate the performance of new homing and/or manoeuvring devices. A point in space, even if moved by computer, is not a source of infrared, nor is it a manoeuvring reflector of radar.

Nevertheless, if clandestine tests with the current Soviet ASAT system are of concern to the USA, it would be reasonable to demand, under article IV.1(b), that there be prior notice of space launches from pads that can launch the ASAT interceptor, so that US surveillance facilities could be on high alert.

Monitoring covert tests of new ASAT types has to be examined on a case-by-case basis. All such tests face an ever-growing battery of surveillance facilities. In particular, the USA has recently upgraded the NORAD radar tracking network, and supplemented it by new radars based in the Pacific; the US ground-based electro-optical deep space surveillance (GEODSS) system, which will provide highly detailed data on even quite small objects at 5 000 km and beyond, is also expected to be in operation by 1987. Furthermore, in a treaty-constrained era it would be wise to develop highly manoeuvrable space vehicles expressly for the purpose of space surveillance. Such vehicles could carry telescopes to photograph and track manoeuvring space vehicles, measure the infra-red emission of space objects to see whether they were being heated by lasers, monitor legitimate space activities that have a potential for clandestine ASAT tests and so on.

Potential ASAT weapons may be broken down into several categories: fast approach interceptors, slow approach manoeuvring vehicles, directed-energy weapons and space mines. The surveillance systems just discussed should make clandestine tests of fast-approach intercepts visible, and should also reveal telemetry and other signatures emanating from a wide variety of tests. Slow-approach interceptors may be much more difficult to distinguish from objects performing legitimate space activities. On the other hand, satellites that can manoeuvre would make such attacks problematic if the prospective ASAT weapon can only practice docking-like approaches. In any event, such slow-approach ASAT weapons are hardly suitable for a simultaneous surprise attack against a widely dispersed set of satellites.

Nevertheless, the last two paragraphs allude to a number of concerns. If deemed necessary, these could be reduced by rules limiting movements of space vehicles and the encoding of telemetry, requiring prior announcement of certain classes of space activities, and permitting certain close approaches by the other party's surveillance vehicles. Such measures could be worked out in the SCC. Alternatively, the Draft Treaty test itself could be suitably expanded under article IV.2(a), provided that it does not moor the treaty to the technology that can be foreseen at the time of signature.

Laser ASAT weapons face such serious technical problems, and have such visible external characteristics, that we would argue that their clandestine development to the stage of an effective operational weapon system would be an unproductive undertaking.

Space mines pose a very serious potential threat to satellites at all altitudes, and it is one of the principal aims of the Draft Treaty to impede their deployment. This threat can be significantly reduced, but not eliminated, by a test ban. The evolution of space mine technology would be greatly hampered by the ban, while monitoring facilities would steadily improve, as would satellite manoeuvrability and onboard surveillance. A mine that can persistently follow a manoeuvring LEO satellite is a suspicious object. If it can also close in rapidly for the kill, it is a sophisticated device indeed. Only if it had been tested under reasonably realistic circumstances could a military commander place much confidence in it.

GEO space mines would have the advantage of a stationary victim. However, if they could not be successfully hidden close to their eventual target they would have to close in for the kill over distances of hundreds of kilometres because of the international rules that prescribe the angular separation between objects in space. The tracking and homing capabilities that would be entailed would be difficult to confirm by clandestine tests.

Protective measures

There have already been a number of allusions to protective measures that are being planned for, or that should be undertaken. These would diminish whatever risks that remained because the ability to verify an ASAT test ban is imperfect and because the Soviet Union would retain some remnants of an ASAT capability.

The most important protective measures are satellite manoeuvrability and redundancy. Manoeuvrability has been mentioned repeatedly, and detailed elaboration of its value is beyond the scope of this paper. By redundancy one can mean one or more of several things; spare satellites ready to launch which are of great military importance and thought to be vulnerable, such as LEO electronic intelligence (ELINT) satellites; ballistic missiles with payloads that can perform satellite functions at far less cost during a critical period; decoy satellites; and replacement satellites already in orbit but that only begin functioning when a similar satellite is damaged or destroyed; and diversification of satellite functions, so that another satellite can assume a task that it does not ordinarily perform. Another strategy would have the USA move to a larger number of operational satellites, each of which carries out a smaller set of functions, and has a shorter lifespan.

V. Conclusions

No arms control agreement can be verified to perfection. One must not only assess the risk posed by activities that may escape surveillance, but also compare their threat to the level of threat that a treaty-free regime would produce.

Satellites are intrinsically vulnerable objects. They are costly to manufacture and to place in orbit. In an unrestrained competition with weapons specifically designed to destroy them they would stand little chance of retaining anything close to their present level of security. The United States cannot protect its space assets by threatening attack against Soviet satellites, since the Soviet Union is less dependent on space-based C^3I systems. Nor can the F-15 ASAT weapon be counted on to attack the Soviet ASAT interceptor, since the latter could be embellished with decoys during the rather short time that it spends in space.

Hence the choice is between two regimes. In the first, constrained by treaty, satellites would be at a small but non-zero risk which is quite well understood, and which can be effectively countered with measures well within the constraints set by budgets and technology. The second is marked by all-out and very costly competition, in which everyone's satellites would become increasingly vulnerable to prompt destruction, and in which crisis stability would be significantly less secure than it presently is. The choice would seem to be clear.

Notes and references

1. *Controlling Weapons in Space*, Hearings before the Committee on Foreign Relations, US Senate, 98th Congress, 1st Session, 14 April and 18 May 1983.
2. *Anti-Satellite Weapons: Arms Control or Arms Race?* (Union of Concerned Scientists, Cambridge, MA, 1983). The other Panel members are Hans A. Bethe, Henry W. Kendall, Franklin A. Long, Leonard C. Meeker, Carl Sagan, Herbert Scoville, Jr and John Steinbruner.
3. We shall, without examination, adopt the standard assumption that no militarily decisive threat is posed by a weapon system that has not undergone field tests.
4. Ball, D., *Can Nuclear War be Controlled?*, Adelphi Paper 169 (International Institute for Strategic Studies, London, 1981).
5. For a similar argument, see Walter Slocombe, paper 10, page 145.
6. Holloway, D., *The Soviet Union and the Arms Race* (Yale University Press, New Haven, 1983), Chapter 2.
7. Interview with Robert Scheer, *Los Angeles Times*, 4 April 1982.
8. US Senate, Committee on Commerce, Science, and Transportation, *Soviet Space Programs: 1976–80*, 97th Congress, 2nd Session; Committee Print presented at the request of the Honorable Bob Packwood, Chairman; December 1982.
   Meyer, S. M., 'Soviet military programs and the "new high ground"', *Survival*, Vol. 25, No. 5, September/October 1983, pp. 204–215.

Johnson, N. L., *The Soviet Year in Space* (Teledyne-Brown Engineering, Colorado Springs, CO, January 1982 and January 1983).

Jasani, B. (ed.), *Outer Space—a New Dimension of the Arms Race* (Taylor & Francis, London, 1982), p. 80 [a SIPRI book].

9. DeLauer, R. D., *FY 84 Department of Defense Program for Research, Development, and Acquisition*, Report to 98th Congress, 1st Session, 2 March 1983.

10. Smith, R. J., 'The search for a nuclear sanctuary', *Science,* Vol. 221, 1 July 1983. Gray, C., *American Military Policy: Information Systems, Weapon Systems and Arms Control* (Abt Books, Cambridge, MA, 1983).

11. See also Part I, pages 19, 26.

12. US Senate Resolutions 28 and 43, 2 February 1983. House Resolution 120, 2 February 1983. Senate Joint Resolution 129, 14 July 1983.

13. The effectiveness of the Soviet ASAT system has been characterized as follows by General Lew Allen, Air Force Chief of Staff, in testimony on 11 July 1979 before the US Senate Foreign Relations Committee: "So, I think our general opinion is that we give it a very questionable operational capability for a few launches. In other words, it is a threat that we are worried about, but they have not had a test program that would cause us to believe it is a very credible threat". (96th Congress, 1st Session, *The SALT II Treaty*, p. 423.) Since that day the USSR has conducted four ASAT tests. According to both Johnson and Meyer (note 8), three of these, using an optical sensor, were failures, the only success being with the older radar sensor. It would therefore seem that Gen. Allen's assessment should still hold. For another recent assessment of the US and Soviet ASAT systems, see Smith, R. J., *Science*, Vol. 222, 14 October 1983, p. 142.

Annex 9.1. A treaty limiting anti-satellite weapons*

Preamble

Article I

Each Party undertakes not to destroy, damage, render inoperable or change the flight trajectory of space objects of other States.

Article II

1. Each Party undertakes not to place in orbit around the earth weapons for destroying, damaging, rendering inoperable, or changing the flight trajectory of space objects, or for damaging objects in the atmosphere or on the ground.
2. Each Party undertakes not to install such weapons on celestial bodies, or station such weapons in outer space in any other manner.
3. Each Party undertakes not to test such weapons in space or against space objects.

Article III

1. For the purpose of providing assurance of compliance with the provisions of this treaty, each Party shall use national technical means of verification at its disposal in a manner consistent with generally recognized principles of international law.
2. Verification by national technical means shall be supplemented, as appropriate, by such cooperative measures for contributing to the effectiveness of verification by national technical means as the Parties shall agree upon in the Standing Consultative Commission.
3. Each Party undertakes not to interfere with the national technical means of verification of the other Party operating in accordance with paragraph 1 of this Article.
4. Each Party undertakes not to use deliberate concealment measures which impede verification by national technical means of compliance with this treaty.

Article IV

1. To promote the objectives and implementation of the provisions of this treaty, the Parties shall use the Standing Consultative Commission, established by the Memorandum of Understanding Between the Government of the United States of

*Source: Anti-Satellite Weapons: Arms Control or Arms Race? (Union of Concerned Scientists, Cambridge, MA, 1983), pp. 33–35.

142

America and the Government of the Union of Soviet Socialist Republics regarding the Establishment of a Standing Consultative Commission of December 21, 1972.

2. Within the framework of the Standing Consultative Commission, with respect to this treaty, the Parties will:

(*a*) consider questions concerning compliance with the obligations assumed and related situations which may be considered ambiguous;

(*b*) provide on a voluntary basis such information as either Party considers necessary to assure confidence in compliance with the obligations assumed;

(*c*) consider questions involving unintended interference with national technical means of verification, and questions involving unintended impeding of verification by national technical means of compliance with the provisions of this treaty;

(*d*) consider, as appropriate, cooperative measures contributing to the effectiveness of verification by national technical means;

(*e*) consider possible changes in the strategic situation which have a bearing on the provisions of this treaty, including the activities of other States;

(*f*) consider, as appropriate, possible proposals for further increasing the viability of this treaty, including proposals for amendments in accordance with the provisions of this treaty.

Article V

The Parties undertake to begin, promptly after the entry into force of this treaty, active negotiations with the objective of achieving, as soon as possible, agreement on further measures for the limitation and reduction of weapons subject to limitation in Article II of this treaty.

Article VI

In order to ensure the viability and effectiveness of this treaty, each Party undertakes not to circumvent the provisions of this treaty, through any other State or States, in any other manner.

Article VII

Each party undertakes not to assume any international obligation which would conflict with this treaty.

Article VIII

1. Each Party may propose amendments to this treaty.

2. Agreed amendments shall enter into force in accordance with the procedures governing the entry into force of this treaty.

Article IX

This treaty shall be of unlimited duration.

Article X

Each Party shall, in exercising its national sovereignty, have the right to withdraw from this treaty if it decides that extraordinary events related to the subject matter of this treaty have jeopardized its supreme interests. It shall give notice of its decisions to the other Party six months prior to withdrawal from the treaty. Such notice shall include a statement of the extraordinary events the notifying Party regards as having jeopardized its supreme interests.

Article XI

1. This treaty shall be subject to ratification in accordance with the constitutional procedures of each Party.

2. This treaty shall enter into force on the day of the exchange of instruments of ratification.

Article XII

1. Done in two copies, each in the English and Russian languages, both texts being equally authentic.

2. This treaty shall be registered pursuant to Article 102 of the Charter of the United Nations.

Paper 10. Approaches to an ASAT treaty

Walter Slocombe

Caplin & Drysdale, 1101 17th Street NW, Washington, DC 20036, USA

I. Military uses of space

Despite the broadening military use of outer space, it has not so far proved a militarily satisfactory place for the deployment of weapons. The Soviet fractional orbit bombardment system (FOBS) tested in the 1960s has been terminated; ideas for orbiting 'battlestars' as space bases for anti-ballistic missile systems, much less attacks on the Earth's surface, remain very much in the conceptual stages.

However, satellites, in the quarter century of their development, have become major collectors and transmitters of militarily important information and critical links in the military communications systems of both superpowers and both major alliances. Satellites also form the backbone of the complex and sophisticated surveillance and intelligence systems of the two sides, and satellite-based navigation systems are of increasing importance, not only for ships and aircraft but for weapon guidance as well.

It is important in the context of arms control to recognize that the critical, and potentially vulnerable, elements in these military information systems are by no means the satellites alone. Without ground stations and without effective and secure communications between those stations and the satellites, often including interconnections between satellites, these space systems are utterly ineffective, whatever the condition of the satellites. Even if the satellites were fully protected, these non-satellite elements are subject to disruption and attack by a variety of means. Analysis of threats to the systems and of the effects of arms control measures intended to protect them have to take into account the vulnerabilities of those other elements as well as of the satellites themselves.

ASAT developments and deployments

Lagging behind but stimulated by the growing use of space for military communications, surveillance and navigation purposes have been efforts by

145

both sides to develop systems capable of destroying orbiting satellites. During the 1960s the United States deployed a nuclear-armed satellite interceptor system, long since decommissioned, at Johnston Island in the Pacific. The USSR, beginning in 1968, has conducted a series of some 20 tests of a co-orbital, conventional explosive anti-satellite (ASAT) system (see paper 5, page 83). The USA, spurred by the Soviet ASAT programme, and by recognition of growing Soviet military use of space especially for monitoring ship movements, embarked in the mid-1970s on an active programme to develop a non-nuclear ASAT system. The major current US programme, the direct-ascent miniature homing vehicle, launched by a small rocket from a high altitude F-15 aircraft is scheduled to be operationally ready in the mid-1980s (see also Part I, page 13).

ASAT threats to stability

The ability of the superpowers to threaten each other's space communications and intelligence systems poses unique threats to stability. These stability concerns are not based on abstract objections to the militarization of space or to the idea of a war in space. No doubt it is regrettable that man is using space and space technology—as he has used practically every other medium and technology—for military purposes, but space would be a better place than the surface of the Earth to conduct a war, if that were the only issue. Rather, from a strategic point of view, the significance of the impending vulnerability of military space systems arises from the special challenges to stability that would arise from attacks on intelligence and communications satellites.

On the whole, these stability threats arise at the lower rungs of the ladder of confrontation and violence. In a general nuclear war, space systems and their ground stations would, like everything else, be highly vulnerable to attack if only because under those conditions nuclear weapons could be used against them. Correspondingly, efforts to enhance the endurance of satellite communication systems that support strategic nuclear forces and to reduce the potential of a surprise attack that could eliminate the communications needed to retaliate for a nuclear attack can only marginally be assisted by arms control because such attacks would be unlikely to use conventional ASAT systems.

However, in the twilight situation of crisis or limited non-nuclear war the potential vulnerability of satellites used for command, control, communications and intelligence (C^3I) poses a serious, if specialized, threat to stability. Under crisis or limited war conditions, space-reliant C^3I systems would remain generally operable and they would have great importance for tactical operations. Vulnerable to small-scale ASAT attack, they would present a very tempting target. In such conditions, in which both sides continued to be highly dependent on satellite systems for operational communications, tactical intelligence, navigation of combat units and strategic warning, each would also be extraordinarily sensitive to any attack on those systems. The type of anti-satellite systems deployed by the Soviet Union and about to be tested by the United States might, in such crises, offer both a temptation and, especially as capabilities improve, a means for a precise, low collateral damage attack aimed at substantial immediate military advantage. An attack on intelligence and communications satellites, however tempting, would, if successful, destroy one of the major mechanisms by which the superpowers could obtain enough information about and exercise enough control over events to restrain escalation. Moreover, the attack would itself represent a significant escalation, as would the likely response. If the greatest possibility of a nuclear war arises from the gradual, and in a sense unintended, escalation of a conventional war, then the threat of using anti-satellite systems in such crisis conditions ranks among the conditions more conducive to the outbreak of a nuclear war.

II. Non-arms control means to diminish the threat

Alternative ways to control vulnerability of space systems are not so promising that the potential of agreements can be ignored, but they do exist.

Deterrence by threat of retaliation (replying to attacks on space systems by counter-attacks on the other side's space systems) would not necessarily be adequate. Given the disruptive effect on other operations of loss of critical space assets, there might be high rewards for striking first, which could not be negated by a subsequent loss of the initial attacker's own space-dependent communications. Moreover, there seem likely to be differences in the degree to which the two sides would depend on space assets for military purposes in particular situations. In such circumstances, denial to both sides of all space systems following an ASAT exchange would favour the less dependent side. Most US observers argue, for example, that the United States is substantially more dependent on sophisticated communications based in space than is the Soviet Union. If this is true, excellent US ASAT systems would be only a weak deterrent if the Soviet Union believed an ASAT attack could succeed. To be sure, there are important qualifications to the generalization of greater US space dependence. For example, the USSR appears to rely heavily on radar satellites to observe the position of US naval vessels. However, it is not important from the point of view of deterrence which side is in fact the more dependent on space in particular circumstances; threats by the more dependent to eliminate the other's space assets will not necessarily prove an effective deterrent to an attack on its own more critical space facilities. Further, the idea of ASAT systems serving a retaliatory purpose is unsatisfactory in crisis conditions where an important, independent interest would be avoiding pressures for further expansion of the conflict by responding to attacks.

Nor is *defence of satellites* by rendering them less vulnerable an entirely satisfactory answer. A great deal can be, and to some degree is being, done to reduce the more obvious vulnerabilities of existing and future systems (e.g., by hardening the satellites or giving them capability to take evasive action, or reducing the value of the target by providing for redundant capability or easy replacement). Such measures are relatively costly and in at least some instances are of uncertain effectiveness.

In short, ASAT threats are serious and the available unilateral ways of meeting those threats uncertain. Therefore it is appropriate to conclude that arms control limitations on ASAT systems—focused especially on reducing the capability for successful limited and precise, but highly escalatory, disruption of space assets in crisis or limited war—is a useful objective in traditional strategic stability terms, because it could ease escalation temptations and pressures.

III. Existing legal limitations on ASAT systems

Rules of conduct established under international law lack enforcement mechanisms to ensure their observance, so their potential for protecting satellites, or anything else, is limited. Nonetheless, by establishing legal norms of conduct, agreed standards of behaviour may inhibit acts that would otherwise be taken without reserve. Accordingly, one area for consideration is the international legal status of satellites. Certain internationally agreed legal inhibitions already exist with respect to carrying out attacks on satellite systems. These inhibitions are, however, sufficiently ambiguous and/or limited in scope that further restrictions, whatever their other utility, would clearly not be legally redundant.

The Outer Space Treaty of 1967 bars nuclear weapons and 'weapons of mass destruction' from orbit—not the core of the problem—and in rather complex terms it limits interference with other countries' satellites. These provisions afford satellites some measure of legally protected status against attack. However, this Treaty is not aimed at the problem of deliberately hostile activities and it does not even purport to limit or affect development, testing or deployment of means of interference, in contrast to actual interference. Important as it has been in expressing a general aspiration for legal sanctuary for space activities, the particular rules of the Outer Space Treaty can hardly be said to render superfluous more precise definition of the status of satellites.

The SALT Treaties ban deliberate interference with 'national technical means of verification' (NTM), a term understood (though not explicitly specified) as embracing certain intelligence-collecting satellite systems. The SALT agreements provide an important legitimization of one key peace-time role of military space systems—the collection of intelligence on strategic programmes—but they do not even purport to restrict possession of the means of carrying out attack. Moreover, whatever legal protection they provide from actual attack extends only to systems used for verification of arms control agreements and operating "in a manner consistent with generally recognized principles of international law". The conditions could reasonably be interpreted as permitting attacks not only on military communications and/or navigation satellites that have never been used in any meaningful sense for arms control verification, but even on recognized NTM in a wartime situation, at least, when, as would often be the case, those NTM were being used to support combat operations.

IV. The 1978–79 negotiations

In 1978 and 1979 there was a brief but suggestive effort by the USA and the USSR at reaching an ASAT agreement. Three negotiating sessions conducted between US and Soviet diplomats, supported by scientific and military experts, produced an extended discussion of a variety of issues.

The talks focused on two types of agreement, one dealing with use of ASAT systems, the second with ASAT means, i.e., the barring or at least imposition of a limitation, or moratorium, on testing systems as a prelude to a more far-reaching agreement restricting capabilities to attack satellites. But while the talks showed that the two sides were capable of carrying on a dialogue on the subject and had some interest in reaching agreements in limited areas, a number of potentially serious areas of difference were exposed.

Differences emerged even with respect to the very modest use agreement on which the talks chiefly focused. The overall idea was to agree that attacks on satellites were, in effect, acts of war, thereby clarifying that another nation's satellites, including those used for military and intelligence purposes, could be attacked only under conditions in which that nation's other military forces, such as its naval vessels on the high seas, could be attacked. The points of dispute were numerous, even with respect to this modest step. For example, the Soviet negotiators were unwilling to agree that *all* attacks on *all* foreign satellites should automatically be declared acts of war, arguing that such protection should not be extended by a US–Soviet agreement to satellites of third states, at least in the absence of an agreement by such states to refrain from using their wholly hypothetical ASAT capability against Soviet satellites. Even as to satellites owned by parties to the agreement, the USSR was reluctant to agree to an entirely comprehensive protection, insisting that there were, at least in theory, certain uses of satellites which were so objectionable as not to deserve protection. Their only explicit example of such an 'illegal' use justifying attack was the highly implausible one of a satellite being used to spray poison gas on the surface of the Earth. The traditional Soviet position that direct broadcast satellites violate the rights of states to whose populations they broadcast suggested they might have had intellectual, as much as chemical, poisons in mind. For both sides, the problems of defining what acts with respect to satellites should be covered was a difficult and sensitive one; for example, a use agreement which affected only the physical destruction of satellites would still leave open a variety of ways to render satellite systems incapable of performing their normal function.

With respect to means limitations, the different state of the two sides' programmes seemed likely to prove a major obstacle. The Soviet ASAT system, capable of intercepts against a restricted (but highly important) class of targets, was already operational; the more sophisticated and capable US system was still to be tested. Thus it was not surprising that the USA supported a limited test moratorium, the USSR an indefinite test ban. The USSR also argued that the US space shuttle had ASAT potential, though the implications of this assertion for the shuttle (or, for that matter, for the Soviet Progrez space resupply programme) were obscure.

The US–Soviet ASAT talks were not resumed after the third session ended in June 1979, initially because the US Administration wanted to devote full effort to ratifying the SALT II Treaty signed that month, later because of the general breakdown in arms negotiations after the Soviet invasion of Afghanistan.

Interest in the topic continued. A UN General Assembly resolution assigned high priority to consideration of ASAT prohibitions. In 1982 the USSR tabled in the UN a draft treaty on space warfare which called for a comprehensive ban on all weapons in space (not just nuclear weapons and weapons of mass destruction) and legal protection for satellites from attack if operating in accordance with the limits of the treaty. The Soviet treaty proposal did not suggest limiting testing or possession of non-orbited means to carry out the anti-satellite attacks it proclaimed generally illegal. In August 1983 the USSR proposed a different draft treaty, discussed in paper 13, page 185 and Part I.

Although both sides have proclaimed readiness to discuss ASAT limitations further, agreement has not been reached on procedures for resuming the talks.

V. Verification

Looming over any serious negotiations on limiting the testing or deployment of ASAT systems, or on the dismantling of already tested and deployed ASATs, is the difficult question of verification. Accepting the definition of adequate verification advanced, for example, by US Secretary of Defense Harold Brown during the SALT II debate as the ability for timely detection of violations which would be militarily significant, ASAT arms control poses special verification difficulties. In the SALT situation, where numbers are large enough and the balance stable enough, small violations by one side or the other would be of only the most marginal military significance. However, it can be argued that the number of critically important satellite targets is small enough that successful concealment of even a few operationally effective anti-satellite systems in violation of a limitation could give a highly significant military advantage.

Such an advantage could, of course, only be obtained if the other side had operated on the assumption that the limitations were being observed. Survivability and defensive measures could—and probably should—be pursued even with an agreement. But if the verification of an agreement is so uncertain that the parties cannot afford to rely on its being observed it has only limited relevance as arms control.

The verification uncertainties in an ASAT agreement arise not only because of the relatively small size of ASAT systems, but because both the current US and Soviet systems use as their launchers equipment widely applied for non-ASAT uses—heavy ICBMs in the case of the Soviet ASAT system and F-15 interceptors in the case of the US. More generally, ASAT operations ultimately require only that one space object be brought into a defined proximity

150

with another; once that is done the mechanics of kill are straightforward. ASAT manoeuvres are therefore sufficiently similar to the anti-ballistic missile (ABM) interceptor tests permitted by the 1972 ABM Treaty and to certain legitimate space activities (including some civilian space activities such as satellite docking) that defining the boundary between permitted and prohibited activities would be extremely difficult during negotiations. Furthermore, it would be a source of potential controversy afterwards, because of fear that permitted conduct just on the safe side of the border represented a clandestine effort to create potential ASAT capability. These difficulties of detecting and regulating 'research' activities with potential ASAT application are still more severe for non-interception attack methods, such as lasers.

However, the scale of verification concerns must be seen in perspective. To some degree the problem of a high reward for small-scale cheating will be reduced by the greater efforts on which the USA (and presumably the USSR) has embarked to ensure the survivability and redundancy of critical satellite systems—efforts that would certainly have to be undertaken without an agreement. With regard to the development of means for attacking satellites, by such subterfuges as ABM or clandestinely exploited 'civil' space programmes, systems which are optimized for other tasks and which have not been able to be fully tested in an ASAT role (and indeed have had to be tested only in a different, 'cover' role) would probably not be thought adequate for the kind of 'high-confidence, low-escalation' attack on a handful of critical satellites which seems to be the most serious stability threat from ASAT weapons.

VI. Possible forms of limitation

Use agreements

One modest but still useful initial step would be the completion of efforts to reach an agreement defining an attack on satellites as a hostile act. As noted above, a measure along these lines was intensively discussed in the 1978–79 negotiations. This measure would substitute for the current unsettled legal situation an explicit protection under international law of satellites in orbit from attack during peace-time. Even if such an agreement did no more than codify what many would argue is already an implicit rule of international law, it would have some marginal inhibiting effect on willingness to use interceptors against satellites in a crisis before hostilities had broken out on the Earth's surface, and perhaps even for some further period of low-intensity conflict.

'Rules of the road'

A rules-of-the-road limitation would require that satellites of different countries maintain a separation sufficient to protect against the possibility of implantation of so-called space mines, that is, attack satellites placed in orbit near target satellites, waiting to be activated on command. As such, it would represent a transition from limiting 'use' to limiting 'means' or at least testing. (To inhibit testing, such an agreement would have to be joined to explicit test limitations since tests would normally use one's own, not another country's, space objects as targets.)

Such an agreement has some theoretical attraction, but it would face formidable definitional difficulties. For example, the lethal distance (or required orbital relationship) of ASAT systems varies tremendously according to the characteristics of the target and the attacker. There would also be great enforcement problems, given the large number of objects in orbit—by no means all of them active, working satellites. Tracking capabilities are improving, but, even assuming no effort at concealment, the task of keeping track of whether the many objects in orbit were complying with the agreed rules would be complex and expensive. Like other operational agreements, any such 'keep out zone' arrangement could be rapidly abrogated. Direct launches would be unaffected. Even as to space mines, satellites parked just outside the permitted zone could, either overtly or covertly, be manoeuvred close enough to target satellites to attack immediately or after an interval. However, the additional complexity and the untested character of such manoeuvres might prove a useful inhibition in a crisis.

Test limitations

Applying the generally accepted principle—relied on extensively both in military intelligence and in arms control verification—that only systems that are tested to the full extent of their intended capability will be relied upon in wartime for that capability (at least where the issue is deliberate initiation, not improvisation out of necessity), many proposals to limit ASAT means, as contrasted to actual use of ASAT systems, focus on test limitations. A broad menu of variations has been discussed. The limitation could be a complete ban on all ASAT tests; different altitude regimes could be established; quotas could be provided for certain types of tests, or specific test methods could be prohibited.

From a political point of view, the existence of a fully tested and operational Soviet low-orbit system, while the United States is still testing a better system (see Part I), creates an asymmetry in the two sides' programmes which is likely to make negotiation of a test limit difficult. A comprehensive test ban of long duration would permanently block the United States from having a reliable interceptor ASAT system equivalent to the fully-tested Soviet system, giving the USSR a *breakout* advantage. On the other hand, the better quality of the new US system makes it unlikely that the Soviet Union would agree to an arrangement under which the USA would be permitted to 'catch up' with the USSR while the USSR was restricted from testing a replacement for its current system.

Because both the US and the Soviet systems are lower orbit systems, limitations framed in terms of the altitude of the target, permitting (though perhaps restricting) tests below that altitude have received considerable attention, and may be the most promising among the possibilities. Of particular interest would be a limitation on tests aimed at making intercepts at geosynchronous orbit infeasible, because some key communications satellites and early warning satellites are at that altitude. Neither the operational Soviet system nor the US system under development has this capability, and significant modifications, probably requiring substantial testing for confidence, would be required to obtain it.

The usual litany of verification concerns applies to test limits: tests at lower altitudes may be adequate to demonstrate a capability for a fundamentally similar operation at a somewhat higher altitude, although not necessarily at greatly increased altitudes. Given the highly elliptical character of many satellite orbits, the altitude of a test is far from self-defining. So long as non-ASAT space activities that involve close approaches of one satellite to another are permitted (as they probably must be for perfectly legitimate civil and military space programmes to continue), there will necessarily be substantial testing of the critical element of co-orbital interceptors—the ability to reach a certain position relative to another satellite at a specified time. Similarly, ABM tests and other space activities offer opportunities to demonstrate an ability to make direct ascents to predefined points. However, the issue for ASAT development is not the general capability to accomplish close encounters in space—which both sides have demonstrated routinely—but to do so with equipment that is in other respects effective and efficient for ASAT purposes. A set of test limits that impairs confidence in ASAT attacks—even if it does not make such attacks impossible in all circumstances—could be sufficiently useful to be worth having, given that a principal objective is to make it hard to have high confidence in the reliability of ASAT attacks in a crisis.

Dismantling existing systems and systems under development

In obtaining a truly comprehensive agreement covering testing, development and operational practices, intended to eliminate ASAT interceptor capability altogether, an attempt might be made to require dismantling of existing systems. The commonality of launchers for existing systems—the SL-11 and the F-15—with non-ASAT applications and the significance of limited numbers of clandestinely retained ASAT systems present formidable objections to relying on the success of a dismantling agreement.

No new types

An effort might be made to avoid the dismantling problem by making each side maintain its current system while banning any new type. The term 'new type' would obviously have to be defined, and access to test information secured to enforce the limitation. A constraint on these lines would not meet the asymmetry problem, that is, the greater capability of the new US system relative to the deployed Soviet system.

Ban on new intercept technologies

Another approach, which could be combined with some of the other more limited possible agreements, would seek to block the application for ASAT purposes of certain novel technologies, such as lasers, space mines or particle beam weapons, which have been discussed but, so far, not developed or tested for such purposes. Formidable definition and verification problems would exist, for example, in distinguishing ASAT lasers from space research laser work, but as in other areas the ability to restrict tests of optimized (as contrasted to adaptable) systems could be a useful measure. A useful precedent for dealing with restrictions on unknown technologies is in the 1972 ABM Treaty's treatment of unorthodox ABM technologies, barring their deployment except as subsequently agreed.

Confidence-building measures

Possibly as an adjunct to testing limitations and as a means of reducing the feasibility of using civil and non-ASAT military space activities to evade ASAT agreements, special notification and observation rights must be required for such permitted activities.

Bilateral or multilateral?

A matter of some controversy during the 1978–79 talks was the multilateral or bilateral character of the agreement. For all practical purposes the only countries likely to have ASAT interceptor capabilities in the indefinite future are the United States and the Soviet Union. However, increasing numbers of other countries are beginning to operate satellites of their own. The most logical treaty regime—a multilateral treaty protecting only parties to it—has the very considerable defect of legitimating the development and possession of ASAT capabilities to attack non-parties. Moreover, it makes even comprehensive legal protection against use dependent on a decision to participate by states, like China and France, that have political objections to joining in US–Soviet arms limitations efforts.

Formal or tacit?

A further question is the importance of a formal, explicit agreement. Undoubtedly, informal bilateral undertakings to restrict the pace and scale of ASAT development would be—or more precisely would have been—in the interest of international stability. However, both sides seem to be far enough along the road that tacit bilateral restraint scarcely appears an attractive or effective approach. In any event, tacit agreements affecting use of capabilities would be most useful precisely in those periods of crisis and confrontation when informal restraint would be least likely to be maintained.

VII. Conclusion

Arms control can provide no more than a limited part of a comprehensive effort to reduce the instabilities inherent in satellite vulnerability. Indeed, arms control and defensive measures (survivability and redundancy) would each be most effective used in conjunction. Arms control also offers only marginal hope of limitations on the ability to interfere with satellite communication links, to attack their ground stations, or to use nuclear weapons to attack them. However, precise interceptor attacks in crises are perhaps the most serious threat to stability. The verification problems are formidable. Further, the fact that the USSR has already developed a limited ASAT capability while the US system is still untested creates an asymmetry that could be difficult both militarily and politically. Nevertheless, a US conclusion that it has little use for ASAT systems—a conclusion that would be sharply disputed by some—might make limits on its own ASAT capability worthwhile if Soviet capability were at least significantly reduced, even if it were not eliminated entirely and even if certain verification concerns remained. In any event, the comparison must be to a world without limitations on use, testing and development of ASAT systems and not, for example, to one with perfect defensive measures and unilaterally constrained threats.

Paper 11. Approaches to prevent an arms race in outer space

Sune Danielsson*

Swedish UN Mission, 825 Third Ave, 39th floor, New York, NY 10022, USA

I. Introduction

While satellites enhance the military capability of the major space powers, they also make them more dependent on space-based systems and more suspicious about the space potential and intentions of the adversary. This tends to create a demand for protection of one's own vulnerable space capacity and an offensive potential against the space resources of the other side. Thus, the basis is laid for increased efforts to establish anti-satellite (ASAT) capability, which might lead to the development of a capacity for anti-ballistic missile (ABM) warfare in outer space, possibly through the use of beam weapons. Such a development could have far-reaching implications for peace and security. Many military space systems are so important that an attack on them could be a *casus belli*. The effect on the strategic balance of beam weapons for ABM purposes would be such that even research and development could lead to nervousness and tension. Furthermore, the introduction of space weapons would have negative effects on civilian space programmes, national as well as international. Therefore, something has to be done to prevent the introduction of weapons into outer space.

Although international law contains a number of provisions dealing with certain military uses of outer space, it seems that those provisions are not sufficient to prevent an arms race and armed conflicts in outer space. Thus, further measures are needed. When considering what approach will be the best to cope with the most immediate problems, in particular those raised by ASAT systems, it does not seem sufficient to limit the discussion to specific space weapons. It seems necessary to consider also if broader approaches can be

*This paper contains the views of the author and does not necessarily reflect the views of the Swedish government.

helpful. Proposals made and different approaches will be discussed below, as well as some factors which should be taken into account in this context.

First, however, some brief comments on military space activities will be made. (For a fuller description of the military use of space, see Part I.) Also, existing international law will be reviewed to find out what additional regulation is needed to ensure that outer space does not become a new battlefield.

II. Military uses of outer space

It is important to differentiate between 'force amplifiers'—military space systems which perform a support function, such as communication, information gathering, navigation and so on—and actual and conceivable weapons.

To attack or hinder the functioning of a spacecraft it is not an absolute necessity to use weapons specially designed for use in outer space. In general, space systems, both military and civilian, depend on radio communications with ground stations. Thus, an attack on a ground station can incapacitate a space system guided by it; also, radio signals between the Earth and a satellite can be jammed.

If we turn to actual attacks on satellites, it should first be pointed out that a satellite could very well be made useless by a mere collision (see Part I, page 11). Thus the simplest form of space warfare would be—as in the early days of naval warfare—to ram the target. But the simple technique of ramming probably lacks the precision and speed for carrying out an effective attack in outer space. For this reason efforts are being made to develop systems specifically for use against satellites. The Soviet Union, which has been testing ASAT systems since the end of the 1960s, uses an interceptor which hunts the target during a few orbits before it closes in (see Paper 5, page 83). During the last few years the US interest in ASAT systems has been revived following reports of successful tests by the Soviet Union. In January 1984 the first test took place of a direct-ascent system which will use a miniature homing intercept vehicle (see Part I, page 13).

The present ASAT systems in existence or planned are aimed at targets in low Earth orbits, such as various reconnaissance satellites. However, does a capacity to launch objects into geostationary orbit not also imply the technological capacity to damage or disturb a geostationary satellite by colliding with it? Whether this is a militarily attractive method for attacking these satellites is another question. This might be one of the reasons for the interest in beam weapons.

Both the USA and the USSR are investigating the possibility of using directed-energy or high-energy beam weapons not only for space warfare but also for ballistic missile defence (BMD) and other applications (see Paper 7, page 107). Even if scientists disagree whether it is possible to place beam weapons in space, the mere possibility that this would happen is a sufficient reason to consider such weapons in the context of disarmament. The discussion before World War II about the impossibility of producing nuclear weapons should serve as a reminder in this context.

Finally, mention should be made of two other types of weapon which have a close relationship with space technology: ballistic missiles and fractional orbit bombardment systems (FOBS). The satellite launchers of the space powers were based on ballistic missiles used for carrying nuclear weapons. This merits two reflections. First, today the development of satellite launchers could be used for launching nuclear warheads. Second, ballistic missiles do not enter into an orbit around the Earth but fly in ballistic trajectories which go up to altitudes which are normally considered as outer space. (See below under Multilateral treaties, concerning the Outer Space Treaty.) FOBS, however, enter into Earth orbit but descend onto the target on the Earth before completing a full orbit (hence fractional orbit). This kind of weapon will also be mentioned below under Bilateral agreements.

III. Existing rules of international law relevant to space weapons

The rules of international law relevant to the use of weapons in space can be found in international treaties both in those of a general nature, in particular the United Nations Charter, and in those containing specific rules, especially those which apply to space activities.

The Charter of the United Nations

Article 2.4 of the Charter of the United Nations prohibits the use of force or the threat of use of force. An attack on a spacecraft belonging to another country must be forbidden according to this article. An explicit reference to the UN Charter is included in article III of the 1967 Outer Space Treaty.

Could an attack be justified as a measure of self-defence in accordance with article 51 of the Charter? It is inconceivable that this article could be referred to as far as an attack on non-military systems is concerned. For military systems it might be different. It would seem far-fetched, however, to justify an attack on force amplifiers (e.g., a communication satellite or early warning satellite) as self-defence. In addition, surveillance satellites used for verification are protected as national technical means of verification under the SALT Agreements and early warning satellites under the Accident Measures Agreement (see below under Bilateral agreements). If arms were placed in space the situation could change.

Multilateral treaties

Turning to specific rules of international law relating mainly to space activities, a number of multilateral treaties contain regulations of interest.

1. The 1963 Partial Test Ban Treaty prohibits the testing of nuclear weapons in outer space (article 1, paragraph 1(a)).

159

2. The 1967 Outer Space Treaty has several provisions of fundamental importance.

Article IV.1 of that Treaty prohibits the placing "in orbit around the earth any objects carrying nuclear weapons or any other kinds of weapons of mass destruction" and the installation of such weapons on celestial bodies, or stationing of such weapons in outer space in any other manner. This provision does not, however, impose restrictions on other kinds of weapon, that is, conventional weapons, or on military space systems of the kind referred to above as force amplifiers.

The second paragraph of that article states that the Moon and other celestial bodies shall be used *exclusively* for peaceful purposes and prohibits all kinds of military activities on those bodies (see also below concerning the Agreement relating to the Moon).

According to article I of the Outer Space Treaty, space activities "shall be carried out for the benefit and in the interest of all countries, regardless of their degree of economic or scientific development, and shall be the province of all mankind". According to article III, space activities shall be carried out in accordance with international law, including the UN Charter, and "in the interest of maintaining international peace and security and promoting international co-operation and understanding". It has been said that these provisions are only of a declaratory nature. Even if this is the case they should at least mean, especially in conjunction with the UN Charter, that an attack on the space object of another country is forbidden.

In article IX, it is stated that states shall conduct their activities in outer space "with due regard to corresponding interests of all other States Parties". If space activities could cause potentially harmful interference with peaceful activities of other states, international consultations should be held. This article does not, however, contain a clear prohibition of harmful interference with the functioning of a spacecraft.

The Outer Space Treaty also contains certain provisions which are of interest as regards verification. Article X relates to the observation of space flights but states that the conditions for such observations should be agreed between the states concerned. Article XI deals with giving information to the UN and the general public "to the greatest extent feasible" and article XII with visits to installations on the Moon and other celestial bodies. These three provisions have one thing in common; they do not contain any clear obligation to give information or allow inspection.

3. In this context it is worth mentioning the provisions on notification which are contained in the 1975 Registration Convention. According to article IV of this Convention, certain general data about space missions should be sent to the Secretary-General of the United Nations as soon as practicable. However, the information supplied to the UN is so general that it can only be guessed what purpose the mission has and often several months pass between the launch and the notification.

4. The latest of the international agreements which have been elaborated by the UN is the 1979 Agreement Governing the Activities of States on the Moon

160

and other Celestial Bodies. Article 3 confirms and expands article IV of the Outer Space Treaty. Since orbits around or trajectories to these bodies are included in the terms "the moon and other celestial bodies" (article 1.2), article 3 is also applicable as regards these orbits and trajectories. It can be concluded that the Moon Agreement demilitarizes all of outer space except that part in proximity to the Earth, or, more precisely, orbits around the Earth.

5. In connection with article IX of the Outer Space Treaty it can be mentioned that the International Telecommunication Convention of 1973 contains in article 35 a prohibition of harmful interference with other countries' radio communications that are operated in accordance with the Radio Regulations of the International Telecommunication Union (ITU). The ITU has adopted such rules regarding most of the space-based communications. Signals to and from satellites are thus protected according to this provision. This is of particular importance since radio communication is a vital factor for the functioning and use of a spacecraft.

6. Finally, in this context should be mentioned the Environmental Modification Agreement of 1977 which prohibits the use of some environmental warfare techniques which *inter alia* could involve outer space.

Bilateral agreements

Certain bilateral arms control agreements between the United States and the Soviet Union contain provisions which relate to space activities.

1. The two SALT Agreements (the Interim Agreement of 1972 and the SALT II Agreement of 1979, with which the Soviet Union and United States abide unilaterally awaiting ratification or new negotiations) contain similar provisions about verification (articles V and XV, respectively). According to these provisions the contracting parties shall use "national technical means of verification" to monitor the adherence to the provisions of the agreements. Furthermore, it is stated that these national means of verification must not be disturbed or "interfered with", to use the language of the Agreements. It is assumed that surveillance satellites are among those 'means'. The SALT Agreements also prohibit "deliberate concealment measures which impede verification by national technical means". Thus, the national technical means of verification have been given a protected status: not only should they not be interfered with (e.g., attacked, moved or 'jammed') but their operation should not be hindered by concealment measures on the ground.

Article IX of the SALT II Agreement contains a relatively unnoticed expansion of the prohibition in article IV of the Outer Space Treaty which only prohibits the placement of nuclear weapons or other weapons of mass destruction in outer space. SALT II also forbids the development, testing and deployment of systems for placing in orbit nuclear weapons and so on. Since there is no mention of outer space in this context this prohibition must also extend to the development, testing and deployment of such systems on the ground. In addition, this article prohibits the testing, development and deployment of

FOBS. It might have been argued that FOBS with nuclear warheads are not prohibited under article IV of the Outer Space Treaty, however the prohibition contained in article IX of the SALT Agreement makes the situation regarding FOBS clear.

2. According to the ABM Treaty of 1972, article V.1: "Each party undertakes not to develop, test or deploy ABM systems or components which are sea-based, air-based, *space-based* or mobile land-based" (emphasis added). It is thus clear that the placing of ABM systems in outer space is prohibited.

3. The Accident Measures Agreement (1971) and the Prevention of Nuclear War Agreement (1974) together oblige the Soviet Union and the United States to refrain from interfering with or attacking early warning systems of either side, which would include satellites that are components of such warning systems.

4. In this context can also be mentioned the Hot Line Agreement (1963) and the Hot Line Modernization Agreement (1971), where the United States and the Soviet Union undertake to maintain two direct communication links at all times using satellite communication networks.

IV. ASAT negotiations between the USA and the USSR

The bilateral negotiations between the Soviet Union and the United States about ASAT systems in 1978 and 1979 covered both limits on actions against satellites and limits on capabilities for attacking satellites. During the first round of negotiations, the sides outlined their general concerns, and during the second and third rounds some progress was made in examining and clarifying key issues. However, important areas of disagreement emerged, both with regard to limits on actions against satellites and with regard to limits on ASAT verification.[1]

The negotiations did not end in any agreement. The two parties now quarrel over who is to blame that these negotiations did not continue. Regardless of whose fault it is, it can only be regretted that it was not possible to achieve an agreement that would put a stop to the development of arms for use in space.

V. Proposals for the prevention of an arms race in outer space

Two draft agreements have been presented in intergovernmental fora with concrete proposals to stop the arms race in outer space, the first one in 1979 by Italy in the Committee on Disarmament (CD) and the second one in 1981 by the Soviet Union in the UN General Assembly. (This paper was written before the Soviet proposal on a treaty on the prohibition of the use of force in outer space and from space against the Earth could be evaluated. See Paper 13, page 185 and Part I, page 33.)

Italian proposal in 1979

The proposal by Italy was a draft Additional Protocol to the 1967 Outer Space Treaty.[2] As a first proposal it was an important contribution to the efforts by the international community to take measures to prevent an arms race in outer space. However, since it was presented before the discussions had evolved further in the UN and the CD, the proposed Additional Protocol does not take into account some important aspects.

Looking at some of the shortcomings of the Italian proposal, it seems to be both too general and too specific. It proposes that outer space should be used for peaceful purposes only, that is, all military space activities would be forbidden. This may cause problems because of the military satellites used for verification and early warning. It may also be too general since countries could claim that their military space activities only have peaceful purposes.

The prohibition on stationing and testing in outer space of weapons other than those of mass destruction is too limited since the proposal does not, for example, forbid deployment of ASAT systems on the ground or in the atmosphere.

Finally, the proposal does not contain any provisions regarding verification, and the complaints procedure in the Security Council would not be very effective since those two countries which today have the possibility of breaching the suggested undertakings are also in a position to put an effective stop to any investigation by using their veto.

Soviet proposal in 1981

The proposal by the Soviet Union in 1981 is a Draft Treaty on the prohibition of the stationing of weapons of any kind in outer space.[3] This proposal reflected a change of attitude. Up to then both the major space powers seemed to be content to limit the discussion on space weapons to bilateral talks. The initiative of the Soviet Union could be seen as a response to the concern expressed by many countries in the UN about the militarization of outer space. It is to be welcomed that one of the major space powers has taken this action. This, however, does not mean that the proposal by the Soviet Union contains no shortcomings. Indeed, some of them are as fundamental as those which were mentioned regarding the Italian proposal.

Article 1 suffers from a lack of definition or an explanation of what is meant by the term 'weapons of any kind'. Since almost any manoeuvrable space object—military or non-military—can be used to collide with another satellite, a non-military space object could also be considered a weapon. This lack of precision becomes even more important in view of the provision proposed in article 3 (see below).

Another shortcoming is that the prohibition proposed only relates to the placing or stationing of weapons in orbit around the Earth. This means that the ASAT systems in existence or planned today would be covered only to a certain extent. Their establishment would not be forbidden and only the use of certain types of ASAT system would be prohibited. The ASAT systems we know of today are not stationed in outer space but are (or will be) stationed at bases on the ground or on aircraft where they are kept until they are launched. This goes for the 'hunter-killer' type of ASAT system as well as direct-ascent systems. Hunter-killers could only be considered stationed when they enter into orbit. Direct-ascent systems do not even enter Earth orbit but attack the target at the end of a ballistic trajectory which starts on the ground or in the atmosphere. The use of this latter type of ASAT system does not seem to be covered at all by the proposed prohibition to station weapons in Earth orbit.

The same problem relates to the stationing of weapons 'in any other manner'. The reason is that the proposed prohibition is related to stationing which seems to imply that the object in question has to enter Earth orbit.

The proposed prohibition does not mention development, testing and deployment which should be important ingredients in any effort to prevent the use of arms in outer space.

The next question relating to article 1 is whether there is any need to mention reusable space vehicles. Weapons could be mounted on different kinds of space vehicle, reusable or disposable, manned or unmanned. It seems questionable that reusable space vehicles are more useful as platforms for weapons than disposable ones. The military implications of new space transportation systems are rather that an increased transportation capacity can be used for military purposes. Of more immediate importance seems to be, however, to determine whether a spacecraft—reusable or not, unmanned or manned—can be used for aggressive purposes. A decisive factor in this context seems to be whether it can be manoeuvred. However, these questions are of a nature best solved during negotiations.

The proposed article 2 is slightly different from a similar provision (article III) in the Outer Space Treaty. But since there are differences their implications should be clarified.

The proposed article 3 presents a major problem in that it permits the use of force and interference against space objects since the undertaking not to destroy and so on is limited to objects placed in orbit in strict accordance with article 1.1. As has been pointed out above, the lack of definition of 'weapons of any kind' leaves open to interpretation what is to be considered a weapon. One state could describe another state's space object, which it for some reason or another does not like, as a weapon. The proposed article 3 would then give it the right to intervene with force or in some other manner against that space object. This would make legal actions which are now forbidden. It would be contrary to article 2.4 of the UN Charter which prohibits the use of force. It would have implications for the provisions of the Outer Space Treaty and it would undermine article 35 of the International Telecommunication Convention which prohibits harmful interference with radio communications. Because of these limitations this article could well create international problems or lead to tension instead of solving problems and easing tension.

The proposed article 4 on verification is an improvement on the Italian

164

proposal in that it attempts to take care of the problem of verification. In addition, it is an improvement on that proposal because it does not refer to the Security Council in the 'complaints procedure' described in paragraph 3 and thus does not subject complaints to the possibility of a veto. However, verification by national technical means does not seem to be sufficient because of difficulties such as distinguishing a launcher for a non-military satellite from an ASAT system or monitoring aircraft-borne ASAT missiles. On-site inspection appears to be necessary for this. The complaints procedure proposed contains an obligation to supply information and this should be welcomed. The absence of a mechanism which is more effective than consultations in solving disputes, however, seems to weaken the procedure to make the proposed provisions work.

VI. Approaches to and other considerations regarding the prevention of an arms race in outer space

Timing

The development of specific arms for use in outer space has accelerated during the last few years and consideration is even being given to the possibility of using exotic weapons in space such as beam weapons, *inter alia* for ballistic missile defence. The development and/or testing of ASAT systems is far advanced. However, such arms do not seem to have been deployed on any scale as yet. It is always easier to take disarmament measures before weapon systems have been deployed. Therefore, it is urgent to start negotiations and conclude agreements on disarmament measures regarding outer space before irreversible actions have been taken and decisive investments made in weapon systems aimed for use in outer space.

Ban on all or certain military uses of outer space

The interest in space weapons has developed because of the operation of different kinds of space systems for military purposes. It is mainly—but not only—these military systems which would be the target of an attack in outer space.

One approach to avoid an arms race in outer space could be to prohibit all military uses of space systems. In this way there would be no potential targets for space weapons, which in turn would not be needed. This objective would, however, be difficult to achieve without a complete general disarmament and could even present disadvantages.

A ban on all military space systems would include such satellites as surveillance satellites used to verify arms control agreements and early warning satellites which have a vital stabilizing effect. This may not be in the interests of disarmament and international peace and security.

Important non-military systems such as those for communication could be of interest in a conflict because they support important functions in modern societies. Also, civil communications satellites may well be used to transmit military messages. Therefore, a total ban on military satellites may not completely eradicate the temptation to develop space weapons or, indeed the use of non-military satellites to ram other satellites.

Another great disadvantage is that it would be unrealistic to expect a total ban on military activities in outer space in the short term. It would, thus, not solve the immediate problems of today. Could it then be possible to restrict certain military uses of outer space to diminish the temptation to introduce weapons for use in outer space? This might be a possibility if these efforts were to be concentrated in particular on those satellites which are integral parts of terrestrial weapons or warfare systems, but it would probably be difficult to find agreement on what space systems should be prohibited. Therefore, it might take time to achieve results and meet the most urgent needs with this approach. And the temptation to develop space weapons will always be there as long as any space system of military use or interest exists. However, this approach would have one important advantage: it would contribute to the halting of the qualitative arms race on Earth.

Ban on certain arms

Another approach could be to look at the means for attacking space objects: the weapons, both conventional ASAT systems and exotic weapons such as beam weapons.

To be effective a prohibition of ASAT systems must cover not only their use in outer space but also their deployment on the ground, on aircraft or in outer space. The ASAT systems, at least the ones we know of today, are not deployed in outer space; they are only to be used there.

To prohibit the deployment of ASAT systems would, however, not be sufficient. If a weapon had been developed, tested and put into production it would be easy to deploy it rapidly and use it. Therefore, an ASAT ban would have to include a prohibition on the development, testing and production of such weapons. Furthermore, to the extent that ASAT systems have been developed and deployed, they would have to be dismantled and abolished.

If exotic weapons, such as beam weapons, are developed they could be used against satellites from the ground, the air or from outer space. Therefore, an ASAT ban should also cover such weapons. This is particularly important in order to ensure that beam weapons intended for ABM use are not disguised as ASAT systems. Futhermore, the prohibition in the US–Soviet ABM Treaty of development, testing and deployment of *inter alia* space-based ABM systems must be upheld. A confirmation at the international level of this ban on ABM systems would not only serve as a reassurance for the international community, but also prevent the possibility of other countries developing such ABM systems.

To be complete, a prohibition of space weapons should also include space-based weapons directed against the Earth, to complement the ban on weapons of mass destruction in the Outer Space Treaty.

The shortcoming with this approach is that even the total suppression of ASAT systems and other types of space weapons does not exclude the possibility of hostile acts against space objects using other means.

Prohibition of hostile acts

It has been mentioned above that the Charter of the United Nations in article 2.4 contains a prohibition on the use or threat of use of force, but that Article 51 gives states the right to use force in self-defence. If there had been any doubts that states have to observe these provisions in outer space also, the Outer Space Treaty explicitly states in article III that space activities shall be carried out in accordance with international law, including the Charter of the United Nations. The ITU Convention also prohibits (in article 35) harmful interference with radio communications.

One possible approach is, therefore, to confirm that the use of force, harmful interference, and similar acts against space objects are forbidden. The advantage with this approach is that all hostile acts against space systems would be included, whether they are carried out by specific weapons, by or from non-military space objects from the Earth, or otherwise. The disadvantage is that it would not halt the present trend in space weapons since these could not only be developed and tested but also be deployed without contravening such a ban.

Proliferation of space technology

The two major space powers have had the capability to build, launch and operate their own spacecraft for 25 years. Today, the space-faring capacity of other countries is rapidly increasing and a number of countries have already established themselves as independent space nations, for example, China, Japan and India. Ten European countries have developed a space capacity together under the European Space Agency (ESA). Does this mean that the risks of an arms race in outer space are increasing?

It is difficult to give an answer to this question without sufficient information about national space programmes. It can, however, be noted that the Convention on the establishment of ESA states clearly that the purpose of the Agency is to promote, for exclusively peaceful purposes, co-operation among European states in space research and development.

One aspect that seems to warrant increased attention is the use of launching capabilities for the purpose of carrying weapons. To what extent does the proliferation of such capabilities entail a risk of proliferation of missiles with nuclear warheads? States which have not developed nuclear missiles could be asked to declare that their satellite launchers are not to be used for carrying weapons.

In the long term the proliferation of space activities may also have implications for the arms race in outer space. As long as only two nations have the possibility to develop or have developed a capability for warfare in outer space it should be easier to come to an agreement. If nothing is done, however, the proliferation of such capabilities may create further problems in the future. In this context it is obvious that accession to the Outer Space Treaty by those states which have not yet joined it would be a very important first step.

Verification

A treaty concerning space weapons must be possible to verify sufficiently. National technical means of verification are probably insufficient but they also have the disadvantage of not being available to all potential parties to such a treaty. A limitation of verification to such means could, therefore, negatively influence universal adherence to it. This would be unfortunate, especially since a space potential is growing in many countries outside the two major space powers. International verification would thus be necessary. To solve the technical problems of verification it seems that some kind of on-site inspection would be necesssary.

Openness

In order to build up confidence on all sides it is important that information is available on what is actually taking place. The mere suspicion that the adversary is about to develop space weapons can create a demand for developing an offensive potential. Increased transparency of national and international space activities would contribute to stability. Openness would be of great importance for verification of compliance with disarmament measures concerning outer space. Furthermore, the availability of information would be an important contribution to solving problems concerning proliferation.

The present rules in the Outer Space Treaty and the Registration Convention about notification to the UN and information to the public need to be improved and made more comprehensive in order to complement and facilitate measures to prevent an arms race in outer space, especially verification of such measures.

A step-by-step approach

It seems clear that it would be very difficult to achieve demilitarization of outer space in one stroke, *inter alia* because of the complex relationship between military space systems and terrestrial warfare capability. To achieve progress before it is too late, the best approach would be to try to solve the most urgent problems—ASAT systems—first and then to continue with other aspects to try to reach results progressively.

Bilateral or multilateral agreements?

The number of countries with a direct interest in what takes place in outer space is already large and their space activities, and consequently their interests, are increasing. For this reason the appropriate approach would be to elaborate multilateral agreements in this area. It could be said in favour of this approach that the likelihood of a wide accession to such agreements increases if the potential parties have a say in their elaboration. This is of particular importance to prevent problems of proliferation in the future. From a legal standpoint, it can also be argued that outer space according to the Outer Space Treaty is *res communes* and should be used in the interest of all states.

Two states, the Soviet Union and the United States, are most directly involved and can claim to have special interests in this area. They would probably prefer to deal with these problems on a bilateral basis. This can be illustrated by the bilateral ASAT negotiations in 1978–1979. The situation may have changed with the proposal in the UN by the Soviet Union in 1981.

On balance, the arguments in favour of multilateral negotiations should be given more weight. It is important to add that because of their special interests the two major space powers should be encouraged to hold bilateral talks in order to settle certain questions of particular interest to them. This would certainly be of great importance if rapid progress is to be achieved.

VII. Possible measures to revert the trend towards an arms race in outer space

From the above review of some possible approaches to the prevention of an arms race in outer space it seems clear that there is no single approach which will solve all problems. Therefore, it is necessary to combine different approaches to achieve results. But it is also important to initiate a process through which step after step could be taken to develop further measures progressively, in parallel with terrestrial disarmament measures, to reduce militarization of outer space and as a final goal put a halt to the possibility of an arms race in outer space. In this process it may well be necessary to elaborate more than one agreement.

In the near future

Time is of the essence. Therefore, certain measures should be taken as soon as possible.

The elaboration of such measures should be done on a multilateral basis, but the United States and the Soviet Union should resume bilateral talks to facilitate a solution of the most pressing problems, notably the prevention of anti-satellite warfare. Some measures which can and should be taken now and included in a multilateral treaty are mentioned below.

1. A ban should be adopted regarding certain activities. Thus, hostile activities and the threat of such activities against spacecraft should be prohibited as well as the use of force from outer space to the ground. This would be in line with article 2.4 of the UN Charter and of articles I and III of the Outer Space Treaty. Furthermore, damage, disturbance and harmful interference with the normal functioning of space objects should be forbidden. This would strengthen article IV of the Outer Space Treaty and confirm article 35 of the ITU convention. Any limitation of this prohibition should not go beyond the UN Charter (article 51).

2. This should be complemented with a ban on particular weapon systems meant to be used for the activities mentioned above. This ban would have to include the development, testing and deployment of such systems on or under the ground or the surface of the sea, in the atmosphere or in outer space. Such a measure would be a complement to article IV of the Outer Space Treaty.

To this ban would also have to be added a provision on the dismantling of any such system in existence as well as putting a stop to any development, testing and production under way at present.

A confirmation of the ban on space-based ABM systems in the 1972 ABM treaty should also be included and comprise, as in that treaty, the development, testing and deployment of such systems.

A prohibition of FOBS should likewise be included in line with SALT II.

3. Provisions would have to be adopted regarding verification of compliance with such a treaty. The best method in this respect would be international on-site inspection of some kind.

4. A procedure to settle disputes with regard to the application of the treaty should also be included and refer matters which cannot be solved by negotiation to the International Court of Justice or to arbitration.

5. Finally, the duration of the treaty should be unlimited and it should be made very difficult to withdraw from it.

The measures mentioned above would ban ASAT systems but would also prohibit the use of non-military space objects for hostile purposes, thus meeting what today can be considered to be the most urgent needs.

The fact that these measures would draw to a great extent on existing rules of international law already in force should contribute to speeding up negotiations. To complement the above measures, those states which have not yet joined the Outer Space Treaty should accede to it. This is important not only in the context of proliferation but also to avoid any fears that space technology could be used to place nuclear weapons in orbit by states that do not feel bound by the Outer Space Treaty. Such fears could make countries less willing to agree to the measures described above.

In the longer term

The measures mentioned above do not completely rule out the risk of an arms race in outer space. They should rather be seen as the beginning of a process to achieve this objective. Additional measures would have to be studied and discussed: for example, how to reduce military activities in outer space. It should be investigated whether restrictions on certain systems can be introduced but it should also be determined which of them have an important stabilizing effect and can contribute to disarmament measures. Since many force amplifiers in outer space are used and will be used to enhance the terrestrial warfare capacity, this discussion would be of particular importance as a means of reducing the qualitative arms race on Earth.

The solution of problems relating to verification, not only with regard to space weapons but also in connection with existing or future disarmament agreements, would be facilitated by international satellite verification through an international satellite monitoring agency. The proposal by France for the establishment of such an agency should be further considered.

It would seem advisable to discuss if there are any risks of expanding the arms race—not only in outer space but also on Earth—in the proliferation of such space technologies as those related to the launching of space vehicles.

Measures should be undertaken to increase openness on all kinds of space activities, both military and non-military. The notification procedures in the 1975 Registration Convention should be further developed. Such measures would facilitate the prevention of an arms race in outer space, lead to increased confidence and make it easier to assess the risk of proliferation.

An increased involvement by more countries in peaceful outer space activities would strengthen the interest in keeping outer space free from armed conflicts. International co-operative efforts for this purpose should be stimulated.

VIII. Conclusion

The present trend towards an extension of the arms race into outer space are disturbing. They could severely hamper or endanger very considerable civilian use of outer space for a variety of purposes, both international and national. They could, furthermore, become destabilizing as far as the superpower nuclear weapon relationship is concerned. This may lead to a wasteful and futile arms race in outer space, which could easily become unmanageable. This would be in nobody's interest.

It is not yet too late to preclude such a development. But time is running short and some measures must be taken urgently.

References

1. Testimony before the Arms Control Sub-Committee of the US Senate Foreign Relations Committee by Eugene V. Rostow, Director of ACDA, 20 September 1982.
2. UN Document CD/9 of 26 March 1979.
3. UN Document A/36/192.

Paper 12. Arms control in outer space: the need for new legal action

Peter Jankowitsch*

Parlement, A1017 Vienna, Austria

I. Arms control in outer space: a short history

When the exploration of outer space demonstrated the attractiveness of its use for terrestrial purposes and the first space applications became feasible, an awareness immediately arose that space was to play an important part in matters connected with international peace and security.

The International Treaty Banning Nuclear Weapon Tests in the Atmosphere, in Outer Space and Under Water concluded in August 1963 is the first legally binding international instrument which acknowledges the fact that outer space constitutes a new dimension in international security, deserving attention not less than that given to terrestrial dimensions.

An even clearer link of this kind was created by the Treaty on Principles Governing the Activities of States in the Exploration and Use of Outer Space, Including the Moon and Other Celestial Bodies, concluded in 1967. Prohibiting the placing in orbit around the Earth or stationing in outer space of any objects carrying nuclear weapons or other weapons of mass destruction, it subjected outer space—in a manner relevant to its special nature—to a new body of arms control measures designed to limit the use of nuclear weapons as well as weapons of mass destruction.

While these treaty obligations certainly go some way towards creating a special status for outer space and could be seen as a first element in the building of a new and at least nuclear weapon-free 'sanctuary', they are not much more than an extraterrestrial extension of arms control measures designed for more traditional theatres of warfare. They are therefore only to

*Ambassador Jankowitsch is the Chairman of the Committee on the Peaceful Uses of Outer Space (COPUOS). The opinions expressed in this paper are those of the author and should not therefore be regarded as statements of policy of COPUOS, the Federal Government of Austria or other bodies to which the author is associated.

a minor degree addressed to the new technological possibilities offered by this medium.

A somewhat larger perspective is offered by the further provisions of article IV of the 1967 Outer Space Treaty, which explicitly outlaws "the establishment of military bases, installations and fortifications, the testing of any kinds of weapons and the conduct of military manoeuvres on celestial bodies". These provisions—although limited to celestial bodies, in particular the Moon— constitute a somewhat rudimentary but conceptually hopeful design of an outer space environment placed outside conventional terrestrial battlegrounds.

In particular, the 1967 Treaty appears as the fruit of international legislative procedures, conceived and negotiated *multilaterally* in the Committee on the Peaceful Uses of Outer Space of the UN General Assembly and later adopted by the Assembly itself. Two further international agreements that have added to the existing body of arms control provisions for outer space differ from the previous ones not only because they have resulted from bilateral arms control negotiations between the United States and the Soviet Union. They are the US–Soviet Treaty of 1972 on the limitation of anti-ballistic missile (ABM) systems, which also prohibits the deployment of ABM systems in outer space, and the SALT I Agreement. They both establish the principle of 'non-interference' with the so-called national technical means of verification.

The provisions contained in these two bilateral agreements constitute a new step in arms control for outer space, as for the first time they address themselves not only to the extension of weapon systems existing on Earth to outer space but also to the protection of technologies which—if we assume that national technical means of verification includes satellites—are typical for the space environment only.

Of the other international agreements and conventions relating to outer space—concerning the rescue of astronauts, international liability for damage caused by space objects, registration of space objects and the Moon Treaty[1]— the latter is of particular relevance for the subject under consideration. As far as arms control on the Moon—and other celestial bodies—is concerned it confirms and even somewhat extends the principles contained in the 1967 Outer Space Treaty.

A look at this existing body of space arms control provisions shows a picture which is certainly incomplete, and lacks a coherent approach; this becomes obvious when one considers that none of the treaties and agreements mentioned above is specifically and exclusively directed at arms control in space but contains such provisions rather as by-products of other concepts.

A critique of this body of law will also have to focus on the philosophy and motivation which lie behind these provisions. Here again, it is difficult to identify a unifying concept.

As pointed out above, some elements of these provisions suggest that there may indeed have been some effort towards the concept of a fully demilitarized 'sanctuary' totally removed from terrestrial concepts of arms control, deterrence and military balance. While also incomplete and not devoid of loopholes—which will be discussed below—the provisions relating to the

Moon and other celestial bodies perhaps bear closest resemblance to the concept of sanctuarization.

Other provisions, however, suggest the idea that outer space has rather been regarded as a kind of support area for Earth-based military—and, of course, civilian—activities but that at least some specific rules and regulations should serve to govern its uses.

This conceptual ambiguity is hardly surprising if one considers the diversity of the actors concerned, a diversity clearest not perhaps among the architects of multilateral treaties but between the two major space powers themselves.

Difficult as it may be to identify some coherent concept or philosophy behind these various provisions, it appears, all the same, that—with all caution that has to be taken offering judgement in such matters—they all suggest a measure of restraint in the military uses of outer space; even the incomplete measures adopted originally were supposed to rule out the conversion of outer space into a full-scale battlefield of the future.

While an assessment of this nature would allow for some optimism—especially as it would suggest a possibility to build on this existing body of law—a number of reservations have to be made which produce a picture of a much less benevolent nature.

First of all, it is striking that progress in concluding new agreements in this field has been virtually nil for over a decade. In particular, talks between the United States and the Soviet Union on ASAT weapons, which were conducted in three rounds from June 1978 to June 1979, were suspended without a tangible result. It was hoped at the time that an ASAT agreement would be reached that could be signed at the same time as the SALT II Treaty.

While the suspension of these talks owed perhaps more to the world political atmosphere of the times—in particular the Soviet invasion of Afghanistan—than to the subject matter itself, the fact remains that no serious effort has since been made to reopen these negotiations.

The same lack of progress has characterized the various multilateral fora which have been landed with the problem of arms control in outer space. Chief among them, the two Special Sessions of the General Assembly of the United Nations devoted to Disarmament, while not failing to "recognize the dangers of a potential arms race in Outer Space" and while "calling for further measures to be taken and international negotiations to be held in order to prevent such a development", did not produce any new agreements on the matter.

In view of the remarkable reluctance of many of those concerned to seriously tackle the issue of arms control in outer space, it is not surprising that it was only in 1982 that the Committee on Disarmament finally came to the conclusion that the question of "prevention of an arms race in Outer Space" should be put on its agenda.

The Committee on the Peaceful Uses of Outer Space, while inhibited by its present mandate from taking up matters of arms control in space, became in the meantime one of the main fora for the expression of international concern on developments in the less peaceful uses of outer space. Similarly, the Second

United Nations Conference on the Exploration and Peaceful Uses of Outer Space, held in Vienna in August 1982, urged in its report "all nations, in particular those with major space capabilities . . . to contribute actively to the goal of preventing an arms race in Outer Space and to refrain from any action contrary to that aim".

These concerns are easily explained. While, on the one hand, no progress concerning new arms control was achieved, developments of an ominous nature began to cast strong doubt on the willingness of the main space powers to adhere to the doctrine of restraint in military matters which had heretofore characterized their behaviour in outer space. These doubts arise as much in view of concrete developments as in view of plans and concepts which are the subject of public debate in various major countries.

II. Military uses of outer space: a step into the unknown?

Present public concern about the militarization of outer space has its roots more in the future than in the past.

While military use has been made of outer space for nearly a quarter of a century, superpower competition was not conducted with weaponry but rather with a wide variety of military support systems. Almost as soon as satellites were put into orbit, important military applications were found for them. In many cases they offered possibilities not realizable by any other means.

As a paper presented by Canada to the Committee on Disarmament in August 1982[2] points out, one of the most important military uses of space consists of warning systems against ballistic missiles, especially those with intercontinental range. The most effective of these systems depend on satellites able to detect heat from the launching rocket. Today, three geostationary satellites can cover nearly all of the Earth's area.

Photoreconnaissance satellites provide the most effective means of verifying arms control agreements but also of observing military deployments and operations.

For a number of years, these and similar space programmes have assumed major significance for strategic deterrence. However, more recently—as the Canadian paper points out—there have been important new advances in the military uses of outer space.

While some of these developments can perhaps still be categorized as more sophisticated support systems for global deterrence (such as systems which increase the accuracy of ballistic missiles, whether ground-, air- or sea-launched, or systems which increase the reliability of warning systems), others bear an unmistakably offensive character, which makes it difficult to perceive them as elements of stabilization.

This is not only true of anti-satellite (ASAT) satellites but, in particular, of new technologies which may have great potential as strategic weaponry, especially in space, and which can be combined under the heading of directed-energy weapons. The most advanced and the one with probably the highest potential is the high-energy laser; the other type of directed energy weapon is the particle beam.

Both of these weapons have potential uses for defence against ballistic missiles as well as for the destruction of satellites and in both cases the weapon could be mounted on a space vehicle or on the surface of the Earth.

In general, many military as well as civilian functions are coming to depend more and more on Earth satellites for their operation. This is particularly true for the function of long distance communications.

It therefore does not come as a surprise that both the United States and—perhaps to a somewhat lesser degree—the Soviet Union have developed a high degree of dependence on space systems for command and control functions. It is estimated that approximately 70 per cent of US overseas military communications are transmitted via satellite and that consequently both countries' war-fighting capabilities are strongly affected by space systems.

For the purposes of this discussion it is not very relevant to what extent the USA and the USSR exhibit what has been called an 'asymmetry of dependence' regarding space systems and which country appears to be more vulnerable against attack on its space-based systems. Discussion of these facts might certainly be relevant if one merely wished to explain why one country has preceded the other in the development of ASAT systems. In the present circumstances, it is important to note, however, that military uses of outer space have reached a qualitatively new dimension and are about to take a dangerous turn. From a basically stabilizing function these uses are about to assume destabilizing characteristics with immensely hazardous consequences not only on outer space itself.

The question therefore arises what action can be taken to avert a trend that has already become firmly established. The central problem seems to be one of security—or perhaps immunity—for modern space-based systems, which have assumed such importance for international peace and security.

The conventional response to this question seems to be one of a purely military character, namely to prevent a threat to these systems by devising new and potentially threatening systems of 'space deterrence'.

While this does not, on the surface, seem to be a major departure from other systems of deterrence, especially the ones operating on Earth, the particular qualities of outer space and the increasing sophistication of systems now in the research and planning stages cast a deep shadow of doubt on these developments.

Other avenues have to be explored, therefore, to ascertain by what other means not only the required degree of security can be found but, even more importantly, what can be done to preserve outer space as the predominantly peaceful environment that it has been so far.

III. Space security through treaty: the unexplored avenue

If an arms race in outer space is now clearly in sight, much of the blame must certainly go to the inadequacy of existing international treaties. This inadequacy results not only from the fact that the area of weapons deployment they cover is insufficient, but also from a number of in-built ambiguities. Thus the only serious limitation placed on military activity in outer space by the 1967 Outer Space Treaty concerns nuclear weapons or other weapons of mass destruction. This limitation, important as it may seem in a general context, appears of reduced value in a space context as it has now been clearly established that any nuclear explosion in space would not only cripple or destroy enemy satellites but also the satellites of the aggressor.

It can therefore be argued that, quite to the contrary, the Treaty authorizes—or at least tolerates—other military uses of outer space.

As far as the principle of 'non-interference' with national technical means of verification of arms control treaties is concerned, it is shrouded in a mass of ambiguity which greatly reduces its usefulness. First of all, it is not clear from this terminology whether satellites can indeed be safely included in such a category. While a declaration by President Carter of 1 October 1978 establishes an unequivocal link between military observation satellites and national means of verification, the position of the other contracting partner remains in doubt.

But even if the Soviet position were in complete harmony with the position of the United States many more questions would remain. Some of these questions are discussed in a chapter entitled 'Immunity of Space Vehicles' of paper CD/375 presented by France to the Committee on Disarmament.[3]

In particular, the question is raised whether such immunity is subject to any restrictive interpretations concerning the scope of acceptable verification or whether any type of observation capability would thus be protected.

A further question of a perhaps more hypothetical character is the one concerning the effect on third countries of this US–Soviet understanding on the inviolability of national technical means of verification.

A satisfactory reply to these questions—one that basically confirms legitimacy of these satellite observation activities—appears of interest also in view of the provisions of article I and article III of the Outer Space Treaty, which state that outer space should be used in accordance with international law, in conformity with the Charter of the United Nations and in the interest of international peace and security. Insofar as the role they play can be considered as one of a legitimate nature, they would certainly enjoy a higher degree of protection through international law.

There is no doubt therefore that specific new treaty provisions are required to supplement the existing body of law and introduce what is lacking at present in security for conduct of activities in outer space that serve international peace and security.

Before discussing the most appropriate form such a treaty could take it also seems imperative to have a very clear idea of the overall objectives of a new body of international space law.

In defining the objectives of new principles of space law designed to prevent an arms race in outer space, it seems imperative to combine pragmatism with a more long-range view of the problem. The pragmatic view certainly commends an avenue in which a major focus would be put on the most immediate threat, that constituted by the imminence of ASAT weapons. The long-term view would, however, also be required to deal with a next generation of space weapons, such as directed-energy weapons, which appear to be far advanced on the drawing board.

Inclusion of such types of weapons in new arms control treaties seems indicated even if one were to come to the conclusion that at least some of them could be considered 'weapons of mass destruction' and would therefore already have been banned from space by the 1967 Outer Space Treaty.

But in the last analysis, what new space legislation should aim at is certainly more than the explicit banning from outer space of the weapon systems that are at present known. The ultimate objective should be as close as possible to the one that the 1967 Outer Space Treaty—in spirit if not in letter—has been trying to achieve but with limited success: the establishment of outer space as an environment dedicated to activities which lead to an increase in international security, rather than becoming an additional source of instability.

As a letter from Dean Rusk to the Chairman of the Sub-Committee on Arms Control, Oceans, International Operations and Environment of the Committee on Foreign Relations of the US Senate suggests, international law-makers in the mid-1960s effectively thought that through adoption of the Outer Space Treaty they had "gone a long way toward removing Outer Space from Military competition", much as they had succeeded in removing a large chunk of the Earth from the arms race through the conclusion of the Antarctic Treaty.

Adhering to considerations of this kind would certainly increase the scope of new treaties and make the negotiation process more complex and more lengthy. On the other hand, the history of previous space treaties not only demonstrates the gravity of loopholes which are left open if only partial solutions are sought, it also provides evidence that it is not easy to supplement one treaty by another in chronological order, as negotiation processes might easily be interrupted by changes in the international atmosphere and other adverse factors.

Divorcing outer space from the arms race, both now and in the future, therefore appears to be a task of considerable magnitude. Moving beyond the ASAT threat to space weapons and weapons which can be operated in space would certainly place enormous strain on the future negotiator who might have to include a wide variety of options. Such a treaty might have to include—as was pointed out in testimony before the Arms Control Sub-Committee of the US Senate—both "broad prohibitions and careful functional prohibitions".

Among such prohibitions are those concerning the testing, production, deployment or use of any space-based, air-based, sea-based or ground-based weapon system that might be designed to damage, destroy or interfere with the functioning of spacecraft.

Conversely, such a treaty might also prohibit the stationing in orbit around the Earth, on any celestial body or at any other location in outer space, of any weapon that has been designed to inflict injury or cause damage on the Earth, in the atmosphere or on objects placed in space.

Explosions, collisions, close approaches, electromagnetic interferences and perhaps even atomic power sources in space would become the object of further prohibitions and limitations.

While some case can be made against a treaty that appears to have been weighted down too heavily by detail, expanding technologies in outer space certainly require a considerable broadening of legislative targets as against the more limited possibilities that existed at the time of the drafting of the Outer Space Treaty in the mid-1960s.

While a new treaty—or a series of new treaties to be negotiated and concluded contemporaneously—will therefore require a considerable degree of sophistication in addressing the elimination of present and future weapon systems from space, most of the broad political or philosophical objectives which should be inherent in new space legislation can already be found in the 1967 Outer Space Treaty, as well as in the Moon Treaty, the last—for the time being—in the series of multilateral treaties governing the activities of states in outer space.

IV. Treaty alternatives for a new security in space

In order to build a coherent new body of space law that can assure a new quality of security in space, various steps, for which various alternatives exist, have to be taken. In the first place, it seems imperative to consolidate and fortify elements of security that already exist in present treaties. One such element is the immunity of satellites, embodied in the principle of non-interference with national technical means of verification. That, however, for the present, rests exclusively on bilateral agreements. This immunity should be made more specific and should be broadened and extended beyond the scope of bilateral agreements to apply to all satellites that respond to the basic criteria of space security.

In this case, as in others, it therefore appears that there should be a movement towards a multilateral approach as opposed to a purely bilateral one. While there may be virtue—especially in the short run and in order to operate against time constraints—in occasionally adopting the bilateral approach, a long-range solution will certainly have to be built on the broad basis of international consensus that only the lengthier but more solid multilateral negotiation processes can provide.

In this regard the 1967 Outer Space Treaty appears as the convenient point of departure for any new legislative effort. A first effort has been made by Italy in proposing—for some years now—an Additional Protocol to the Treaty. The virtues of this proposal are that it leaves the Treaty intact over wide areas and merely seeks to add such new elements as would effectively prevent an arms race in outer space.

An updating of this proposal, which further seeks to link the Outer Space Treaty with other relevant international instruments such as the Convention on the prohibition of military and any other hostile use of environmental modification techniques, would certainly constitute an interesting avenue which merits further enquiry. An Additional Protocol could also endeavour to bring into the multilateral realm pertinent provisions of existing bilateral treaties.

A further avenue would be an even wider and more ambitious drafting of the Treaty—whether in the form of different Additional Protocols or by an entirely new draft. Such a redraft might seek to expand existing guarantees for the peaceful uses of outer space by adopting language similar to the one used in articles I and VII.3 of the 1959 Antarctic Treaty.

Article I of that agreement provides that: "Antarctica shall be used for peaceful purposes only. There shall be prohibited, *inter alia*, any measures of a military nature, such as the establishment of military bases or fortifications, the carrying out of military manoeuvres, as well as the testing of any kinds of weapons". As a verification measure, article VII.3 stipulates that "all areas of Antarctica including all stations, installations and ... points of discharging cargos or personnel in Antarctica, shall be open at all times to inspection by any ... observers ...".

While there are certainly striking differences—in strategic terms as well— between Antarctica and outer space, which explain the willingness of the major powers to subject Antarctica to a regime much more advanced than the one at present operating for outer space, there is still some reason to pursue the possibility of aligning arms control measures for these two areas.

New international legislation should also build on experience and proposals that have emerged over the last decade with a view to strengthening various security arrangements.

In the field of verification, which remains a centrepiece of any new treaty system, alternatives to purely national technical means of verification (i.e., more advanced forms involving a higher degree of international co-operation), should be explored. Such an alternative is offered by the proposal to establish an international satellite monitoring agency, designed *inter alia* for the verification of compliance with arms limitation agreements and for purposes of crisis control. The positive effects of the establishment of such an agency have been underlined by a report of a group of experts to the Second Special Session on Disarmament. This report also concluded that its installation would be technically, legally and financially feasible.

While we are certainly still a long way from achieving international consensus on such a proposal, a new treaty could create a legal basis for the Agency's establishment while at the same time keeping the national forms of verification, which might gradually be superseded by international forms of verification.

There is also a case for incorporating various confidence-building measures into new treaty arrangements: such measures could include increased international transparency of national space activities by requiring more precise information on the characteristics and missions of space objects and by encouraging a resumption of genuine international co-operation in outer space, such as joint missions, sharing of research data, and so on.

New legislation should also draw relevant conclusions from the much increased human presence in space: too much emphasis has been placed in previous space treaties on technology rather than on the human presence, which needs adequate protection to harness its potential for initiative and judgement.

Finally, it is possible to supplement the present provisions of the Outer Space Treaty on arms control with a separate agreement of the kind proposed to the General Assembly by the Soviet Union in 1981. A similar approach—although limited to ASAT weapons—is contained in a draft treaty presented by the Union of Concerned Scientists.[4]

Criticism of the Soviet draft has centred less on its methodological approach than on the contents of its provisions, which seem to leave considerable liberty to states to deploy anti-satellite systems. In its paper presented to the Committee on Disarmament, France, for one, charged that the present wording of the draft would "have the effect of authorizing states to take the law into their own hands in Outer Space on the basis of their suspicions, thus creating mistrust and insecurity for all ...".

At the present time there is no US draft before the Committee on Disarmament, although the USA supported Resolution 37/83 adopted by the General Assembly in December 1982, which centred on the question of negotiating effective and verifiable agreements aimed at preventing an arms race in outer space, taking into account all existing and future proposals designed to meet this objective. It further requested the Committee on Disarmament to continue substantive consideration, as a matter of priority, of the question of negotiating an effective and verifiable agreement to prohibit anti-satellite systems.

Both the Soviet draft and the draft of the Union of Concerned Scientists, as well as the resolutions addressed by the General Assembly to the Committee on Disarmament, therefore seem to favour an approach that would separate general legislation on the nature and function of outer space—such as is constituted by the 1967 Outer Space Treaty—from treaties limited to arms control aspects only. One reason for this approach might be a purely functional one in that the competence of a body such as the Committee on Disarmament is clearly needed to elaborate arms control provisions which are closely linked to overall arms control considerations.

On the other hand, a strong case can be made for a single, unified instrument encompassing all relevant provisions of international law relating to outer space.

The way to achieve this might be an expanded Outer Space Treaty comprising general rules for the conduct of activities of states in outer space with reviewed and modernized arms control provisions. As no single forum of the United Nations appears to be in a position to draft such a Treaty, such a task might be given to a Review Conference, once the Committee on Disarmament and, concerning other aspects, the Committee on the Peaceful Uses of Outer Space have completed their respective tasks.

While there are therefore a considerable number of alternatives which can be pursued to reach the goal of new space security through universally accepted broadly based treaties, there are also a number of contingencies which favour a short-term approach. This is the imminence of the introduction of permanent ASAT systems into space which would heavily prejudice any further negotiations and create entirely new, unfavourable conditions for the preservation of outer space as a peaceful environment.

It is here that the bilateral alternative might have to be adopted, even on a temporary basis and with a view to later incorporation in a multilateral system of treaties. The time still available to negotiate even such an alternative might be too short. Non-binding norms or codes might be resorted to which might facilitate subsequent treaty negotiations.

One such alternative would be an agreed short-term moratorium, such as the one used prior to the negotiation of the 1963 Partial Test Ban Treaty. The development and testing of new technology could be placed under such a moratorium until negotiations on a treaty have made sufficient progress.

Another avenue which has also been used in the past is the adoption of unilateral initiatives in anticipation of a similar response by the other side.

Finally, there is a possibility—less accessible perhaps in the present case—of voluntary acceptance of informal restraints related to non-binding norms, codes or unratified treaties. Such a course was chosen in the past when the USA and the USSR chose to adhere to the terms of the SALT II Treaty, although it never formally came into force.

In any case, past international practice is certainly not devoid of means that the main actors concerned could adopt if mutually inspired by willingness to refrain from irreversible steps towards an arms race in outer space.

V. Conclusions

The 1967 Outer Space Treaty, often called the 'Magna Charta' of outer space, while not having outlived its usefulness, is now clearly in need of fundamental overhaul.

A new 'Magna Charta' has to be drafted which not only encompasses what has happened in outer space over the last 20 years but which can also avert the imminent danger of an arms race in outer space.

On the way to this new instrument of law, which will also bring a new sense of security to this environment and ensure man's presence there, a number of contingency measures will have to be taken to leave the option of peaceful development open.

Such a course of action will require vigorous interaction between various fora in the United Nations system and also between the main actors on the space scene today, who bear for the time being a disproportionate amount of responsibility.

Their best interests, however, will not be served by the mindless translation of conventional means to achieve security in outer space but by the patient search for a new security agenda which will bear dividends not only for themselves but also for the rest of mankind. In this search they will not be alone but assisted by many nations which have begun to share a burning concern for the future of one of the great new fields of human endeavour, which still offers such enormous promise.

References

1. *Agreement Govering the Activities of States on the Moon and Other Celestial Bodies*, UN Document, General Assembly Resolution 34/68, Annex (1979).
2. 'Arms Control and Outer Space', paper presented to the Committee on Disarmament, CD/320, August 1982, pp. 4–5.
3. 'Prevention of an arms race in outer space', a working document submitted by France to the Committee on Disarmament, CD/375, 14 April 1983.
4. *Anti-Satellite Weapons: Arms Control or Arms Race*? (Union of Concerned Scientists, Cambridge, MA, 1983).

Paper 13. Averting a new round in the militarization of outer space: an urgent problem and goal

Evgeniy Velikhov,* Andrei Kokoshin† and Alexei Vassiliev‡

I. Introduction

The military use of space in the West began with the deployment of satellites for communication, navigation, early warning, surveillance, and so on (see Part I). In some cases, taking into account the realities of the present strategic balance, such a use of outer space can be of deterrent, stabilizing character because it provides verification of strategic arms control agreements and early warning.

However, the early 1980s are characterized by the beginning of a new, more dangerous stage in the military use of space. For example, from our point of view, there is a clearly destabilizing aspect to the deployment (by 1987) of a constellation of NAVSTAR satellites, aimed at increasing the accuracy of intercontinental ballistic missiles (ICBMs), submarine-launched ballistic missiles (SLBMs) and other nuclear-capable missiles up to 10 m circular error probable. The incorporation of this satellite system into the structure of the US strategic forces cannot be explained from the point of view of strengthening second-strike forces, which do not need the degree of accuracy that the NAVSTAR system would provide. It appears that the capability to carry out a pre-emptive first strike is being created, which can lead the US leadership to increased illusions that it is possible to 'win' a nuclear war.

There is growing concern over plans for the intensified use of satellites by the United States as one of the most important components of anti-submarine

*Vice-President, USSR Academy of Sciences; Chairman, Committee of Soviet Scientists Against Nuclear War.
†Deputy Director and Head of the Political-Military Department, Institute of US and Canadian Studies of the USSR Academy of Sciences; Vice-Chairman, Committee of Soviet Scientists Against Nuclear War.
‡Head of Section, Political-Military Department of the Institute of US and Canadian Studies; Senior Expert, Committee of Soviet Scientists Against Nuclear War.

forces, the uncontrolled development of which can, at least, raise doubts over survivability of the sea leg of the strategic triad and thus lessen strategic stability.

Lately the US militarization of outer space has gained a qualitatively new and more menacing dimension with the possibility of launching offensive weapons into space which can be used to hit a wide range of space, air and ground targets.

II. *Space-based anti-missile systems: a grave threat*

The greatest long-term threat lies in the possible creation by the United States of a wide-scale anti-missile system based on outer space echelons. The supporters of this system in the USA assert that it will create an effective defence against massive nuclear attack and allow escape from the 'balance of terror', that is, the strategic situation characterized by the ability of the confronting sides to inflict 'mutual assured destruction'. They say an intention of such a system is to shift the centre of gravity of military rivalry into outer space and thus deliver people on Earth from the role of nuclear hostages, moving possible war activities far from the Earth's biosphere.

The Working Group of the Committee of Soviet Scientists Against Nuclear War has carried out special research into this problem. Attention was focused on analysing the capability of different kinds of directed-energy weapon (using electromagnetic waves or particle beams) to destroy ICBMs and SLBMs in a single hit. As possible components of a space-based anti-missile system (SBAMS), US political, military and academic circles have studied lasers in the infra-red, visible or ultra-violet range, X-ray lasers powered by nuclear explosion, high-energy particle accelerators and ultra-high frequency generators. These potential weapon systems are, evidently, at substantially different stages of technical development.

A most likely candidate for a potential US SBAMS in the near future is the hydrogen fluoride chemical laser. The creation of military space stations carrying chemical lasers will be very difficult and labour-consuming, both scientifically and technologically. According to our calculations, 60 MW lasers will be needed, not the 5–10 MW lasers that have been mentioned; accordingly, the mirror should be 15 m instead of 4 m in diameter. Such a station (taking into account the necessary supplies of fuel for the laser) would weigh about 800 tonnes.

A lot of unsolved problems are connected with the creation of a reliable system for target searching, tracking and aiming and also with determining if the target has been destroyed. Moreover, there are problems with the directed-energy source operation system.

More than 40 flights of the US space shuttle would be needed to assemble an 800-tonne military station in polar orbit. It was calculated that an additional protection of ICBMs against laser beams would necessitate increasing the power of the laser by a factor of three to four and the diameter of the mirror by a factor of two to three, and it would mean an accordingly drastic increase in the weight of the station or the number of stations comprising the SBAMS. (If only 800-tonne military laser stations are taken into consideration, their number should be about 50.) The creation and deployment of such a system using a chemical laser, intended for defence against a massive nuclear first strike, would cost about 500 billion dollars. But it would form only one layer of defence and could let through a lot of missiles carrying hundreds of powerful nuclear warheads, even if it functions perfectly well and there are no anti-SBAMS. Theoretically it is possible to lower the number of penetrating warheads by making a multi-layered anti-missile system, which would also include a land-based component, but this would only occur if (and this is absolutely impossible) during the several decades necessary to create and deploy the anti-missile system the strategic forces of the other side were frozen. A lot of facts and calculations prove that any outer space anti-missile system—whether it is based on chemical lasers, X-ray lasers or neutral particle accelerators—will be vulnerable to different combinations of countermeasures, both active and passive. Thus the system capable of neutralizing even the multi-layered SBAMS will cost 1–2 per cent of the SBAMS, according to the preliminary calculations of the Working Group of the Committee of Soviet Scientists.

All the above-mentioned facts lead to the quite definite conclusion that a large-scale anti-missile system cannot be taken as an effective means of defence against a massive first strike. It can spawn only unfounded hopes that it can lessen damage caused by a retaliatory strike (second strike).

This justifies our assertion that the creation of a large-scale anti-missile system, together with the development of such systems as MX, Trident II (D-5), Pershing II, NAVSTAR and so on, is another big and dangerous step in the direction of creating a first-strike capability.

The examination of a prospective US anti-missile weapon system as a means to achieve first-strike capabilities is also stimulated by the fact that the USA still refuses to make a commitment of no-first-use of nuclear weapons.[1] The Soviet Union, realizing the importance of strengthening strategic stability in the worsening international politico-military situation, pledged in July 1982, unilaterally, not to be the first to use nuclear weapons. This has become an integral part of Soviet military doctrine. According to this commitment, even greater attention is being given to training the Soviet military forces with the goals of preventing the escalation of a military conflict into a nuclear one: for example, stricter parameters in defining the personnel of military forces; and organizing stricter control to prevent unauthorized launching of a nuclear weapon, from tactical to strategic.

It is worth mentioning that the various US outer space echelons of an anti-missile system (with beam and missile weapons), which are under active consideration in the circles close to the Reagan Administration, can be taken not only as means of destroying strategic missiles of the other side after their launching, but also as direct weapons for destroying land-based targets. They can be seen, in fact, as first-strike weapons.

An outer space anti-missile weapon system, deployed even on a relatively small scale, can be treated also as an anti-satellite (ASAT) weapon. The creation and the deployment of ASAT weapon systems (both outer space and land-based) can also affect strategic stability and the politico-military situation in a negative way.

III. Anti-satellite weapons

The deployment of US anti-satellite weapons will negatively affect the prospects of achieving agreements between the Soviet Union and the United States on a freeze, limitation and radical reductions of nuclear weapons.

One of the main arguments put forward by the US proponents of ASAT systems is based on the allegation that the Soviet Union, by rapidly developing such systems, is forcing the United States to follow suit.

But numerous facts contradict this assertion. Development of anti-satellite weapons began in the United States in the late 1950s. Due to guidance system inefficiency, the first US land-based ASAT missiles were supposed to be equipped with nuclear warheads that were to affect, in the first place, space vehicle electronic systems. In early 1963 President Kennedy approved plans for developing "active anti-satellite forces". From 1963 to 1966 the US Army deployed several Nike-Zeus missiles within the framework of Program 505, capable of destroying satellites at a height of several hundred kilometres. In 1964 President Johnson declared that the USA had another operational anti-satellite system deployed on the Johnston atoll in the Pacific Ocean. By this he meant the Air Force system based on the Thor missile and developed within the framework of Program 437. The system was of a longer range. It is known that it was tested at least 16 times and was on a five-minute alert up to 1975. According to some information, it can be reactivated within six months.

Information is available on at least two more US systems of that time. In April 1959, the Air Force started to test the ASAT missile Bold Orion which was launched from a B-47 bomber, and in 1962 Naval Forces carried out two similar launches from F-4 fighters within Program Hi-Ho.

The above-mentioned argument of the US anti-satellite proponents looks even less persuasive if one takes into account the clear position of the Soviet Union: the Soviet leadership declared in August 1983 that it first, unilaterally pledged not to test and deploy anti-satellite weapons and second, proposed to reach an agreement on complete renunciation of new anti-satellite systems and the elimination of all the existing ones.

Estimating possible strategic consequences of ASAT weapon deployment, it should be mentioned that, if they are used, the attacked side will not see this as an isolated act of aggression but would expect massive use of different kinds of nuclear weapons to follow. An attempt to destroy satellites of the other side (or even an attempt to blind them for some time), can be treated as the first step in waging an unlimited nuclear war. The destruction of satellites gives the attacked side the right, without waiting for nuclear attacks at launching complexes and other targets, to hit all possible targets of the side that started military actions against satellites.

The situation of constant threat to the existence of satellites caused by ASAT deployments can negatively affect the prospects of achieving agreements on the freeze of nuclear weapons, their meaningful reduction, and the prospects of the verification of these agreements.

The beginning of the testing of the components of the F-15 launched ASAT system in the USA means that the Reagan Administration, initiating an arms race in this field, is, in fact, making basic national technical means less reliable. It serves as further proof that it is not seeking to reach an agreement on nuclear arms limitation and reduction. Examination of the US plans for the deployment of offensive weapons in outer space shows that they are not based on an objective consideration of the present balance of forces in the international arena nor on the real scientific and technological capabilities of potential enemies; instead they rely on an illusion of scientific and technological superiority over the Soviet Union and its allies. The Socialist countries have proved many times that their existing economic and scientific-technological capacities enable them in the shortest possible time to build any weapon system which potential enemies stake their hopes on. There can be no monopoly on this or that weapon system, and to hope that the Soviet Union will let any country be superior is a dangerous miscalculation.

IV. A treaty prohibiting the use of force in and from outer space

Fully aware of the scale of the threat being caused by the militarization of outer space in the 1980s, the Soviet Union, in 1981, put forward a proposal for an international agreement on the prohibition on the deployment of any weapon system in outer space. In the draft treaty submitted by the Soviet Union to the 36th Session of the General Assembly of the UN there were provisions that the states parties pledge (a) not to put into outer space any type of weapon, (b) not to place these weapons on the celestial bodies and (c) not to station them in any other possible way in outer space, including on reusable manned space vehicles of an existing type or of any other types which may be developed in the future.

On 9 December 1981 the 36th Session of the General Assembly adopted Resolution 36/99 on this issue on the basis of the Draft Resolution submitted by Angola, Bulgaria, Cuba, the German Democratic Republic, Hungary, Laos, Mongolia, Poland, the Soviet Union and Viet Nam; 123 countries voted for it and 21 (the USA, its NATO allies and others) abstained. The resolution calls on the Committee on Disarmament to start negotiations on working out an appropriate agreement to avert the spread of the arms race into outer space. Because of the negative position of the United States and its allies in 1982, the Committee could neither start the negotiations nor form a working organ of the Committee to hold the negotiations.

At the 37th Session of the General Assembly this issue was raised for the second time. As a result, in December 1982, on the basis of the Joint Draft Resolution of the Socialist and non-aligned countries, Resolution 37/83 was adopted: 'Prevention of an arms race in outer space'. The resolution was supported by 138 countries, and 7 abstained. The USA voted against it and continued to block the work of the Committee on this issue.

Taking into account that time waits for no-one, the Soviet Union decided not to stand still and to move further. It proposed a treaty prohibiting the use or threat of force in outer space and by space objects against targets on Earth, which was submitted in August 1983 to the 38th Session of the General Assembly.

An important feature of the Draft Treaty is the combination of politico-legal obligations of states not to use force against one another in outer space and from outer space with concrete measures directed at prohibiting the introduction of weapons into outer space.

Article 1 prohibits "the use or threat of force against space objects in orbit around the Earth, on celestial bodies or stationed in outer space in any other manner".[2] Besides, it would be prohibited to use or threaten to use force by utilization of the space objects themselves.

It was also envisaged that the member states pledge not to destroy, damage or interfere with normal functioning and not to change the flight trajectory of other countries' space objects. The commitments would mean prohibiting some actions in outer space and from outer space which are qualified as the use of force in international law. The multilateral treaty proposed by the Soviet Union would make the principle of no-use of force in outer space more concrete.

The new Draft contains wider concrete measures, the realization of which would make it impossible for the arms race to extend into outer space and become a source of military threat. While in 1981 the Soviet Union proposed that the member states pledge not to place, station and deploy weapons in outer space, in the new Draft Treaty the USSR considers it essential to come to an agreement on a complete prohibition on testing and deploying any space-based weapon to be used against targets on Earth, in the atmosphere or in outer space.

It was proposed not to use as means of destruction the existing space objects in orbit around the Earth, on celestial bodies or stationed in outer space in any other way.

Moreover, according to article 2.4, the parties would undertake not to test or create new anti-satellite systems and to destroy any anti-satellite systems that they may already have.

In such a way, the new Soviet Draft Treaty is aimed at taking more radical measures to prevent an arms race in outer space, because it envisages prohibiting the initial stages in the creation of outer space weapons.

The new Soviet initiative reflects the Soviet position that it is much easier to prohibit weapons that have not yet been created than ones that are already operational. It is more effective to prevent an arms race from spilling over to the regions where it has never been, than struggling for the prohibition on some weapon systems in militarized outer space.

Verification of a potential agreement based on the Soviet Draft Treaty on the prohibition of the use of force in outer space and from outer space against Earth was treated with thorough consideration. It contains the following concrete provisions on verification: (a) it would be by national technical means, and (b) the states would consult and co-operate on any problems which may arise in respect of the goals of the Treaty or connected with the implementation of its provisions. The consultations and co-operation could be undertaken by using appropriate international procedures within the framework of the UN and in accordance with its Charter. These procedures may include the use of the Consultative Committee of the member states; in fact, any member state can appoint a representative to the Committee.

In this way, the Soviet proposals are not confined to national technical means, which are attainable only by certain states, but provide for other means of verification involving all the interested states. Verification is as important for the Soviet Union as for any other country, including the USA and other NATO countries.

V. Conclusion

The world community has demonstrated growing concern over the transition of the military use of space to a more advanced and more dangerous level. Representatives of many countries discussed in a constructive way the Soviet Draft Treaty on the prohibition on the use of force in outer space and from outer space against Earth at the 38th Session of the General Assembly. A resolution was adopted on the 'Prohibition on an arms race in outer space' at the initiative of a group of non-aligned countries, and after some appropriate changes, they were joined as co-sponsors by 20 other states.

The Resolution calls for urgent steps to be taken to avert an arms race in outer space. It suggests that the Conference on Disarmament (formally known as the Committee on Disarmament) consider this issue without any delay and from different angles, taking into account all the proposals as well as the points of view expressed during discussions at the 38th Session. The Resolution also sets a concrete timetable for the creation of a special working group on this issue. It was to be formed by the Conference on Disarmament at the beginning of its 1984 session. The urgent and concrete character of the adopted decisions, as well as the intention to consider this issue in all its aspects, is in contradiction to the US course aimed at accelerating the militarization of outer space; in fact, the USA was the only country that voted against the Resolution.

It is quite clear that a solution must be found to such an extremely important problem as the prevention of an arms race in space. Outer space is the inheritance of all mankind. It is necessary to do everything possible to make it free of all kinds of weapon and to prevent it from becoming an arena of military confrontation. The people on Earth must be relieved of the threat coming from outer space.

Notes

1. *Editors Note*: Since nuclear explosion-generated X-ray lasers are considered as third generation nuclear weapons, the declaration of no-first-use could be taken to include a commitment not to use these ASAT weapons. Such a declaration could be extended to cover all categories of ASAT weapons, particularly in the absence of an ASAT treaty. After all, the USSR has declared a moratorium on ASAT testing.
2. See Appendix 2, page 245 for the official translation of the Soviet treaty proposal.

Paper 14. Verification possibilities should an ASAT treaty materialize

Michel Guionnet

Centre National d'Etudes Spatiales, 129, rue de l'Université, 75007 Paris, France

I. Introduction

A treaty banning the development, manufacture and use of anti-satellite weapons is doubtless extremely desirable, in view of the widespread use of space for peaceful purposes and the considerable cost of a race to 'harden' systems and to build aggressive and defensive weaponry, to say nothing of the destabilizing effect of those developments.

However, the enforcement of such a treaty will be very difficult to verify and it is the limits of possible controls which will define its contours. When a satellite breaks down it will often be difficult to ascertain whether it is as a result of an attack and, if so, who the culprit is. ASAT devices cannot always be distinguished from peaceful systems or systems designated for other applications (anti-aircraft or anti-ballistic missile, for example).

In the paper we shall examine these different aspects in the light of present perspectives of possible ASAT attacks.

II. A satellite failure: the result of aggression or merely a break-down?

Aggression can take many forms: for example, a head-on collision would undoubtedly shatter the target satellite, or alter its trajectory. The accuracy of existing optical or radar observation equipment enables such phenomena to be detected from the ground. To detect pellet spraying, laser beam heating or irradiation, either a 'black box' could be flown on board the satellite (which would detect such events and relay information to the ground) or the satellite could be recovered for a post-mortem analysis.

Some aggression can be temporary in nature; for example, electromagnetic jamming, sensor blinding. The ensuing loss of control would lead to the loss of the satellite, even though all its elements were in working order: this would occur, for instance, if a spacecraft's attitude could no longer be controlled because of jamming on the command up-link and if its antennae were pointed in such a way that it could no longer receive command signals. One can also imagine hostile commands being sent which would deplete the spacecraft's propellant or energy reserves. The telemetry system, if it were still operating, could provide circumstantial evidence but rarely positive proof. The fact that a hostile act can be carried out covertly and anonymously can encourage such practices. Sensitive military satellites are undoubtedly fitted with black boxes hardened against possible attacks and designed to dispel any doubts. The possibilities of a close look, or even recovery (which currently can be contemplated only for spacecraft in low Earth orbit), will deter the two superpowers from conducting an unqualified aggression, at least for as long as they alone are in a position to do so. Building special satellites to spy on other satellites will certainly be envisaged.

However, for civilian purposes it would be unreasonable to start a race to harden satellites and fit them with black boxes, such a procedure being liable to jeopardize the systems' commercial efficiency. It is doubtless these systems which, because they are the most vulnerable, will determine the scope of an agreement banning ASAT systems, even though one can imagine they will not be prime targets.

III. Means of verification

ASAT systems fall into three categories: those which involve a rendezvous between an interceptor and a target satellite, those operating by emitting a beam from the ground and those which do so from space.

ASAT systems of the 'rendezvous' type

These systems are designed so that an interceptor vehicle catches up with the target satellite and either collides with it or explodes in its vicinity. The interceptor can be launched like any other satellite from a launch centre, and the launch has then to be phased with the orbit of the target satellite (the approach used by the Soviet Union). It can also be a rocket launched from an aircraft, to reach satellites in low Earth orbit, with less timing constraints (the US approach). The testing of such systems is detectable and could therefore be subject to verification. At the present time the situation is unequal. The USSR started to develop its system 15 years ago while the USA is just beginning testing. The presumably unsophisticated nature of the Soviet system could justify asking whether or not it would be preferable to ban tests now. An analysis of this question would, however, be outside the scope of this paper (see paper 9, page 131). The limits of possible control have to be borne in mind: a test ban would impede the development of new systems and verification could be achieved with a fair degree of certainty. However, rendezvous manoeuvres for peaceful purposes (the assembly of large communications stations, for example) could be a cover-up for tests on the acquisition of unco-operative objects, a keystone of ASAT systems, and would be difficult to verify, unless one were to look very closely at approach conditions.

Once such an ASAT system has been developed, ground store checks will not be possible: storage conditions for interceptor vehicles are no different from those of other satellites. They use the same launch facilities (except for systems jettisoned from aircraft, which are even more discreet!) and the same ground station network. They are, one might say, quite unremarkable.

Pre-positioned space mines would be noticeable given the performance of existing surveillance systems (it is claimed that the US Ground-based Electro-Optical Deep Space Surveillance system can detect a football in geosynchronous orbit), but ASAT systems can await launch without fear of being detected.

ASAT systems using ground-emitted beams

Two categories of ground-based ASAT beam weapon system can be distinguished: 'disruptive' systems, which prevent the target satellite from operating but do not destroy any part of it, although loss of control can result; and 'destructive' systems, which cause irreversible damage to the target.

That such disruption has been caused deliberately will be hard to ascertain: doubtless a laser designed for geodetic experiments will, when it is aimed at a satellite, cause trouble, the origin of which will remain unidentified if it is the attitude sensors which are affected, or possibly identified if an observation instrument is affected. An electromagnetic jamming station will look very much like a telecom station, but there is perhaps some likelihood that an aggressive action will be detected by electronic intelligence satellite network.

Destructive systems will undoubtedly be much more characteristic as they call for a beam of very high energy. (A laser station next to an electric power station at high altitude would be suspicious.) The deployment of such facilities could be detected by national means of observation and monitored if criteria were drawn up by which such systems could be distinguished from anti-aircraft or anti-missile protection systems. In view of the latter's applications, on-site checks would clearly be impossible.

ASAT systems using space-emitted beams

Such systems currently mentioned in the literature are of the 'destructive' type and involve large spacecraft (between 10 and 100 tonnes or so if they also have an anti-ballistic missile role). They will need large power sources using nuclear reactors and efficient heat dissipating devices. An operational system would call for the deployment of several spacecraft. Currently all these are specific characteristics which render verification feasible.

What about tomorrow, when outer space may be full of material processing stations and space stations? Close-look missions would be the only way of dispelling doubts: laser systems will need to use large focusing mirrors, fairly specific ones no doubt, while systems with an anti-ballistic missile objective as well will probably operate at higher altitudes than other stations if their number is to be kept down. The deployment of less characteristic space-based 'disruptive systems' should not be ruled out and would be more difficult to monitor.

IV. Conclusion

Only ASAT tests, the deployment of space mines or of large radiation transmitters from the ground or from space can be monitored with some degree of confidence. The arsenals of existing ASAT systems cannot be monitored.

Insidious action can be suspected but hardly ever proven, so the enforcement of a treaty banning ASAT systems will not be an easy matter. New means of observation in space as well as on-site checks will be required. Close looks at suspicious objects remains a possibility: the USA and the USSR will no doubt be able to build new satellite surveillance spacecraft should existing systems prove inadequate.

Proof of good faith might be called for, requiring the supply of information regarding the objects launched. At the present time little detailed information is given when a launch is notified. Participating states could be requested on such occasions to supply characteristics which prove that the system to be launched cannot be used as an ASAT device. Lastly, as provided for in the SALT agreements for missiles, it would be compulsory for spacecraft telemetry to be transmitted in uncoded form, thereby enabling valuable information to be gathered regarding the nature of these objects (military missile performances are deduced from the analysis of telemetry data).

An expert in ASAT systems or control problems would doubtless be better able to indicate whether there are other characteristics peculiar to ASAT systems. However, the evolution of aggressive and defensive concepts, or of satellite design, will make the development of such criteria very difficult. Solely the determination to stop this race and to allow co-operative measures and close-look or on-site verification would have any effect. But it would not dispel the threat of systems already developed and stocked whose numbers could not be verified.

Appendix 1. Satellite launches in 1982 and 1983

Appendix 1A. Photographic reconnaissance satellites launched in 1982 and 1983

Country, satellite name and designation	Launch date and time (GMT)	Orbital inclination (deg) and period (min)	Perigee and apogee heights (km)	Comments
USA				
USAF (1982-06A)	21 Jan 1926	97 92	177 550	Lifetime 122 days
USAF (1982-41A)	11 May 1843	96 89	177 262	Big Bird satellite; lifetime 208 days; decayed on 5 Dec 1982
USAF (1982-111A)	17 Nov 2122	97 93	280 520	Probably a KH-11 type satellite
USAF (1983-32A)	15 Apr 1843	97 89	136 297	Lifetime 128 days; high resolution; manoeuvrable; film recovery type
USAF (1983-60A)	20 Jun 1843	97 89	169 229	In orbit at the end of December 1983; Big Bird satellite; manoeuvrable
USSR				
Cosmos 1332 (1982-02A)	12 Jan 1229	82 89	211 250	Lifetime 13 days; geodesy and mapping; TL recovery beacon
Cosmos 1334 (1982-05A)	20 Jan 1131	73 89	196 290	Lifetime 14 days; high resolution
Cosmos 1336 (1982-08A)	30 Jan 1131	70 90	170 352	Lifetime 27 days; fourth generation; high resolution
Cosmos 1338 (1982-11A)	16 Feb 1117	73 90	186 376	Lifetime 14 days; subsequently orbited at high perigee; medium resolution
Cosmos 1342 (1982-18A)	5 Mar 1048	73 90	230 303	Lifetime 14 days; high resolution
Cosmos 1343 (1982-21A)	17 Mar 1033	73 90	229 288	Lifetime 14 days; high resolution; TF recovery beacon
Cosmos 1347 (1982-28A)	2 Apr 1019	70 90	173 340	Lifetime 50 days; fourth generation; high resolution
Cosmos 1350 (1982-32A)	15 Apr 1438	67 90	172 355	Lifetime 31 days; fourth generation; high resolution
Cosmos 1352 (1982-35A)	12 Apr 0922	70 90	209 361	Lifetime 14 days; medium resolution

Country, satellite name and designation	Launch date and time (GMT)	Orbital inclination (deg) and period (min)	Perigee and apogee heights (km)	Comments
Cosmos 1353 (1982-36A)	23 Apr 0950	82 89	212 242	Lifetime 13 days; Earth resources; TF recovery beacon; data received by Priroda Nature Station
Cosmos 1368 (1982-46A)	21 May 1243	70 90	211 341	Lifetime 13 days; high resolution; TF recovery beacon
Cosmos 1369 (1982-48A)	25 May 0853	82 90	269 276	Lifetime 14 days; Earth resources; TF recovery beacon
Cosmos 1370 (1982-49A)	28 May 0907	65 89	197 275	Lifetime 44 days; fourth generation; high resolution
Cosmos 1373 (1982-53A)	2 Jun 1258	70 90	210 347	Lifetime 14 days; medium resolution; TF recovery beacon
Cosmos 1376 (1982-56A)	8 Jun 0755	82 90	261 274	Lifetime 14 days; Earth resources; TF recovery beacon; data received by Priroda Nature Station
Cosmos 1377 (1982-57A)	8 Jun 1200	65 90	173 363	Lifetime 44 days; fourth generation; high resolution
Cosmos 1381 (1982-62A)	18 Jun 1258	70 90	208 374	Lifetime 13 days; medium resolution; TF recovery beacon
Cosmos 1384 (1982-67A)	30 Jun 1507	67 90	170 355	Lifetime 30 days; fourth generation; high resolution
Cosmos 1385 (1982-68A)	6 Jul 0755	82 89	186 237	Lifetime 14 days; Earth resources; data received by Priroda Nature Station
Cosmos 1387 (1982-71A)	13 Jul 0810	82 89	212 243	Lifetime 13 days; Earth resources; data received by Priroda Nature Station
Cosmos 1396 (1982-75A)	27 Jul 1229	73 90	198 298	Lifetime 14 days; high resolution; TF recovery beacon
Cosmos 1398 (1982-77A)	3 Aug 1131	82 89	216 234	Lifetime 10 days; geodesy and mapping; TL recovery beacon
Cosmos 1399 (1982-78A)	4 Aug 1131	65 90	171 344	Lifetime 43 days; fourth generation; high resolution
Cosmos 1401 (1982-81A)	20 Aug 0950	82 90	261 274	Lifetime 14 days; Earth resources
Cosmos 1403 (1982-85A)	1 Sep 0907	70 92	354 416	Lifetime 14 days; medium resolution; TF recovery beacon
Cosmos 1404 (1982-86A)	1 Sep 1146	73 92	358 416	Lifetime 14 days; medium resolution; TF recovery beacon
Cosmos 1406 (1982-89A)	8 Sep 1019	82 89	211 230	Lifetime 13 days; Earth resources; data received by Priroda Nature Station
Cosmos 1407 (1982-91A)	15 Sep 1536	67 90	173 339	Lifetime 31 days; fourth generation; high resolution
Cosmos 1411 (1982-98A)	30 Sep 1200	73 90	197 358	Lifetime 14 days; high resolution
Cosmos 1416 (1982-101A)	14 Oct 0922	70 90	231 278	Lifetime 14 days; high resolution; TF recovery beacon

Country, satellite name and designation	Launch date and time (GMT)	Orbital inclination (deg) and period (min)	Perigee and apogee heights (km)	Comments
Cosmos 1419 (1982-108A)	2 Nov 0936	70 90	230 282	Lifetime 14 days; high resolution; TF recovery beacon
Cosmos 1421 (1982-112A)	18 Nov 0936	70 90	231 282	Lifetime 14 days; high resolution
Cosmos 1422 (1982-114A)	3 Dec 1148	73 89	228 288	Lifetime 13 days; high resolution
Cosmos 1424 (1982-117A)	16 Dec 0952	65 90	171 349	High resolution
Cosmos 1425 (1982-119A)	23 Dec 1203	70 90	348 416	Medium resolution; only second flight from Tyuratam at this inclination (compare Cosmos 609)
Cosmos 1438 (1983-05A)	27 Jan 0838	70 89	209 230	Lifetime 11 days; high resolution
Cosmos 1439 (1983-07A)	6 Feb 1131	70 89	170 251	Lifetime 16 days; high resolution; fourth generation
Cosmos 1440 (1983-09A)	10 Feb 0712	82 90	260 275	Lifetime 14 days; Earth resources; high resolution
Cosmos 1442 (1983-12A)	25 Feb 1243	67 90	170 367	Lifetime 45 days; high resolution; fourth generation
Cosmos 1444 (1983-14A)	2 Mar 1048	73 92	358 416	Lifetime 14 days; medium resolution
Cosmos 1446 (1983-18A)	16 Mar 0853	70 89	222 242	Lifetime 14 days; high resolution
Cosmos 1449 (1983-24A)	31 Mar 1048	73 92	357 416	Lifetime 15 days; medium resolution
Cosmos 1451 (1983-29A)	8 Apr 0838	82 90	227 323	Lifetime 14 days; only one that was not announced as Earth resources
Cosmos 1454 (1983-36A)	22 Apr 1438	67 90	171 343	Lifetime 30 days; high resolution; fourth generation
Cosmos 1457 (1983-39A)	26 Apr 1005	70 90	171 349	Lifetime 43 days; high resolution; fourth generation
Cosmos 1458 (1983-40A)	28 Apr 0824	82 89	212 240	Lifetime 13 days; Earth resources; data received by Priroda Nature Station; high resolution
Cosmos 1460 (1983-43A)	6 May 0907	70 92	351 417	Lifetime 14 days; TF; medium resolution
Cosmos 1462 (1983-45A)	17 May 0810	82 90	259 275	Lifetime 14 days; Earth resources; data received by Priroda Nature Station; high resolution
Cosmos 1466 (1983-50A)	26 May 1200	65 90	174 345	Lifetime 41 days; high resolution; fourth generation
Cosmos 1467 (1983-52A)	31 May 1146	73 92	357 417	Lifetime 12 days; medium resolution
Cosmos 1468 (1983-55A)	7 Jun 0755	82 90	255 280	Lifetime 14 days; Earth resources; TF; data received by Priroda Nature Station; high resolution
Cosmos 1469 (1983-57A)	14 Jun 1214	73 90	232 344	Lifetime 10 days; high resolution

Country, satellite name and designation	Launch date and time (GMT)	Orbital inclination (deg) and period (min)	Perigee and apogee heights (km)	Comments
Cosmos 1471 (1983-64A)	28 Jun 1507	67 90	185 344	Lifetime 30 days; high resolution; fourth generation
Cosmos 1472 (1983-68A)	5 Jul 0755	82 92	338 362	Lifetime 14 days; Earth resources; TF; high perigee flight; medium resolution
Cosmos 1482 (1983-71A)	13 Jul 0936	70 92	352 413	Lifetime 14 days; TF; announced as Earth resources; only one at 70°; high perigee flight; medium resolution
Cosmos 1483 (1983-74A)	20 Jul 0755	82 90	260 275	Lifetime 14 days; TF; Earth resources; high resolution
Cosmos 1485 (1983-76A)	26 Jul 1200	73 92	358 416	Lifetime 14 days; TF; medium resolution
Cosmos 1487 (1983-80A)	5 Aug 0922	82 90	261 275	Lifetime 14 days; TF; Earth resources; data received by Priroda Nature Station; high resolution
Cosmos 1488 (1983-82A)	9 Aug 1131	73 92	358 416	Lifetime 14 days; medium resolution
Cosmos 1489 (1983-83A)	10 Aug 1258	65 90	171 365	Lifetime 44 days; high resolution; fourth generation
Cosmos 1493 (1983-87A)	23 Aug 1102	73 92	360 414	Lifetime 14 days; medium resolution
Cosmos 1495 (1983-92A)	3 Sep 1019	82 89	215 236	Lifetime 13 days; TK; Earth resources; high resolution
Cosmos 1496 (1983-93A)	7 Sep 1326	67 90	170 341	Lifetime 42 days; high resolution; fourth generation
Cosmos 1497 (1983-95A)	9 Sep 1102	73 92	357 416	Lifetime 14 days; medium resolution
Cosmos 1498 (1983-96A)	14 Sep 1033	82 90	261 275	Lifetime 14 days; Earth resources; high resolution
Cosmos 1499 (1983-97A)	17 Sep 1117	73 92	357 416	Lifetime 14 days; medium resolution
Cosmos 1504 (1983-104A)	14 Oct 1005	65 89	173 305	Lifetime 53 days; high resolution; fourth generation
Cosmos 1505 (1983-107A)	21 Oct 1214	75 92	358 415	Lifetime 14 days; medium resolution
Cosmos 1509 (1983-112A)	17 Nov 1214	73 90	227 292	Lifetime 14 days; high resolution
Cosmos 1511 (1983-117A)	30 Nov 1341	67 90	172 343	Lifetime 44 days; high resolution; fourth generation
Cosmos 1512 (1983-119A)	7 Dec 1241	73 92	356 418	Lifetime 14 days; medium resolution
Cosmos 1516 (1983-124A)	27 Dec 0936	65 89	197 275	Lifetime 44 days; high resolution; fourth generation; no signals received by the Kettering Group; probably similar to Cosmos 1426; manoeuvred[b]

Country, satellite name and designation	Launch date and time (GMT)	Orbital inclination (deg) and period (min)	Perigee and apogee heights (km)	Comments
People's Republic of China				
China 12 (1982-90A)	9 Sep 0726	63 90	174 385	A capsule was recovered on 14 Sep 1982
China 13 (1983-86A)	19 Aug 0600	63 90	173 382	Lifetime 15 days

[a] Morse code recovery beacon data supplied by the Kettering Group.
[b] G. E. Perry, private communication.

Appendix 1B. Electronic reconnaissance satellites launched in 1982 and 1983

Country, satellite name and designation	Launch date and time (GMT)	Orbital inclination (deg) and period (min)	Perigee and apogee heights (km)	Comments
USA				
USAF (1982-41C)	11 May 1843	96 99	701 707	This satellite was ejected into an independent orbit from the Big Bird satellite 1982-41A
USAF (1983-60C)	20 Jun 1843	97 111	1 289 1 291	Satellite was ejected from the Big Bird satellite 1983-60A
USSR				
Cosmos 1335[a] (1982-07A)	29 Jan 1102	74 95	482 518	Lifetime 2 years
Cosmos 1340 (1982-13A)	19 Feb 0141	81 98	626 654	Lifetime 60 years; replaced Cosmos 1206[b]
Cosmos 1345 (1982-26A)	31 Mar 0907	74 95	504 547	Lifetime 5 years; replaced Cosmos 1222[b]
Cosmos 1346 (1982-27A)	31 Mar 1634	81 98	622 661	Lifetime 60 years; replaced Cosmos 1184[b]
Cosmos 1356 (1982-39A)	5 May 0810	81 98	632 671	Lifetime 60 years; replaced Cosmos 1315[b]
Cosmos 1400 (1982-79A)	5 Aug 0658	81 98	630 653	Lifetime 60 years
Cosmos 1437 (1983-03A)	20 Jan 1731	81 98	628 658	Lifetime 60 years
Cosmos 1441 (1983-10A)	16 Feb 1005	81 98	631 642	Lifetime 60 years
Cosmos 1453 (1983-34A)	19 Apr 1200	74 95	471 517	Lifetime 4 years; orbital period lower than usual
Cosmos 1455 (1983-37A)	23 Apr 1424	83 98	637 665	Lifetime 60 years
Cosmos 1470 (1983-61A)	23 Jun 0000	83 98	635 670	Lifetime 60 years
Cosmos 1500 (1983-99A)	28 Sep 0755	83 98	635 667	Lifetime 60 years
Cosmos 1515 (1983-122A)	15 Dec 1229	83 98	638 665	Lifetime 60 years; scientific oceanographic mission announced; TCE survey possibly with side-looking radar

[a] Orbital period lower than usual.
[b] These are not exact replacements; the whole system appears to be being redistributed some 20° off (G. E. Perry, private communication).

Appendix 1C. Ocean surveillance and oceanographic satellites launched in 1982 and 1983

Country, satellite name and designation	Launch date and time (GMT)	Orbital inclination (deg) and period (min)	Perigee and apogee heights (km)	Comments
USA				
NOSS-4 (1983-08A)	9 Feb 1355	63 108	1 063 ⎫ 1 186 ⎪	
SSU-D (1983-08B)	9 Feb 1355	63 108	1 047 ⎪ 1 184 ⎪	
SSU-A (1983-08E)	9 Feb 1355	63 108	1 052 ⎬ 1 168 ⎪	Navy ocean-surveillance satellites; five sub-satellites and SSU satellites
SSU-B (1983-08F)	9 Feb 1355	63 108	1 052 ⎪ 1 168 ⎪	
SSU-C (1983-08H)	9 Feb 1355	63 108	1 052 ⎭ 1 167	
NOSS-5 (1983-56A)	10 Jun 0307	63 107	1 048 ⎫ 1 168 ⎪	
GB 1 (1983-56C)	10 Jun 0307	63 108	1 051 ⎬ 1 171 ⎪	Navy ocean-surveillance satellites; only three payloads launched
GB 2 (1983-56D)	10 Jun 0307	63 108	1 051 ⎭ 1 170	
USSR				
Cosmos 1337 (1982-10A)	11 Feb 0112	65 93	429 447	Passive satellite with ion thruster
Cosmos 1355 (1982-38A)	29 Apr 1005	65 93	425 443	Passive satellite with ion thruster
Cosmos 1365 (1982-43A)	14 May 1926	65 90	252 264	Nuclear-powered radar; manoeuvred into higher orbit on 27 Sep 1982
Cosmos 1372 (1982-52A)	1 Jun 1355	65 90	246 270	Nuclear-powered radar; manoeuvred into higher orbit on 11 Aug 1982
Cosmos 1378[a] (1982-59A)	10 Jun 1746	83 98	634 663	Presumed to be oceanographic
Cosmos 1402 (1982-84A)	30 Aug 1005	65 90	251 265	Nuclear-powered radar; attempts to manoeuvre into higher orbit appeared to have failed; satellite broke up; power reactor entered the Earth's atmosphere on 7 Feb 1983
Cosmos 1405 (1982-88A)	4 Sep 1746	65 93	429 445	Passive satellite with ion thruster
Cosmos 1408[a] (1982-92A)	16 Sep 0502	83 98	633 667	Presumed to be oceanographic; replaced Cosmos 1378
Cosmos 1412 (1982-99A)	2 Oct 0000	65 90	251 266	Nuclear-powered radar; manoeuvred into higher orbit on 10 Nov 1982
Cosmos 1461 (1983-44A)	7 May 1033	65 93	429 445	Passive satellite with ion thruster
Cosmos 1507 (1983-110A)	29 Oct 0824	65 93	435 443	Passive satellite with ion thruster

[a] Probably heavier Elint (electronic intelligence) type (G. E. Perry, private communication).

Appendix 1D. Early warning satellites launched in 1982 and 1983

Country, satellite name and designation	Launch date and time (GMT)	Orbital inclination (deg) and period (min)	Perigee and apogee heights (km)	Comments
USA				
IMEWS-13	6 Mar	2	35 520	
(1982-19A)	2015	1 424	35 598	
USSR				
Cosmos 1341	3 Mar	63	631	Replaced Cosmos 1247
(1982-16A)	0546	708	39 251	
Cosmos 1348	7 Apr	63	593	Replaced Cosmos 1172
(1982-29A)	1341	709	39 316	
Cosmos 1367	20 May	63	581	Filled the empty ninth location
(1982-45A)	1312	707	39 264	
Cosmos 1382	25 Jun	63	592	Replaced Cosmos 1223
(1982-64A)	0224	711	39 436	
Cosmos 1409	22 Sep	63	613	Replaced Cosmos 1217
(1982-95A)	0629	717	39 690	
Cosmos 1456	25 Apr	63	622	Replaced Cosmos 1191
(1983-38A)	1938	717	39 716	
Cosmos 1481	8 Jul	63	643	Replaced Cosmos 1285
(1983-70A)	1926	707	39 200	
Cosmos 1518	28 Dec	63	585	Replaced Cosmos 1341
(1983-126A)	0350	709	39 348	

Appendix 1E. Communications satellites launched in 1982 and 1983

Country, satellite name and designation	Launch date and time (GMT)	Orbital inclination (deg) and period (min)	Perigee and apogee heights (km)	Comments
USA				
DSCS II-15	30 Oct	3	35 772	
(1982-106A)	—	1 438	35 865	
DSCS III-16	30 Oct	3	35 845	
(1982-106B)	—	1 440	35 877	
TDRS 1	4 Apr	2	35 763	Tracking and Data Relay Satellite
(1983-26B)	1829	1 436	35 805	launched from space shuttle STS 6 to provide spacecraft-to-ground communications; located about 40° W longitude
USAF SDS 8	31 Jul	—	—	Satellite Data System; orbit similar
(1983-78A)	—	—	—	to 1980-100A
USSR				
Cosmos 1331	7 Jan	74	774	Possibly store-dump
(1982-01A)	1536	101	812	communications satellite; replaced Cosmos 1302
Molniya 1-53	26 Feb	63	476	Replaced Molniya 1-47
(1982-15A)	2010	735	40 743	
Cosmos 1354	28 Apr	74	794	Possibly store-dump
(1982-37A)	0253	101	815	communications satellite; replaced Cosmos 1190
Cosmos 1358–	6 May	74	1 400	Octuple launch
Cosmos 1364 (1982-40A–H)	1800	115	1 480	
Cosmos 1366	17 May	2	35 803	Experimental communications
(1982-44A)	2346	1 437	35 803	satellite
Molniya 1-54	28 May	63	627	Replaced Molniya 1-44
(1982-50A)	2248	763	40 631	
Cosmos 1371	1 Jun	74	790	Possibly store-dump
(1982-51A)	0434	101	812	communications satellite; replaced Cosmos 1140
Cosmos 1388–	21 Jul	74	1 395	Octuple launch
Cosmos 1395 (1982-73A–H)	0629	115	1 518	
Molniya 1-55	21 Jul	63	617	Replaced Molniya 1-46
(1982-74A)	0950	701	38 917	
Cosmos 1420	11 Nov	74	780	Possibly store-dump
(1982-109A)	0614	101	811	communications satellite; replaced Cosmos 1331
Cosmos 1423	9 Dec	63	405	Should have replaced Molniya 1-48;
(1982-115A)	0346	94	515	broke up at the time of injection into elliptic orbit[a]
Cosmos 1429–	19 Jan	74	1 401	Octuple launch
Cosmos 1436 (1983-02A–H)	0224	116	1 521	
Molniya 1-56	16 Mar	63	453	Replaced Molniya 1-50
(1983-19A)	1814	737	40 825	

Country, satellite name and designation	Launch date and time (GMT)	Orbital inclination (deg) and period (min)	Perigee and apogee heights (km)	Comments
Molniya 1-57 (1983-25A)	2 Apr 0210	63 700	470 39 006	Replaced Molniya 1-52
Cosmos 1452 (1983-31A)	12 Apr 1814	74 101	785 810	Possibly store-dump communications satellite; replaced Cosmos 1317?[b]
Cosmos 1473– Cosmos 1480 (1983-69A–H)	6 Jul 0029	74 116	1 397 1 484	Octuple launch
Molniya 1-58 (1983-73A)	19 Jul 1522	63 700	459 39 014	Replaced Molniya 1-49
Cosmos 1486 (1983-79A)	3 Aug 1243	74 101	784 806	Possible store-dump communications satellite; replaced Cosmos 1354
Cosmos 1503 (1983-103A)	12 Oct 0014	74 101	790 810	Possibly store-dump communications satellite; replaced Cosmos 1486
Molniya 1-59 (1983-114A)	23 Nov 1648	63 702	442 39 145	Replaced Molniya 1-48 and Cosmos 1423, 11 months after failure to replace Molniya 1-48 with Cosmos 1423, which exploded[a]

[a] G. E. Perry, private communication.
[b] Not in exactly the same orbital planes (G. E. Perry, private communication).

Appendix 1F. Navigation satellites launched in 1982 and 1983

Country, satellite name and designation	Launch date and time (GMT)	Orbital inclination (deg) and period (min)	Perigee and apogee heights (km)	Comments
USA				
USAF/ NAVSTAR 8 (1983-72A)	14 Jul 1019	63 726	19 952 20 798	No. 8 in a network of 18 satellites; NAVSTAR 7 launched on 18 Dec 1981 failed
USSR				
Cosmos 1333 (1982-03A)	14 Jan 0755	83 105	971 1 017	Replaced Cosmos 1153; No. 3[c]
Cosmos 1339 (1982-12A)	17 Feb 2150	83 105	955 1 018	Replaced Cosmos 1092; No. 14; civil navigation
Cosmos 1344 (1982-24A)	24 Mar 1938	83 105	971 1 012	Replaced Cosmos 1244; No. 1
Cosmos 1349 (1982-30A)	8 Apr 0014	83 105	970 1 014	Replaced Cosmos 1153[a]; No. 4
Cosmos 1380 (1982-61A)	18 Jun 1200	83 93	145 659	Should have replaced Cosmos 1225 but failed to reach required orbit
Cosmos 1383 (1982-66A)	29 Jun 2150	83 105	991 1 029	Replaced Cosmos 1168; part of a civil system
Cosmos 1386 (1982-69A)	7 Jul 0950	83 105	955 1 011	Replaced Cosmos 1225 and Cosmos 1380; No. 2
Cosmos 1413– Cosmos 1415 (1982-100A, D,E)	12 Oct 1507	65 673	19 069 19 070	Triple GLONASS (Global Navigation Satellite System); nearly semi-synchronous orbit; experimental; initially satellites were close together then gradually separated[b]
Cosmos 1417 (1982-102A)	19 Oct 0600	83 105	962 1 012	Replaced Cosmos 1308
Cosmos 1428 (1983-01A)	12 Jan 1355	83 105	957 1 006	Replaced Cosmos 1333; No. 3; Cosmos 1333 became No. 7 transmitting at the end of 1983
Cosmos 1448 (1983-23A)	30 Mar 0112	83 105	963 1 006	Replaced Cosmos 1344; No. 1; Cosmos 1344 not transmitting
Cosmos 1459 (1983-42A)	6 May 0253	83 105	947 1 019	Replaced Cosmos 1349; No. 4
Cosmos 1464 (1983-48A)	24 May 0253	83 105	968 1 011	Replaced Cosmos 1295; No. 5
Cosmos 1513 (1983-120A)	8 Dec 0614	83 105	963 1 019	Replaced Cosmos 1417; No. 6; Cosmos 1417 no longer in operation

[a] Cosmos 1153 has been renumbered No. 7, and Cosmos 1184 renumbered No. 8 (G.E. Perry, private communication).
[b] In 1983 two more sets of triple GLONASS satellites, Cosmos 1490–1492 and Cosmos 1519–1521, were launched. These are 120° out of phase with the previous launch signifying operational capability. These and Cosmos 1506 are, however, from the civil navigation system (G.E. Perry, private communication). They are therefore omitted from this table.
[c] These numbers are identity numbers used by the Soviet Union.

Appendix 1G. Meteorological satellites launched in 1982 and 1983

Country, satellite name and designation	Launch date and time (GMT)	Orbital inclination (deg) and period (min)	Perigee and apogee heights (km)	Comments
USA				
DMSP 2-01	21 Dec	99	816	First of the Defense Meteorological
(1982-118A)	0238	101	827	Satellite Program 2 series
NASA/				
NOAA 8	28 Mar	99	808	National Oceanographic and
(1983-22A)	1550	101	830	Atmospheric Administration satellite; includes SARSAT (Search and Rescue Satellite-Aided Tracking) of the joint Cospas project
NASA/				
GOES 6	28 Apr	15	33 367	Geostationary Operational
(1983-41A)	2219	1 704	48 390	Environmental Satellite
DMSP 2-02	18 Nov	99	816	
(1983-113A)	0629	101	833	
USSR				
Meteor 2-08	25 Mar	83	942	
(1982-25A)	0950	104	964	
Meteor 2-09	14 Dec	81	812	
(1982-116A)	2359	102	892	
Meteor 2-10	28 Oct	81	754	Only ones in operation are
(1983-109A)	0907	101	890	Meteors 2-07, 2-08 and 2-10

208

Appendix 1H. Interceptor/destructor satellites launched in 1982

Country, satellite name and designation	Launch date and time (GMT)	Orbital inclination (deg) and period (min)	Perigee and apogee heights (km)	Comments
USSR				
Cosmos 1375 (1982-55A)	6 Jun 1702	66 105	981 1 011	ASAT target; orbital height similar to Soviet navigation satellites
Cosmos 1379 (1982-60A)	18 Jun 1102	65 91	144 546	Interceptor passed close to Cosmos 1375 on 18 Jun 1982; de-orbited and burnt up on re-entry

Appendix 2. Treaties and treaty proposals which contain provisions aimed at some form of arms control in space

Treaty banning nuclear weapon tests in the atmosphere, in outer space and under water

SIGNED: Moscow, 5 August 1963
ENTERED INTO FORCE: 10 October 1963
DEPOSITARIES: UK, US and Soviet governments
PARTIES: 112

The Governments of the United States of America, the United Kingdom of Great Britain and Northern Ireland, and the Union of Soviet Socialist Republics, hereinafter referred to as the "Original Parties",

Proclaiming as their principal aim the speediest possible achievement of an agreement on general and complete disarmament under strict international control in accordance with the objectives of the United Nations which would put an end to the armaments race and eliminate the incentive to the production and testing of all kinds of weapons, including nuclear weapons,

Seeking to achieve the discontinuance of all test explosions of nuclear weapons for all time, determined to continue negotiations to this end, and desiring to put an end to the contamination of man's environment by radioactive substances,

Have agreed as follows:

Article I

1. Each of the Parties to this Treaty undertakes to prohibit, to prevent, and not to carry out any nuclear weapon test explosion, or any other nuclear explosion, at any place under its jurisdiction or control:

(*a*) in the atmosphere; beyond its limits, including outer space; or under water, including territorial waters or high seas; or

(*b*) in any other environment if such explosion causes radioactive debris to be present outside the territorial limits of the State under whose jurisdiction or control such explosion is conducted. It is understood in this connection that the provisions of this subparagraph are without prejudice to the conclusion of a treaty resulting in the permanent banning of all nuclear test explosions, including all such explosions underground, the conclusion of which, as the Parties have stated in the Preamble to this Treaty, they seek to achieve.

2. Each of the Parties to this Treaty undertakes furthermore to refrain from causing, encouraging, or in any way participating in, the carrying out of any nuclear weapon test explosion, or any other nuclear explosion, anywhere which would take place in any of the environments described, or have the effect referred to, in paragraph 1 of this Article.

Article II

1. Any Party may propose amendments to this Treaty. The text of any proposed amendment shall be submitted to the Depositary Governments which shall circulate it to all Parties to this Treaty. Thereafter, if requested to do so by one-third or more of the Parties, the Depositary Governments shall convene a conference, to which they shall invite all the Parties, to consider such amendment.

2. Any amendment to this Treaty must be approved by a majority of the votes of all the Parties to this Treaty, including the votes of all of the Original Parties. The amendment shall enter into force for all Parties upon the deposit of instruments of ratification by a majority of all the Parties, including the instruments of ratification of all of the Original Parties.

Article III

1. This Treaty shall be open to all States for signature. Any State which does not sign this treaty before its entry into force in accordance with paragraph 3 of this Article may accede to it at any time.

2. This Treaty shall be subject to ratification by signatory States. Instruments of ratification and instruments of accession shall be deposited with the Governments of the Original Parties—the United States of America, the United Kingdom of Great Britain and Northern Ireland, and the Union of Soviet Socialist Republics—which are hereby designated the Depositary Governments.

3. This Treaty shall enter into force after its ratification by all the Original Parties and the deposit of their instruments of ratification.

4. For States whose instruments of ratification or accession are deposited subsequent to the entry into force of this Treaty, it shall enter into force on the date of the deposit of their instruments of ratification or accession.

5. The Depositary Governments shall promptly inform all signatory and acceding States of the date of each signature, the date of deposit of each instrument of ratification of and accession to this Treaty, the date of its entry into force, and the date of receipt of any requests for conferences or other notices.

6. This Treaty shall be registered by the Depositary Governments pursuant to Article 102 of the Charter of the United Nations.

Article IV

This Treaty shall be of unlimited duration.

212

Each Party shall in exercising its national sovereignty have the right to withdraw from the Treaty if it decides that extraordinary events, related to the subject matter of this Treaty, have jeopardized the supreme interests of its country. It shall give notice of such withdrawal to all other Parties to the Treaty three months in advance.

Article V

This Treaty, of which the English and Russian texts are equally authentic, shall be deposited in the archives of the Depositary Governments. Duly certified copies of this Treaty shall be transmitted by the Depositary Governments to the Governments of the signatory and acceding States.

IN WITNESS WHEREOF the undersigned, duly authorized, have signed this Treaty.

DONE in triplicate at the city of Moscow the fifth day of August, one thousand nine hundred and sixty-three.

For the Government of the United States of America:	*For the Government of the United Kingdom of Great Britain and Northern Ireland:*	*For the Government of the Union of Soviet Socialist Republics:*
Dean Rusk	Home	A. Gromyko

Treaty on principles governing the activities of states in the exploration and use of outer space, including the Moon and other celestial bodies

SIGNED: London, Moscow and Washington, 27 January 1967
ENTERED INTO FORCE: 10 October 1967
DEPOSITARIES: UK, US and Soviet governments
PARTIES: 85

The States Parties to this Treaty,

Inspired by the great prospects opening up before mankind as a result of man's entry into outer space,

Recognizing the common interest of all mankind in the progress of the exploration and use of outer space for peaceful purposes,

Believing that the exploration and use of outer space should be carried on for the benefit of all peoples irrespective of the degree of their economic or scientific development,

Desiring to contribute to broad international co-operation in the scientific as well as the legal aspects of the exploration and use of outer space for peaceful purposes,

Believing that such co-operation will contribute to the development of mutual understanding and to the strengthening of friendly relations between States and peoples,

Recalling resolution 1962 (XVIII), entitled "Declaration of Legal Principles Governing the Activities of States in the Exploration and Use of Outer Space", which was adopted unanimously by the United Nations General Assembly on 13 December 1963,

Recalling resolution 1884 (XVIII), calling upon States to refrain from placing in orbit around the earth any objects carrying nuclear weapons or any other kinds of weapons of mass destruction or from installing such weapons on celestial bodies, which was adopted unanimously by the United Nations General Assembly on 17 October 1963,

Taking account of United Nations General Assembly resolution 110 (II) of 3 November 1947, which condemned propaganda designed or likely to provoke or encourage any threat to the peace, breach of the peace or act of aggression, and considering that the aforementioned resolution is applicable to outer space,

Convinced that a Treaty on Principles Governing the Activities of States in the Exploration and Use of Outer Space, including the Moon and Other Celestial Bodies, will further the Purposes and Principles of the Charter of the United Nations,

Have agreed on the following:

Article I

The exploration and use of outer space, including the moon and other celestial bodies, shall be carried out for the benefit and in the interests of all countries, irrespective of their degree of economic or scientific development, and shall be the province of all mankind.

214

Outer space, including the moon and other celestial bodies, shall be free for exploration and use by all States without discrimination of any kind, on a basis of equality and in accordance with international law, and there shall be free access to all areas of celestial bodies.

There shall be freedom of scientific investigation in outer space, including the moon and other celestial bodies, and States shall facilitate and encourage international co-operation in such investigation.

Article II

Outer space, including the moon and other celestial bodies, is not subject to national appropriation by claim of sovereignty, by means of use or occupation, or by any other means.

Article III

States Parties to the Treaty shall carry on activities in the exploration and use of outer space, including the moon and other celestial bodies, in accordance with international law, including the Charter of the United Nations, in the interest of maintaining international peace and security and promoting international co-operation and understanding.

Article IV

States Parties to the Treaty undertake not to place in orbit around the earth any objects carrying nuclear weapons or any other kinds of weapons of mass destruction, install such weapons on celestial bodies, or station such weapons in outer space in any other manner.

The moon and other celestial bodies shall be used by all States Parties to the Treaty exclusively for peaceful purposes. The establishment of military bases, installations and fortifications, the testing of any type of weapons and the conduct of military manoeuvres on celestial bodies shall be forbidden. The use of military personnel for scientific research or for any other peaceful purposes shall not be prohibited. The use of any equipment or facility necessary for peaceful exploration of the moon and other celestial bodies shall also not be prohibited.

Article V

States Parties to the Treaty shall regard astronauts as envoys of mankind in outer space and shall render to them all possible assistance in the event of accident, distress, or emergency landing on the territory of another State Party or on the high seas. When astronauts make such a landing, they shall be safely and promptly returned to the State of registry of their space vehicle.

In carrying on activities in outer space and on celestial bodies, the astronauts of one State Party shall render all possible assistance to the astronauts of other States Parties.

States Parties to the Treaty shall immediately inform the other States Parties to the Treaty or the Secretary-General of the United Nations of any phenomena they discover in outer space, including the moon and other celestial bodies, which could constitute a danger to the life or health of astronauts.

Article VI

States Parties to the Treaty shall bear international responsibility for national activities in outer space, including the moon and other celestial bodies, whether such activities are carried on by governmental agencies or non-governmental entities, and for assuring that national activities are carried out in conformity with the provisions set forth in the present Treaty. The activities of non-governmental entities in outer space, including the moon and other celestial bodies, shall require authorization and continuing supervision by the appropriate State Party to the Treaty. When activities are carried on in outer space, including the moon and other celestial bodies, by an international organization, responsibility for compliance with this Treaty shall be borne both by the international organization and by the States Parties to the Treaty participating in such organization.

Article VII

Each State Party to the Treaty that launches or procures the launching of an object into outer space, including the moon and other celestial bodies, and each State Party from whose territory or facility an object is launched, is internationally liable for damage to another State Party to the Treaty or to its natural or juridical persons by such object or its component parts on the Earth, in air space or in outer space, including the moon and other celestial bodies.

Article VIII

A State Party to the Treaty on whose registry an object launched into outer space is carried shall retain jurisdiction and control over such object, and over any personnel thereof, while in outer space or on a celestial body. Ownership of objects launched into outer space, including objects landed or constructed on a celestial body, and of their component parts, is not affected by their presence in outer space or on a celestial body or by their return to the Earth. Such objects or component parts found beyond the limits of the State Party to the Treaty on whose registry they are carried shall be returned to that State Party, which shall, upon request, furnish identifying data prior to this return.

Article IX

In the exploration and use of outer space, including the moon and other celestial bodies, States Parties to the Treaty shall be guided by the principle of co-operation and mutual assistance and shall conduct all their activities in outer space, including the moon and other celestial bodies, with due regard to the corresponding interests of all other States Parties to the Treaty. States Parties to the Treaty shall pursue studies of outer space, including the moon and other celestial bodies, and conduct exploration of them so as to avoid their harmful contamination and also adverse changes in the environment of the Earth resulting from the introduction of extraterrestrial matter and, where necessary, shall adopt appropriate measures for this purpose. If a State Party to the Treaty has reason to believe that an activity or experiment planned by it or its nationals in outer space, including the moon and other celestial bodies, would cause potentially harmful interference with activities of other States Parties in the peaceful exploration and use of outer space, including the moon and other celestial bodies, it shall undertake appropriate international consultations before proceeding with any such activity or experiment. A State Party to the Treaty which has reason to believe that an activity or experiment planned by another State Party in outer space, including the moon and other celestial bodies, would cause potentially harmful interference with activities in the peaceful exploration and use of outer space, including the moon and other celestial bodies, may request consultation concerning the activity or experiment.

Article X

In order to promote international co-operation in the exploration and use of outer space, including the moon and other celestial bodies, in conformity with the purposes of this Treaty, the States Parties to the Treaty shall consider on a basis of equality any requests by other States Parties to the Treaty to be afforded an opportunity to observe the flight of space objects launched by those States.

The nature of such an opportunity for observation and the conditions under which it could be afforded shall be determined by agreement between the States concerned.

Article XI

In order to promote international co-operation in the peaceful exploration and use of outer space, States Parties to the Treaty conducting activities in outer space including the moon and other celestial bodies, agree to inform the Secretary-General of the United Nations as well as the public and the international scientific community, to the greatest extent feasible and practicable, of the nature, conduct, locations and results of such activities. On receiving the said information, the Secretary-General of the United Nations should be prepared to disseminate it immediately and effectively.

Article XII

All stations, installations, equipment and space vehicles on the moon and other celestial bodies shall be open to representatives of other States Parties to the Treaty on a basis of reciprocity. Such representatives shall give reasonable advance notice of a projected visit, in order that appropriate consultations may be held and that maximum precautions may be taken to assure safety and to avoid interference with normal operations in the facility to be visited.

Article XIII

The provisions of this Treaty shall apply to the activities of States Parties to the Treaty in the exploration and use of outer space, including the moon and other celestial bodies, whether such activities are carried on by a single State Party to the Treaty or jointly with other States, including cases where they are carried on within the framework of international inter-governmental organizations.

Any practical questions arising in connexion with activities carried on by international inter-governmental organizations in the exploration and use of outer space, including the moon and other celestial bodies, shall be resolved by the States Parties to the Treaty either with the appropriate international organization or with one or more States members of that international organization, which are Parties to this Treaty.

Article XIV

1. This Treaty shall be open to all States for signature. Any State which does not sign this Treaty before its entry into force in accordance with paragraph 3 of this Article may accede to it at any time.

2. This Treaty shall be subject to ratification by signatory States. Instruments of ratification and instruments of accession shall be deposited with Governments of the United Kingdom of Great Britain and Northern Ireland, the Union of Soviet Socialist Republics and the United States of America, which are hereby designated the Depositary Governments.

3. This Treaty shall enter into force upon the deposit of instruments of ratification by five Governments including the Governments designated as Depositary Governments under this Treaty.

4. For States whose instruments of ratification or accession are deposited subsequent to the entry into force of this Treaty, it shall enter into force on the date of the deposit of their instruments of ratification or accession.

5. The Depositary Governments shall promptly inform all signatory and acceding States of the date of each signature, the date of deposit of each instrument of ratification of and accession to this Treaty, the date of its entry into force and other notices.

6. This Treaty shall be registered by the Depositary Governments pursuant to Article 102 of the Charter of the United Nations.

Article XV

Any State Party to the Treaty may propose amendments to this Treaty. Amendments shall enter into force for each State Party to the Treaty accepting the amendments upon their acceptance by a majority of the States Parties to the Treaty and thereafter for each remaining State Party to the Treaty on the date of acceptance by it.

Article XVI

Any State Party to the Treaty may give notice of its withdrawal from the Treaty one year after its entry into force by written notification to the Depositary Governments. Such withdrawal shall take effect one year from the date of receipt of this notification.

Article XVII

This Treaty, of which the English, Russian, French, Spanish and Chinese texts are equally authentic, shall be deposited in the archives of the Depositary Governments. Duly certified copies of this Treaty shall be transmitted by the Depositary Governments to the Governments of the signatory and acceding States.

IN WITNESS WHEREOF the undersigned, duly authorized, have signed this Treaty.

DONE in triplicate, at the cities of London, Moscow and Washington, the twenty-seventh day of January, one thousand nine hundred and sixty-seven.

Treaty between the United States of America and the Union of Soviet Socialist Republics on the limitation of anti-ballistic missile systems

SIGNED: Moscow, 26 May 1972
ENTERED INTO FORCE: 3 October 1972

The United States of America and the Union of Soviet Socialist Republics, hereinafter referred to as the Parties,

Proceeding from the premise that nuclear war would have devastating consequences for all mankind,

Considering that effective measures to limit anti-ballistic missile systems would be a substantial factor in curbing the race in strategic offensive arms and would lead to a decrease in the risk of outbreak of war involving nuclear weapons,

Proceeding from the premise that the limitation of anti-ballistic missile systems, as well as certain agreed measures with respect to the limitation of strategic offensive arms, would contribute to the creation of more favorable conditions for further negotiations on limiting strategic arms,

Mindful of their obligations under Article VI of the Treaty on the Non-Proliferation of Nuclear Weapons,

Declaring their intention to achieve at the earliest possible date the cessation of the nuclear arms race and to take effective measures towards reductions in strategic arms, nuclear disarmament, and general and complete disarmament,

Desiring to contribute to the relaxation of international tension and the strengthening of trust between States,

Have agreed as follows:

Article I

1. Each party undertakes to limit anti-ballistic missile (ABM) systems and to adopt other measures in accordance with the provisions of this Treaty.

2. Each Party undertakes not to deploy ABM systems for a defense of the territory of its country and not to provide a base for such a defense, and not to deploy ABM systems for defense of an individual region except as provided for in Article III of this Treaty.

Article II

1. For the purpose of this Treaty an ABM system is a system to counter strategic ballistic missiles or their elements in flight trajectory, currently consisting of:

(a) ABM interceptor missiles, which are interceptor missiles constructed and deployed for an ABM role, or of a type tested in an ABM mode;

(b) ABM launchers, which are launchers constructed and deployed for launching ABM interceptor missiles; and

(c) ABM radars, which are radars constructed and deployed for an ABM role, or of a type tested in an ABM mode.

2. The ABM system components listed in paragraph 1 of this Article include those which are:

(*a*) operational;

(*b*) under construction;

(*c*) undergoing testing;

(*d*) undergoing overhaul, repair or conversion; or

(*e*) mothballed.

Article III

Each Party undertakes not to deploy ABM systems or their components except that:

(*a*) within one ABM system deployment area having a radius of one hundred and fifty kilometers and centered on the Party's national capital, a Party may deploy: (1) no more than one hundred ABM launchers and no more than one hundred ABM interceptor missiles at launch sites, and (2) ABM radars within no more than six ABM radar complexes, the area of each complex being circular and having a diameter of no more than three kilometers; and

(*b*) within one ABM system deployment area having a radius of one hundred and fifty kilometers and containing ICBM silo launchers, a Party may deploy: (1) no more than one hundred ABM launchers and no more than one hundred ABM radars comparable in potential to corresponding ABM radars operational or under construction on the date of signature of the Treaty in an ABM system deployment area containing ICBM silo launchers, and (3) no more than eighteen ABM radars each having a potential less than the potential of the smaller of the above-mentioned two large phased-array ABM radars.

Article IV

The limitations provided for in Article III shall not apply to ABM systems or their components used for development or testing, and located within current or additionally agreed test ranges. Each Party may have no more than a total of fifteen ABM launchers at test ranges.

Article V

1. Each Party undertakes not to develop, test, or deploy ABM systems or components which are sea-based, air-based, space-based or mobile land-based.

2. Each Party undertakes not to develop, test, or deploy ABM launchers for launching more than one ABM interceptor missile at a time from each launcher, not to modify deployed launchers to provide them with such a capability, not to develop, test, or deploy automatic or semi-automatic or other similar systems for rapid reload of ABM launchers.

Article VI

To enhance assurance of the effectiveness of the limitations on ABM systems and their components provided by the Treaty, each Party undertakes:

(*a*) not to give missiles, launchers, or radars, other than ABM interceptor missiles, ABM launchers, or ABM radars, capabilities to counter strategic ballistic missiles or their elements in flight trajectory, and not to test them in an ABM mode; and (*b*) not to deploy in the future radars for early warning of strategic ballistic missile attack except at locations along the periphery of its national territory and orientated outward.

Article VII

Subject to the provisions of this Treaty, modernization and replacement of ABM systems or their components may be carried out.

Article VIII

ABM systems or their components in excess of the numbers or outside the areas specified in this Treaty, as well as ABM systems or their components prohibited by this Treaty, shall be destroyed or dismantled under agreed procedures within the shortest possible agreed period of time.

Article IX

To assure the viability and effectiveness of this Treaty, each Party undertakes not to transfer to other States, and not to deploy outside its national territory, ABM systems or their components limited by this Treaty.

Article X

Each Party undertakes not to assume any international obligations which would conflict with this Treaty.

Article XI

The Parties undertake to continue active negotiations for limitations on strategic offensive arms.

Article XII

1. For the purpose of providing assurance of compliance with the provisions of this Treaty, each Party shall use national technical means of verification at its disposal in a manner consistent with generally recognized principles of international law.

2. Each Party undertakes not to interfere with the national technical means of verification of the other Party operating in accordance with paragraph 1 of this Article.

3. Each Party undertakes not to use deliberate concealment measures which impede verification by national technical means of compliance with the provisions of this Treaty. This obligation shall not require changes in current construction, assembly, conversion, or overhaul practices.

Article XIII

1. To promote the objectives and implementation of the provisions of this Treaty, the Parties shall establish promptly a Standing Consultative Commission, within the framework of which they will:

(*a*) consider questions concerning compliance with the obligations assumed and related situations which may be considered ambiguous;

(*b*) provide on a voluntary basis such information as either Party considers necessary to assure confidence in compliance with the obligations assumed;

(*c*) consider questions involving unintended interference with national technical means of verification;

(*d*) consider possible changes in the strategic situation which have a bearing on the provisions of this Treaty;

(*e*) agree upon procedures and dates for destruction or dismantling of ABM systems or their components in cases provided for by the provisions of this Treaty;

(*f*) consider, as appropriate, possible proposals for further increasing the viability of this Treaty; including proposals for amendments in accordance with the provisions of this Treaty;

(*g*) consider, as appropriate, proposals for further measures aimed at limiting strategic arms.

2. The Parties through consultation shall establish, and may amend as appropriate, Regulations for the Standing Consultative Commission governing procedures, composition and other relevant matters.

Article XIV

1. Each Party may propose amendments to this Treaty. Agreed amendments shall enter into force in accordance with the procedures governing the entry into force of this Treaty.

2. Five years after entry into force of this Treaty, and at five-year intervals thereafter, the Parties shall together conduct a review of this Treaty.

Article XV

1. This Treaty shall be of unlimited duration.

2. Each Party shall, in exercising its national sovereignty, have the right to withdraw from this Treaty if it decides that extraordinary events related to the subject matter of this Treaty have jeopardized its supreme interests. It shall give notice of its decision to the other Party six months prior to withdrawal from the Treaty. Such notice shall include a statement of the extraordinary events the notifying Party regards as having jeopardized its supreme interests.

Article XVI

1. This Treaty shall be subject to ratification in accordance with the constitutional procedures of each Party. The Treaty shall enter into force on the day of the exchange of instruments of ratification.

2. This Treaty shall be registered pursuant to Article 102 of the Charter of the United Nations.

Done at Moscow on May 26, 1972, in two copies, each in the English and Russian languages, both texts being equally authentic.

For the United States of America   *For the Union of Soviet Socialist Republics*

President of the United States of   General Secretary of the Central
America   Committee of the CPSU

Agreed statements, common understandings, and unilateral statements regarding the treaty between the United States of America and the Union of Soviet Socialist Republics on the limitation of anti-ballistic missile systems

Agreed statements

The document set forth below was agreed upon and initialed by the Heads of the Delegations on May 26, 1972 [letter designations added]:

[A]
The Parties understand that, in addition to the ABM radars which may be deployed in accordance with subparagraph (a) of Article III of the Treaty, those non-phased-array ABM radars operational on the date of signature of the Treaty within the ABM system deployment area for defense of the national capital may be retained.

[B]
The Parties understand that the potential (the product of mean emitted power in watts and antenna area in square meters) of the smaller of the two large phased-array ABM radars referred to in subparagraph (b) of Article III of the Treaty is considered for purposes of the Treaty to be three million.

[C]
The Parties understand that the centre of the ABM system deployment area centered on the national capital and the centre of the ABM system deployment area containing ICBM silo launchers for each Party shall be separated by no less than thirteen hundred kilometers.

[D]
In order to insure fulfillment of the obligation not to deploy ABM systems and their components except as provided in Article III of the Treaty, the Parties agree that in the event ABM systems based on other physical principles and including components capable of substituting for ABM interceptor missiles, ABM launchers, or ABM radars are created in the future, specific limitations on such systems and their components would be subject to discussion in accordance with Article XIII and agreement in accordance with Article XIV of the Treaty.

[E]
The Parties understand that Article V of the Treaty includes obligations not to develop, test or deploy ABM interceptor missiles for the delivery by each ABM interceptor missile of more than one independently guided warhead.

[F]
The Parties agree not to deploy phased-array radars having a potential (the product of mean emitted power in watts and antenna area in square meters) exceeding three million, except as provided for in Articles III, IV, and VI of the Treaty, or except for the purposes of tracking objects in outer space or for use as national technical means of verification.

The Parties understand that Article IX of the Treaty includes the obligation of the US and the USSR not to provide to other States technical descriptions or blue prints specially worked out for the construction of ABM systems and their components limited by the Treaty.

Common understandings

Common understanding of the Parties on the following matters was reached during the negotiations:

A. *Location of ICBM defenses*

The U.S. Delegation made the following statement on May 26, 1972:

Article III of the ABM Treaty provides for each side one ABM system deployment area centered on its national capital and one ABM system deployment area containing ICBM silo launchers. The two sides have registered agreement on the following statement: "The Parties understand that the centre of the ABM system deployment area centered on the national capital and the center of the ABM system deployment area containing ICBM silo launchers for each Party shall be separated by no less than thirteen hundred kilometers." In this connection, the U.S. side notes that its ABM system deployment area for defense of ICBM silo launchers, located west of the Mississippi River, will be centered in the Grand Forks ICBM silo launcher deployment area. (See Agreed Statement [C].)

B. *ABM test ranges*

The U.S. Delegation made the following statement on April 26, 1972:

Article IV of the ABM Treaty provides that "the limitations provided for in Article III shall not apply to ABM systems or their components used for development or testing, and located within current or additionally agreed test ranges." We believe it would be useful to assure that there is no misunderstanding as to current ABM test ranges. It is our understanding that ABM test ranges encompass the area within which ABM components are located for test purposes. The current U.S. ABM test ranges are at White Sands, New Mexico, and at Kwajalein Atoll, and the current Soviet ABM test range is near Sary Shagan in Kazakhstan. We consider that non-phased array radars of types used for range safety or instrumentation purposes may be located outside of ABM test ranges. We interpret the reference in Article IV to "additionally agreed test ranges" to mean that ABM components will not be located at any other test ranges without prior agreement between our Governments that there will be such additional ABM test ranges.

On May 5, 1972, the Soviet Delegation stated that there was a common understanding on what ABM test ranges were, that the use of the types of non-ABM radars for range safety or instrumentation was not limited under the Treaty, that the reference in

Article IV to "additionally agreed" test ranges was sufficiently clear, and that national means permitted identifying current test ranges.

C. Mobile ABM systems

On January 29, 1972, the U.S. Delegation made the following statement:

Article V(1) of the Joint Draft Text of the ABM Treaty includes an undertaking not to develop, test, or deploy mobile land-based ABM systems and their components. On May 5, 1971, the U.S. side indicated that, in its view, a prohibition on deployment of mobile ABM systems and components would rule out the deployment of ABM launchers and radars which were not permanent fixed types. At the time, we asked for the Soviet view of this interpretation. Does the Soviet side agree with the U.S. side's interpretation put forward on May 5, 1971?

On April 13, 1972, the Soviet Delegation said there is a general common understanding on this matter.

D. Standing Consultative Commission

Ambassador Smith made the following statement on May 22, 1972:

The United States proposes that the sides agree that, with regard to initial implementation of the ABM Treaty's Article XIII on the Standing Consultative Commission (SCC) and of the consultation Articles to the Interim Agreement on offensive arms and the Accidents Agreement,[1] agreement establishing the SCC will be worked out early in the follow-on SALT negotiations; until that is completed, the following arrangements will prevail: when SALT is in session, any consultation desired by either side under these Articles can be carried out by the two SALT Delegations; when SALT is not in session, *ad hoc* arrangements for any desired consultations under these Articles may be made through diplomatic channels.

Minister Semenov replied that, on an *ad referendum* basis, he could agree that the U.S. statement corresponded to the Soviet understanding.

E. Standstill

On May 6, 1972, Minister Semenov made the following statement:

In an effort to accommodate the wishes of the U.S. side, the Soviet Delegation is prepared to proceed on the basis that the two sides will in fact observe the obligations of both the Interim Agreement and the ABM Treaty beginning from the date of signature of these two documents.

---

[1]See Article 7 of Agreement to Reduce the Risk of Outbreak of Nuclear War Between the United States of America and the Union of Soviet Socialist Republics, signed 30 September, 1971.

In reply, the U.S. Delegation made the following statement on May 20, 1972:

The U.S. agrees in principle with the Soviet statement made on May 6 concerning observance of obligations beginning from date of signature but we would like to make clear our understanding that this means that, pending ratification and acceptance, neither side would take any action prohibited by the agreements after they had entered into force. This understanding would continue to apply in the absence of notification by either signatory of its intention not to proceed with ratification or approval.

The Soviet Delegation indicated agreement with the U.S. statement.

Unilateral statements

The following noteworthy unilateral statements were made during the negotiations by the United States Delegation:

A. Withdrawal from the ABM Treaty

On May 9, 1972, Ambassador Smith made the following statement:

The U.S. Delegation has stressed the importance the U.S. Government attaches to achieving agreement on more complete limitations on strategic offensive arms, following agreement on an ABM Treaty and on an Interim Agreement on certain measures with respect to the limitation of strategic offensive arms. The U.S. Delegation believes that an objective of the follow-on negotiations should be to constrain and reduce on a long-term basis threats to the survivability of our respective strategic retaliatory forces. The USSR Delegation has also indicated that the objectives of SALT would remain unfulfilled without the achievement of an agreement providing for more complete limitations on strategic offensive arms. Both sides recognize that the initial agreements would be steps toward the achievement of more complete limitations on strategic arms. If an agreement providing for more complete strategic offensive arms limitations were not achieved within five years, U.S. supreme interests could be jeopardized. Should that occur, it would constitute a basis for withdrawal from the ABM Treaty. The U.S. does not wish to see such a situation occur, nor do we believe that the USSR does. It is because we wish to prevent such a situation that we emphasize the importance the U.S. Government attaches to achievement of more complete limitations on strategic offensive arms. The U.S. Executive will inform the Congress, in connection with Congressional consideration of the ABM Treaty and the Interim Agreement, of this statement of the U.S. position.

B. Tested in ABM mode

On April 7, 1972, the U.S. Delegation made the following statement:

Article II of the Joint Text Draft uses the term "tested in an ABM mode," in defining ABM components, and Article VI includes certain obligations concerning such testing. We believe that the sides should have a common understanding of this phrase. First, we would note that the testing provisions of the ABM Treaty are intended to apply to testing which occurs after the date of signature of the Treaty, and not to any testing which may have occurred in the past. Next, we would amplify the remarks we have made on this subject during the previous Helsinki phase by setting forth the objectives which govern the U.S. view on the subject, namely, while prohibiting testing of non-ABM components for ABM purposes: not to prevent testing of ABM components, and not to prevent testing of non-ABM components for non-ABM purposes. To clarify our interpretation of "tested in an ABM mode," we note that we would consider a launcher, missile or radar to be "tested in an ABM mode" if, for example, any of the following events occur: (1) a launcher is used to launch an ABM interceptor missile, (2) an interceptor missile is flight tested against a target vehicle which has a flight trajectory with characteristics of a strategic ballistic missile flight trajectory, or is flight tested in conjunction with the test of an ABM interceptor missile or an ABM radar at the same test range, or is flight tested to an altitude inconsistent with interception of targets against which air defenses are deployed, (3) a radar makes measurements on a cooperative target vehicle of the kind referred to in item (2) above during the reentry portion of its trajectory or makes measurements in conjunction with the test of an ABM interceptor missile or an ABM radar at the same test range. Radars used for purposes such as range safety or instrumentation would be exempt from application of these criteria.

C. No-transfer article of ABM Treaty

On April 18, 1972, the U.S. Delegation made the following statement:

In regard to this Article [IX], I have a brief and I believe self-explanatory statement to make. The U.S. side wishes to make clear that the provisions of this Article do not set a precedent for whatever provision may be considered for a Treaty on Limiting Strategic Offensive Arms. The question of transfer of strategic offensive arms is a far more complex issue, which may require a different solution.

D. No increase in defense of early warning radars

On July 28, 1970, the U.S. Delegation made the following statement:

Since Hen House radars [Soviet ballistic missile early warning radars] can detect and track ballistic missile warheads at great distances, they have a significant ABM potential. Accordingly, the U.S. would regard any increase in the defenses of such radars by surface-to-air missiles as inconsistent with an agreement.

Interim Agreement between the United States of America and the Union of Soviet Socialist Republics on certain measures with respect to the limitation of strategic offensive arms

SIGNED: Moscow, 26 May 1972
ENTERED INTO FORCE: 3 October 1972

The United States of America and the Union of Soviet Socialist Republics, hereinafter referred to as the Parties,

Convinced that the Treaty on the Limitation of Anti-Ballistic Missile Systems and this Interim Agreement on Certain Measures with Respect to the Limitation of Strategic Offensive Arms will contribute to the creation of more favorable conditions for active negotiations on limiting strategic arms as well as to the relaxation of international tension and the strengthening of trust between States,

Taking into account the relationship between strategic offensive and defensive arms,

Mindful of their obligations under Article VI of the Treaty of the Non-Proliferation of Nuclear Weapons,

Have agreed as follows:

Article I

The Parties undertake not to start construction of additional fixed land-based intercontinental ballistic missile (ICBM) launchers after July 1, 1972.

Article II

The Parties undertake not to convert land-based launchers for light ICBMs, or for ICBMs of older types deployed prior to 1964, into land-based launchers for heavy ICBMs of types deployed after that time.

Article III

The Parties undertake to limit submarine-launched ballistic missile (SLBM) launchers and modern ballistic missile submarines to the numbers operational and under construction on the date of signature of this Interim Agreement, and in addition to launchers and submarines constructed under procedures established by the Parties as replacements for an equal number of ICBM launchers of older types deployed prior to 1964 or for launchers on older submarines.

Article IV

Subject to the provisions of this Interim Agreement, modernization and replacement of strategic offensive ballistic missiles and launchers covered by this Interim Agreement may be undertaken.

Article V

1. For the purpose of providing assurance of compliance with the provisions of this Interim Agreement, each Party shall use national technical means of verification at its disposal in a manner consistent with generally recognized principles of international law.

2. Each party undertakes not to interfere with the national technical means of verification of the other Party operating in accordance with paragraph 1 of this Article.

3. Each Party undertakes not to use deliberate concealment measures which impede verification by national technical means of compliance with the provisions of this Interim Agreement. This obligation shall not require changes in current construction, assembly, conversion, or overhaul practices.

Article VI

To promote the objectives and implementation of the provisions of this Interim Agreement, the Parties shall use the Standing Consultative Commission established under Article XIII of the Treaty on the Limitation of Anti-Ballistic Missile Systems in accordance with the provisions of that Article.

Article VII

The Parties undertake to continue active negotiations for limitations on strategic offensive arms. The obligations provided for in this Interim Agreement shall not prejudice the scope or terms of the limitations on strategic offensive arms which may be worked out in the course of further negotiations.

Article VIII

1. This Interim Agreement shall enter into force upon exchange of written notices of acceptance by each Party, which exchange shall take place simultaneously with the exchange of instruments of ratification of the Treaty on the Limitation of Anti-Ballistic Missile Systems.

2. This Interim Agreement shall remain in force for a period of five years unless replaced earlier by an agreement on more complete measures limiting strategic offensive arms. It is the objective of the Parties to conduct active follow-on negotiations with the aim of concluding such an agreement as soon as possible.

3. Each Party shall, in exercising its national sovereignty, have the right to withdraw from this Interim Agreement if it decides that extraordinary events related to the subject matter of this Interim Agreement have jeopardized its supreme interests. It shall give notice of its decision to the other Party six months prior to withdrawal from this Interim Agreement. Such notice shall include a statement of the extraordinary events the notifying Party regards as having jeopardized its supreme interests.

DONE at Moscow on May 26, 1972, in two copies, each in the English and Russian languages, both texts being equally authentic.

For the United States of America

President of the United States of America

For the Union of Soviet Socialist Republics

General Secretary of the Central Committee of the CPSU

Protocol to the Interim Agreement between the United States of America and the Union of Soviet Socialist Republics on certain measures with respect to the limitation of strategic offensive arms

The United States of America and the Union of Soviet Socialist Republics, hereinafter referred to as the Parties,

Having agreed on certain limitations relating to submarine-launched ballistic missile launchers and modern ballistic missile submarines, and to replacement procedures, in the Interim Agreement,

Have agreed as follows:

The Parties understand that, under Article III of the Interim Agreement, for the period during which that Agreement remains in force:

The U.S. may have no more than 710 ballistic missile launchers on submarines (SLBMs) and no more than 44 modern ballistic missile submarines. The Soviet Union may have no more than 950 ballistic missile launchers on submarines and no more than 62 modern ballistic missile submarines.

Additional ballistic missile launchers on submarines up to the above-mentioned levels, in the U.S.—over 656 ballistic missile launchers on nuclear-powered submarines, and in the U.S.S.R.—over 740 ballistic missile launchers on nuclear-powered submarines, operational and under construction, may become operational as replacements for equal numbers of ballistic missile launchers of older types deployed prior to 1964 or of ballistic missile launchers on older submarines.

The deployment of modern SLBMs on any submarine, regardless of type, will be counted against the total level of SLBMs permitted for the U.S. and the U.S.S.R.

This Protocol shall be considered an integral part of the Interim Agreement.

DONE at Moscow this 26th day of May, 1972

For the United States of America

President of the United States of America

For the Union of Soviet Socialist Republics

General Secretary of the Central Committee of the CPSU

Agreed statements, common understandings, and unilateral statements regarding the Interim Agreement between the United States of America and the Union of Soviet Socialist Republics on certain measures with respect to the limitation of strategic offensive arms

1. Agreed statements

The document set forth below was agreed upon and initialed by the Heads of the Delegations on May 26, 1972 [letter designations added]:

[A]

The Parties understand that land-based ICBM launchers referred to in the Interim Agreement are understood to be launchers for strategic ballistic missiles capable of ranges in excess of the shortest distance between the northeastern border of the continental U.S. and the northwestern border of the continental U.S.S.R.

[B]

The Parties understand that fixed land-based ICBM launchers under active construction as of the date of signature of the Interim Agreement may be completed.

[C]

The Parties understand that in the process of modernization and replacement the dimensions of land-based ICBM silo launchers will not be significantly increased.

[D]

The Parties understand that during the period of the Interim Agreement there shall be no significant increase in the number of ICBM or SLBM test and training launchers, or in the number of such launchers for modern land-based heavy ICBMs. The Parties further understand that construction or conversion of ICBM launchers at test ranges shall be undertaken only for purposes of testing and training.

[E]

The Parties understand that dismantling or destruction of ICBM launchers of older types deployed prior to 1964 and ballistic missile launchers on older submarines being replaced by new SLBM launchers on modern submarines will be initiated at the time of the beginning of sea trials of a replacement submarine, and will be completed in the shortest possible agreed period of time. Such dismantling or destruction, and timely notification thereof, will be accomplished under procedures to be agreed in the Standing Consultative Commission.

Common understandings

Common understandings of the Parties on the following matters was reached during the negotiations:

A. Increase in ICBM silo dimensions

Ambassador Smith made the following statement on May 26, 1972:

The Parties agree that the term "significantly increased" means that an increase will not be greater than 10–15 percent of the present dimensions of land-based ICBM silo launchers.

Minister Semenov replied that this statement corresponded to the Soviet understanding.

B. Standing Consultative Commission

Ambassador Smith made the following statement on May 22, 1972:

The United States proposes that the sides agree that, with regard to initial implementation of the ABM Treaty's Article XIII on the Standing Consultative Commission (SCC) and of the consultation Articles to the Interim Agreement on offensive arms and the Accidents Agreement,[1] agreement establishing the SCC will be worked out early in the follow-on SALT negotiations; until that is completed, the following arrangements will prevail: when SALT is in session, any consultation desired by either side under these Articles can be carried out by the two SALT Delegations; when SALT is not in session, *ad hoc* arrangements for any desired consultations under these Articles may be made through diplomatic channels.

Minister Semenov replied that, on an *ad referendum* basis, he could agree that the U.S. statement corresponded to the Soviet understanding.

C. Standstill

On May 6, 1972, Minister Semenov made the following statement:

In an effort to accommodate the wishes of the U.S. side, the Soviet Delegation is prepared to proceed on the basis that the two sides will in fact observe the obligations of both the Interim Agreement and the ABM Treaty beginning from the date of signature of these two documents.

In reply, the U.S. Delegation made the following statement on May 20, 1972:

The U.S. agrees in principle with the Soviet statement made on May 6 concerning observance of obligations beginning from date of signature but we would like to make clear our understanding that this means that, pending ratification and acceptance, neither side would take any action prohibited by the agreements after they had entered into force. This understanding would continue to apply in the absence of notification by either signatory of its intention not to proceed with ratification or approval.

The Soviet Delegation indicated agreement with the U.S. statement.

Unilateral statements

(*a*) The following noteworthy unilateral statements were made during the negotiations by the United States Delegation:

A. Withdrawal from the ABM Treaty

On May 9, 1972, Ambassador Smith made the following statement:

The U.S. Delegation has stressed the importance the U.S. Government attaches to achieving agreement on more complete limitations on strategic offensive arms, following agreement on an ABM Treaty and on an Interim Agreement on certain measures with respect to the limitation of strategic offensive arms. The U.S. Delegation believes that an objective of the follow-on negotiations should be to constrain

---

[1]See Article 7 of Agreement to reduce the risk of outbreak of nuclear war between the United States of America and the Union of Soviet Socialist Republics, signed 30 September, 1971.

and reduce on a long-term basis threats to the survivability of our respective strategic relatiatory forces. The USSR Delegation has also indicated that the objectives of SALT would remain unfulfilled without the achievement of an agreement providing for more complete limitations on strategic offensive arms. Both sides recognize that the initial agreements would be steps toward the achievement of more complete limitations on strategic arms. If an agreement providing for more complete strategic offensive arms limitations were not achieved within five years, U.S. supreme interests could be jeopardized. Should that occur, it would constitute a basis for withdrawal from the ABM Treaty. The U.S. does not wish to see such a situation occur, nor do we believe that the USSR does. It is because we wish to prevent such a situation that we emphasize the importance the U.S. Government attaches to achievement of more complete limitations on strategic offensive arms. The U.S. Executive will inform the Congress, in connection with Congressional consideration of the ABM Treaty and the Interim Agreement, of this statement of the U.S. position.

B. Land-mobile ICBM launchers

The U.S. Delegation made the following statement on May 20, 1972:

In connection with the important subject of land-mobile ICBM launchers, in the interest of concluding the Interim Agreement the U.S. Delegation now withdraws its proposal that Article I or an agreed statement explicitly prohibit the deployment of mobile land-based ICBM launchers. I have been instructed to inform you that, while agreeing to defer the question of limitation of operational land-mobile ICBM launchers to the subsequent negotiations on more complete limitations on strategic offensive arms, the U.S. would consider the deployment of operational land-mobile ICBM launchers during the period of the Interim Agreement as inconsistent with the objectives of that Agreement.

C. Covered facilities

The U.S. Delegation made the following statement on May 20, 1972:

I wish to emphasize the importance that the United States attaches to the provisions of Article V, including in particular their application to fitting out or berthing submarines.

D. "Heavy" ICBM's

The U.S. Delegation made the following statement on May 26, 1972:

The U.S. Delegation regrets that the Soviet Delegation has not been willing to agree on a common definition of a heavy missile. Under these circumstances, the U.S. Delegation believes it necessary to state the following: The United States would consider any ICBM having a volume significantly greater than that of the largest light ICBM now operational on either side to be a heavy ICBM. The U.S. proceeds on the premise that the Soviet side will give due account to this consideration.

(b) The following noteworthy unilateral statement was made by the Delegation of the U.S.S.R. and is shown here with the U.S. reply:

On May 17, 1972, Minister Semenov made the following unilateral "Statement of the Soviet Side":

Taking into account that modern ballistic missile submarines are presently in the possession of not only the U.S., but also of its NATO allies, the Soviet Union agrees that for the period of effectiveness of the Interim 'Freeze' Agreement the U.S. and its NATO allies have up to 50 such submarines with a total of up to 800 ballistic missile launchers thereon (including 41 U.S. submarines with 656 ballistic missile launchers). However, if during the period of effectiveness of the Agreement U.S. allies in NATO should increase the number of their modern submarines to exceed the numbers of submarines they would have operational or under construction on the date of signature of the Agreement, the Soviet Union will have the right to a corresponding increase in the number of its submarines. In the opinion of the Soviet side, the solution of the question of modern ballistic missile submarines provided for in the Interim Agreement only partially compensates for the strategic imbalance in the deployment of the nuclear-powered missile submarines of the USSR and the U.S. Therefore, the Soviet side believes that this whole question, and above all the question of liquidating the American missile submarine bases outside the U.S., will be appropriately resolved in the course of follow-on negotiations.

On May 24, Ambassador Smith made the following reply to Minister Semenov:

The United States side has studied the "statement made by the Soviet side" of May 17 concerning compensation for submarine basing and SLBM submarines belonging to third countries. The United States does not accept the validity of the considerations in that statement.

On May 26 Minister Semenov repeated the unilateral statement made on May 17. Ambassador Smith also repeated the U.S. rejection on May 26.

Agreement governing the activities of states on the Moon and other celestial bodies

OPENED FOR SIGNATURE: New York, 5 December 1979
ENTERED INTO FORCE: 11 July 1984
DEPOSITARY: UN Secretary-General

The States Parties to this Agreement,

Noting the achievements of States in the exploration and use of the moon and other celestial bodies,

Recognizing that the moon, as a natural satellite of the earth, has an important role to play in the exploration of outer space,

Determined to promote on the basis of equality the further development of co-operation among States in the exploration and use of the moon and other celestial bodies,

Desiring to prevent the moon from becoming an area of international conflict,

Bearing in mind the benefits which may be derived from the exploitation of the natural resources of the moon and other celestial bodies,

Recalling the Treaty on Principles Governing the Activities of States in the Exploration and Use of Outer Space, including the Moon and Other Celestial Bodies, the Agreement on the Rescue of Astronauts, the Return of Astronauts and the Return of Objects Launched into Outer Space, the Convention on International Liability for Damage Caused by Space Objects, and the Convention on Registration of Objects Launched into Outer Space,

Taking into account the need to define and develop the provisions of these international instruments in relation to the moon and other celestial bodies, having regard to further progress in the exploration and use of outer space,

Have agreed on the following:

Article I

1. The provisions of this Agreement relating to the moon shall also apply to other celestial bodies within the solar system, other than the earth, except in so far as specific legal norms enter into force with respect to any of these celestial bodies.

2. For the purpose of this Agreement reference to the moon shall include orbits around or other trajectories to or around it.

3. This Agreement does not apply to extraterrestrial materials which reach the surface of the earth by natural means.

Article 2

All activities on the moon, including its exploration and use, shall be carried out in accordance with international law, in particular the Charter of the United Nations, and taking into account the Declaration on Principles of International Law concerning Friendly Relations and Co-operation among States in accordance with the Charter of the United Nations, adopted by the General Assembly on 24 October 1970, in the interests of maintaining international peace and security and promoting international co-operation and mutual understanding, and with due regard to the corresponding interests of all other States Parties.

Article 3

1. The moon shall be used by all States Parties exclusively for peaceful purposes.

2. Any threat or use of force or any other hostile act or threat of hostile act on the moon is prohibited. It is likewise prohibited to use the moon in order to commit any such act or to engage in any such threat in relation to the earth, the moon, spacecraft, the personnel of spacecraft or man-made space objects.

3. States Parties shall not place in orbit around or other trajectory to or around the moon objects carrying nuclear weapons or any other kinds of weapons of mass destruction or place or use such weapons on or in the moon.

4. The establishment of military bases, installations and fortifications, the testing of any type of weapons and the conduct of military manoeuvres on the moon shall be forbidden. The use of military personnel for scientific research or for any other peaceful purposes shall not be prohibited. The use of any equipment or facility necessary for peaceful exploration and use of the moon shall also not be prohibited.

Article 4

1. The exploration and use of the moon shall be the province of all mankind and shall be carried out for the benefit and in the interests of all countries, irrespective of their degree of economic or scientific development. Due regard shall be paid to the interests of present and future generations as well as to the need to promote higher standards of living and conditions of economic and social progress and development in accordance with the Charter of the United Nations.

2. States Parties shall be guided by the principle of co-operation and mutual assistance in all their activities concerning the exploration and use of the moon. International co-operation in pursuance of this Agreement should be as wide as possible and may take place on a multilateral basis, on a bilateral basis or through international intergovernmental organizations.

Article 5

1. States Parties shall inform the Secretary-General of the United Nations as well as the public and the international scientific community, to the greatest extent feasible and practicable, of their activities concerned with the exploration and use of the moon. Information on the time, purposes, location, orbital parameters and duration shall be given in respect of each mission to the moon as soon as possible after launching, while information on the results of each mission, including scientific results, shall be furnished upon completion of the mission. In the case of a mission lasting more than thirty days, information on conduct of the mission, including any scientific results, shall be given periodically at thirty days' intervals. For missions lasting more than six months, only significant additions to such information need be reported thereafter.

2. If a State Party becomes aware that another State Party plans to operate simultaneously in the same area or in the same orbit around or trajectory to or around the moon, it shall promptly inform the other State of the timing of and plans for its own operations.

3. In carrying out activities under this Agreement, States Parties shall promptly inform the Secretary-General, as well as the public and the international scientific community, of any phenomena they discover in outer space, including the moon, which could endanger human life or health, as well as of any indication of organic life.

Article 6

1. There shall be freedom of scientific investigation on the moon by all States Parties without discrimination of any kind, on the basis of equality and in accordance with international law.

2. In carrying out scientific investigations and in furtherance of the provisions of this Agreement, the States Parties shall have the right to collect on and remove from the moon samples of its mineral and other substances. Such samples shall remain at the disposal of those States Parties which caused them to be collected and may be used by them for scientific purposes. States Parties shall have regard to the desirability of making a portion of such samples available to other interested States Parties and the international scientific community for scientific investigations. States Parties may in the course of scientific investigations also use mineral and other substances of the moon in quantities appropriate for the support of their missions.

3. States Parties agree on the desirability of exchanging scientific and other personnel on expeditions to or installations on the moon to the greatest extent feasible and practicable.

Article 7

1. In exploring and using the moon, States Parties shall take measures to prevent the disruption of the existing balance of its environment whether by introducing adverse changes in that environment, by its harmful contamination through the introduction of extra-environmental matter or otherwise. States Parties shall also take measures to avoid harmfully affecting the environment of the earth through the introduction of extraterrestrial matter or otherwise.

2. States Parties shall inform the Secretary-General of the United Nations of the measures being adopted by them in accordance with paragraph 1 of this article and shall also, to the maximum extent feasible, notify him in advance of all placements by them of radio-active materials on the moon and of the purposes of such placements.

3. States Parties shall report to other States Parties and to the Secretary-General concerning areas of the moon having special scientific interest in order that, without prejudice to the rights of other States Parties, consideration may be given to the designation of such areas as international scientific preserves for which special protective arrangements are to be agreed upon in consultation with the competent bodies of the United Nations.

Article 8

1. States Parties may pursue their activities in the exploration and use of the moon anywhere on or below its surface, subject to the provisions of this Agreement.

2. For these purposes States Parties may, in particular:

(*a*) Land their space objects on the moon and launch them from the moon;

(*b*) Place their personnel, space vehicles, equipment, facilities, stations and installations anywhere on or below the surface of the moon.

Personnel, space vehicles, equipment, facilities, stations and installations may move or be moved freely over or below the surface of the moon.

3. Activities of States Parties in accordance with paragraphs 1 and 2 of this article shall not interfere with the activities of other States Parties on the moon. Where such interference may occur, the States Parties concerned shall undertake consultations in accordance with article 15, paragraphs 2 and 3 of this Agreement.

Article 9

1. States Parties may establish manned and unmanned stations on the moon. A State Party establishing a station shall use only that area which is required for the needs of the station and shall immediately inform the Secretary-General of the United Nations of the location and purposes of the station. Subsequently, at annual intervals that State shall likewise inform the Secretary-General whether the station continues in use and whether its purposes have changed.

2. Stations shall be installed in such a manner that they do not impede the free access to all areas of the moon by personnel, vehicles and equipment of other States Parties conducting activities on the moon in accordance with the provisions of this Agreement or of article I of the Treaty on Principles Governing the Activities of States in the Exploration and Use of Outer Space, Including the Moon and Other Celestial Bodies.

Article 10

1. States Parties shall adopt all practicable measures to safeguard the life and health of persons on the moon. For this purpose they shall regard any person on the moon as an astronaut within the meaning of article V of the Treaty on Principles Governing the Activities of States in the Exploration and Use of Outer Space, Including the Moon and Other Celestial Bodies and as part of the personnel of a spacecraft within the meaning of the Agreement on the Rescue of Astronauts, the Return of Astronauts and the Return of Objects Launched into Outer Space.

2. States Parties shall offer shelter in their stations, installations, vehicles and other facilities to persons in distress on the moon.

Article 11

1. The moon and its natural resources are the common heritage of mankind, which finds its expression in the provisions of this Agreement and in particular in paragraph 5 of this article.

2. The moon is not subject to national appropriation by any claim of sovereignty, by means of use or occupation, or by any other means.

3. Neither the surface nor the subsurface of the moon, nor any part thereof or natural resources in place, shall become property of any State, international intergovernmental or non-governmental organization, national organization or non-governmental entity or of any natural person. The placement of personnel, space vehicles, equipment, facilities, stations and installations on or below the surface of the moon, including structures connected with its surface or subsurface, shall not create a right

or ownership over the surface or the subsurface of the moon or any areas thereof. The foregoing provisions are without prejudice to the international régime referred to in paragraph 5 of this article.

4. States Parties have the right to exploration and use of the moon without discrimination of any kind, on a basis of equality and in accordance with international law and the terms of this Agreement.

5. States Parties to this Agreement hereby undertake to establish an international régime, including appropriate procedures, to govern the exploitation of the natural resources of the moon as such exploitation is about to become feasible. This provision shall be implemented in accordance with article 18 of this Agreement.

6. In order to facilitate the establishment of the international régime referred to in paragraph 5 of this article, States Parties shall inform the Secretary-General of the United Nations as well as the public and the international scientific community, to the greatest extent feasible and practicable, of any natural resources they may discover on the moon.

7. The main purposes of the international régime to be established shall include:

(*a*) The orderly and safe development of the natural resources of the moon;

(*b*) The rational management of those resources;

(*c*) The expansion of opportunities in the use of those resources;

(*d*) An equitable sharing by all States Parties in the benefits derived from those resources, whereby the interests and needs of the developing countries, as well as the efforts of those countries which have contributed either directly or indirectly to the exploration of the moon, shall be given special consideration.

8. All the activities with respect to the natural resources of the moon shall be carried out in a manner compatible with the purposes specified in paragraph 7 of this article and the provisions of article 6, paragraph 2, of this Agreement.

Article 12

1. States Parties shall retain jurisdiction and control over their personnel, vehicles, equipment, facilities, stations and installations on the moon. The ownership of space vehicles, equipment, facilities, stations and installations shall not be affected by their presence on the moon.

2. Vehicles, installations and equipment or their component parts found in places other than their intended location shall be dealt with in accordance with article 5 of the Agreement on Rescue of Astronauts, the Return of Astronauts and the Return of Objects Launched into Outer Space.

3. In the event of an emergency involving a threat to human life, States Parties may use the equipment, vehicles, installations, facilities or supplies of other States Parties on the moon. Prompt notification of such use shall be made to the Secretary-General of the United Nations or the State Party concerned.

Article 13

A State Party which learns of the crash landing, forced landing or other unintended landing on the moon of a space object, or its component parts, that were not launched by it, shall promptly inform the launching State Party and the Secretary-General of the United Nations.

Article 14

1. States Parties to this Agreement shall bear international responsibility for national activities on the moon, whether such activities are carred on by governmental agencies or by non-governmental entities, and for assuring that national activities are carried out in conformity with the provisions set forth in this Agreement. States Parties shall ensure that non-governmental entities under their jurisdiction shall engage in activities on the moon only under the authority and continuing supervision of the appropriate State Party.

2. States Parties recognize that detailed arrangements concerning liability for damage caused on the moon, in addition to the provisions of the Treaty on Principles Governing the Activities of States in the Exploration and Use of Outer Space, Including the Moon and Other Celestial Bodies and the Convention on International Liability for Damage caused by Space Objects, may become necessary as a result of more extensive activities on the moon. Any such arrangements shall be elaborated in accordance with the procedure provided for in article 18 of this Agreement.

Article 15

1. Each State Party may assure itself that the activities of other States Parties in the exploration and use of the moon are compatible with the provisions of this Agreement. To this end, all space vehicles, equipment, facilities, stations and installations on the moon shall be open to other States Parties. Such States Parties shall give reasonable advance notice of a projected visit, in order that appropriate consultations may be held and that maximum precautions may be taken to assure safety and to avoid interference with normal operations in the facility to be visited. In pursuance of this article, any State Party may act on its own behalf or with the full or partial assistance of any other State Party or through appropriate international procedures within the framework of the United Nations and in accordance with the Charter.

2. A State Party which has reason to believe that another State Party is not fulfilling the obligations incumbent upon it pursuant to this Agreement or that another State Party is interfering with the rights which the former State has under this Agreement may request consultations with that State Party. A State Party receiving such a request shall enter into such consultations without delay. Any other State Party which requests to do so shall be entitled to take part in the consultations. Each State Party participating in such consultations shall seek a mutually acceptable resolution of any controversy and shall bear in mind the rights and interests of all States Parties. The Secretary-General of the United Nations shall be informed of the results of the consultations and shall transmit the information received to all States Parties concerned.

3. If the consultations do not lead to a mutually acceptable settlement which has due regard for the rights and interests of all States Parties, the parties concerned shall take all measures to settle the dispute by other peaceful means of their choice appropriate to the circumstances and the nature of the dispute. If difficulties arise in connexion with the opening of consultations or if consultations do not lead to a mutually acceptable settlement, any State Party may seek the assistance of the Secretary-General, without seeking the consent of any other State Party concerned, in order to resolve the controversy. A State Party which does not maintain diplomatic relations with another State Party shall participate in such consultations, at its choice, either itself or through another State Party or the Secretary-General as intermediary.

Article 16

With the exception of articles 17 to 21, references in this Agreement to States shall be deemed to apply to any international intergovernmental organization which conducts space activities if the organization declares its acceptance of the rights and obligations provided for in this Agreement and if a majority of the States members of the organization are States Parties to this Agreement and to the Treaty on Principles Governing the Activities of States in the Exploration and Use of Outer Space, Including the Moon and Other Celestial Bodies. States members of any such organization which are States Parties to this Agreement shall take all appropriate steps to ensure that the organization makes a declaration in accordance with the foregoing.

Article 17

Any State Party to this Agreement may propose amendments to the Agreement. Amendments shall enter into force for each State Party to the Agreement accepting the amendments upon their acceptance by a majority of the States Parties to the Agreement and thereafter for each remaining State Party to the Agreement on the date of acceptance by it.

Article 18

Ten years after the entry into force of this Agreement, the question of the review of the Agreement shall be included in the provisional agenda of the General Assembly of the United Nations in order to consider, in the light of past application of the Agreement, whether it requires revision. However, at any time after the Agreement has been in force for five years, the Secretary-General of the United Nations, as depositary, shall, at the request of one third of the States Parties to the Agreement and with the concurrence of the majority of the States Parties, convene a conference of the States Parties to review this Agreement. A review conference shall also consider the question of the implementation of the provisions of article 11, paragraph 5, on the basis of the principle referred to in paragraph 1 of that article and taking into account in particular any relevant technological developments.

Article 19

1. This Agreement shall be open for signature by all States at United Nations Headquarters in New York.

2. This Agreement shall be subject to ratification by signatory States. Any State which does not sign this Agreement before its entry into force in accordance with paragraph 3 of this article may accede to it at any time. Instruments of ratification or accession shall be deposited with the Secretary-General of the United Nations.

3. This Agreement shall enter into force on the thirtieth day following the date of deposit of the fifth instrument of ratification.

4. For each State depositing its instrument of ratification or accession after the entry into force of this Agreement, it shall enter into force on the thirtieth day following the date of deposit of any such instrument.

5. The Secretary-General shall promptly inform all signatory and acceding States of the date of each signature, the date of deposit of each instrument of ratification or accession to this Agreement, the date of its entry into force and other notices.

241

Article 20

Any State Party to this Agreement may give notice of its withdrawal from the Agreement one year after its entry into force by written notification to the Secretary-General of the United Nations. Such withdrawal shall take effect one year from the date of receipt of this notification.

Article 21

The original of this Agreement, of which the Arabic, Chinese, English, French, Russian and Spanish texts are equally authentic, shall be deposited with the Secretary-General of the United Nations, who shall send certified copies thereof to all signatory and acceding states.

IN WITNESS WHEREOF the undersigned, being duly authorized thereto by their respective Governments, have signed this Agreement, opened for signature at New York on

Soviet proposal for a draft treaty on the prohibition of the stationing of weapons of any kind in outer space

The States Parties to this treaty,

Guided by the goals of strengthening peace and international security,

Proceeding on the basis of their obligations under the Charter of the United Nations to refrain from the threat or use of force in any manner inconsistent with the Purposes of the United Nations,

Desiring not to allow outer space to become an arena for the arms race and a source of aggravating relations between States,

Have agreed on the following:

Article 1

1. States Parties undertake not to place in orbit around the earth objects carrying weapons of any kind, install such weapons on celestial bodies, or station such weapons in outer space in any other manner, including on reusable manned space vehicles of an existing type or of other types which States Parties may develop in the future.

2. Each State Party to this treaty undertakes not to assist, encourage or induce any State group of States or international organization to engage in activities contrary to the provisions of paragraph 1 of this article.

Article 2

States Parties shall use space objects in strict accordance with international law, including the Charter of the United Nations, in the interest of maintaining international peace and security and promoting international co-operation and mutual understanding.

Article 3

Each State Party undertakes not to destroy, damage, disturb the normal functioning or change the flight trajectory of space objects of other States Parties, if such objects were placed in orbit in strict accordance with article 1, paragraph 1, of this treaty.

Article 4

1. For the purpose of providing assurance of compliance with the provisions of this treaty, each State Party shall use the national technical means of verification at its disposal in a manner consistent with generally recognized principles of international law.

2. Each State Party undertakes not to interfere with the national technical means of verification of other States Parties operating in accordance with paragraph 1 of this article.

3. In order to promote the objectives and provisions of this treaty, the States Parties shall, when necessary, consult each other, make inquiries and provide information in connexion with such inquiries.

Article 5

1. Any State Party to this treaty may propose amendments to this treaty. The text of any proposed amendment shall be submitted to the depositary, who shall promptly circulate it to all States Parties.

2. The amendment shall enter into force for each State Party to this Treaty which has accepted it, upon the deposit with the depositary of instruments of acceptance by the majority of States Parties. Thereafter, the amendment shall enter into force for each remaining State Party on the date of deposits of its instrument of acceptance.

Article 6

This treaty shall be of unlimited duration.

Article 7

Each State Party shall in exercising its national sovereignty have the right to withdraw from this treaty if it decides that extraordinary events related to the subject-matter of this treaty have jeopardized its supreme interests. It shall give notice to the Secretary-General of the United Nations of the decision adopted six months before withdrawing from the treaty. Such notice shall include a statement of the extraordinary events which the notifying State Party regards as having jeopardized its supreme interests.

Article 8

1. This treaty shall be open to all States for signature at United Nations Head-quarters in New York. Any State which does not sign this treaty before its entry into force in accordance with paragraph 3 of this article may accede to it at any time.

2. This treaty shall be subject to ratification by signatory States. Instruments of ratification accession shall be deposited with the Secretary-General of the United Nations.

3. This treaty shall enter into force between the States which have deposited instruments of ratification upon the deposit with the Secretary-General of the United Nations of the fifth instrument of ratification.

4. For States whose instruments of ratification or accession are deposited after the entry into force of this treaty, it shall enter into force on the date of the deposit of their instruments of ratification or accession.

5. The Secretary-General of the United Nations shall promptly inform all signatory and acceding States of the date of each signature, the date of deposit of each instrument of ratification or accession, the date of entry into force of this treaty as well as other notices.

Article 9

This treaty, of which the Arabic, Chinese, English, French, Russian and Spanish texts are equally authentic, shall be deposited with the Secretary-General of the United Nations, who shall send duly certified copies thereof to the Governments of the signatory and acceding States.

Soviet proposal for a draft treaty on the prohibition of the use of force in outer space and from space against the Earth

The States Parties to this Treaty,

Guided by the principle whereby members of the United Nations shall refrain in their international relations from the threat or use of force in any manner inconsistent with the purposes of the United Nations,

Seeking to avert an arms race in outer space and thus to lessen the danger to mankind of the threat of nuclear war,

Desiring to contribute towards attainment of the goal whereby the exploration and utilization of outer space, including the Moon and other celestial bodies, would be carried out exclusively for peaceful purposes,

Have agreed on the following:

Article 1

It is prohibited to resort to the use or threat of force in outer space and the atmosphere and on the Earth through the utilization, as the instruments of destruction, of space objects in orbit around the Earth, on celestial bodies or stationed in space in any other manner.

It is further prohibited to resort to the use or threat of force against space objects in orbit around the Earth, on celestial bodies or stationed in outer space in any other manner.

Article 2

In accordance with the provisions of article 1, States Parties to this Treaty undertake:

1. Not to test or deploy by placing in orbit around the Earth or stationing on celestial bodies or in any other manner any space-based weapons for the destruction of objects on the Earth, in the atmosphere or in outer space.

2. Not to utilize space objects in orbit around the Earth, on celestial bodies or stationed in outer space in any other manner as means to destroy any targets on the Earth, in the atmosphere or in outer space.

3. Not to destroy, damage, disturb the normal functioning or change the flight trajectory of space objects of other States.

4. Not to test or create new anti-satellite systems and to destroy any anti-satellite systems that they may already have.

5. Not to test or use manned spacecraft for military, including anti-satellite, purposes.

Article 3

The State Parties to this Treaty agree not to assist, encourge or induce any State, group of States, international organization or natural or legal person to engage in activities prohibited by this Treaty.

Article 4

1. For the purpose of providing assurance of compliance with the provisions of this Treaty, each State Party shall use the national technical means of verification at its disposal in a manner consistent with generally recognized principles of international law.

2. Each State Party undertakes not to interfere with the national technical means of verification of other States Parties operating in accordance with paragraph 1 of this article.

Article 5

1. The States Parties to this Treaty undertake to consult and co-operate with each other in solving any problems that may arise in connection with the objectives of the Treaty or its implementation.

2. Consultations and co-operation as provided in paragraph 1 of this article may also be undertaken by having recourse to appropriate international procedures within the United Nations and in accordance with its Charter. Such recourse may include utilization of the services of the Consultative Committee of States Parties to the Treaty.

3. The Consultative Committee of States Parties to the Treaty shall be convened by the depositary within one month after the receipt of a request from any State Party to this Treaty. Any State Party may nominate a representative to serve on the Committee.

Article 6

Each State Party to this Treaty undertakes to adopt such internal measures as it may deem necessary to fulfil its constitutional requirements in order to prohibit or prevent the carrying out of any activity contrary to the provisions of this Treaty in any place whatever under its jurisdiction or control.

Article 7

Nothing in this Treaty shall affect the rights and obligations of States under the Charter of the United Nations.

Article 8

Any dispute which may arise in connection with the implementation of this Treaty shall be settled exclusively by peaceful means through recourse to the procedures provided for in the Charter of the United Nations.

Article 9

This Treaty shall be of unlimited duration.

Article 10

1. This Treaty shall be open to all States for signature at United Nations Headquarters in New York. Any State which does not sign this treaty before its entry into force in accordance with paragraph 3 of this article may accede to it at any time.

2. This Treaty shall be subject to ratification by signatory States. Instruments of ratification and accession shall be deposited with the Secretary-General of the United Nations.

3. This Treaty shall enter into force between the States which have deposited instruments of ratification upon the deposit with the Secretary-General of the United Nations of the fifth instrument of ratification, provided that such instruments have been deposited by the Union of Soviet Socialist Republics and the United States of America.

4. For States whose instruments of ratification or accession are deposited after the entry into force of this Treaty, it shall enter into force on the date of the deposit of their instruments of ratification or accession.

5. The Secretary-General of the United Nations shall promptly inform all signatory and acceding States of the date of each signature, the date of deposit of each instrument of ratification or accession, the date of entry into force of this Treaty as well as other notices.

Article 11

This Treaty, of which the Arabic, Chinese, English, French, Russian and Spanish texts are equally authentic, shall be deposited with the Secretary-General of the United Nations, who shall send duly certified copies thereof to the Governments of the signatory and acceding States.

Italian proposal for an Additional Protocol to the Treaty on Principles Governing the Activities of States in the Exploration and Use of Outer Space Including the Moon and Other Celestial Bodies

The high contracting Parties,

recalling the need to facilitate, in the interest of all mankind, the exploration and use of outer space for exclusively peaceful purposes;

considering the urgent need of adopting further effective measures aimed at preventing an arms race in outer space;

noting the necessity to supplement the provisions of the Treaty on Principles Governing the Activities of States in the Exploration and Use of Outer Space Including the Moon and Other Celestial Bodies of 27 January 1967;

stressing the importance of the latest technological developments for the effective implementation of the principles mentioned in Article 1 of the Treaty;

convinced of the opportunity to prevent any development that might jeopardize the achievement of the aims of the Treaty;

taking note of paragraph 80 of the Final Document adopted by consensus at the Tenth Special Session of the General Assembly of the United Nations Devoted to Disarmament;

have agreed on the following:

Article I

1. Outer space, including the moon and other celestial bodies, shall be used for peaceful purposes only. States Parties to this Protocol undertake to refrain from engaging in, encouraging or authorizing, directly or indirectly, or in any way participating in any measures of a military or other hostile nature, such as the establishment of military bases, installations and fortifications, the stationing of devices having the same effect, the launching into earth orbit or beyond of objects carrying weapons of mass destruction or any other types of devices designed for offensive purposes, the conduct of military manoeuvres, as well as the testing of any type of weapons.

2. The provisions of this Protocol shall not prevent the use of military personnel or equipment for scientific research or for any other peaceful purposes as well as the use of such personnel or equipment for the purpose of participating in any control system to be established in order to ensure compliance with disarmament and security agreements.

Article II

Each State Party to this Protocol undertakes to adopt any measures it considers necessary in accordance with its constitutional processes to prohibit and prevent any activity in violation of the provisions of the Protocol anywhere under its jurisdiction or control.

248

Article III

1. Any State Party to this Protocol which has reason to believe that any other State Party is acting in breach of obligations deriving from the provisions of the Protocol may lodge a complaint with the Security Council of the United Nations. Such a complaint should include all relevant information as well as all possible evidence supporting its validity.

2. Each State Party to this Protocol undertakes to co-operate in carrying out any investigation which the Security Council may initiate, in accordance with the provisions of the Charter of the United Nations, on the basis of the complaint received by the Council. The Security Council shall inform the States Parties of the result of the investigation.

3. Each State Party to this Protocol undertakes to provide or support assistance, in accordance with the provisions of the Charter of the United Nations, to any State Party which so requests, if the Security Council decides that such Party has been harmed or is likely to be harmed as a result of violation of the Protocol.

Article IV

This Protocol shall be of unlimited duration.

Article V

1. This Protocol shall be open for signature to all the Parties of the Treaty on Principles Governing the Activities of States in the Exploration and Use of Outer Space Including the Moon and Other Celestial Bodies. Any State which does not sign it before its entry into force may accede to it at any time;

2. This Protocol shall be subject to ratification by signatory States. Instruments of ratification or accession shall be deposited with the Governments of the United States of America, the United Kingdom of Great Britain and Northern Ireland and the Union of Soviet Socialist Republics in their capacity as Depositaries of the Treaty;

3. This Protocol shall enter into force upon the deposit of instruments of ratification by .... Governments;

4. For those States whose instruments of ratification or accession are deposited after the entry into force of this Protocol, it shall enter into force on the date of the deposit of their instruments of ratification or accession;

5. The Depositaries shall promptly inform all signatory and acceding States of the date of each signature, the date of deposit of each instrument of ratification or accession and the date of the entry into force of this Protocol, as well as of the receipt of other notices;

6. This Protocol shall be registered by the Depositaries in accordance with Article 102 of the Charter of the United Nations.

Article VI

This Protocol of which the English, Arabic, Chinese, French, Russian and Spanish texts are equally authentic, shall be deposited in the archives of the Depositary Governments, who shall send duly certified copies thereof to the Governments of the signatory and acceding States.

Index

Strategic doctrines, space systems and 45–7, 57–61
Submarines, nuclear 67, 94–5, 97
detection of 7

Talon Gold 16, 69, 89, 115, 116
Tcal Ruby 69
Teller Edward 95
Teller-Ulam mechanism 133
Thiokol Altair 13
Thor rocket 12, 86, 113, 188
'Tomato Can' satellite 14
Triad programme 16
Trident II missile 48
Trident submarines 48
Tsongas, Senator 13

U-2 spy plane 62
Union of Concerned Scientists 33, 78, 131, 182
Union of Soviet Socialist Republics
Afghanistan invaded by 150
disarmament issues and 4, 30–1, 33, 37–8, 39–40, 122, 149–50, 162, 163–5, 182, 188, 189–91, 243–4, 245–7
Korean airliner shot down 65
Moscow 84, 111
nuclear build-up, 1970s 46, 47, 109
nuclear weapons, no-first-use pledge 40
Plesetsk 14, 85, 88, 89
strategic doctrines 109–10
Tyuratam 14, 85, 88, 89

UNISPACE conference 37, 175–6
United Kingdom 69
United Nations 37, 39, 76, 129, 150, 162, 189
Charter 70, 159, 167, 178, 191
Committee on the Peaceful Uses of Outer Space 4, 174, 183
Special Sessions on Disarmament 85, 181
United States of America
Air Force 12, 13, 16, 23, 49, 86
Arms Control and Disarmament Agency 128
Army 12, 111, 116
DARPA 16, 86, 115
disarmament issues and 4, 38, 39–40, 149–50, 190
Emergency Action Message 48, 50
Grand Forks 23
laser laboratory, airborne 16
military communications by satellite (% of) 177
Navy 12, 16, 115–16
SAC 44, 59, 60
strategic doctrines 28, 57, 58–61, 69
Vandenberg Air Force Base 24

V-2s 58, 60
VELA satellites 63

Wallop, Senator Malcolm 94, 100
Weinberger, Caspar 44, 47
White Horse programme 116